A Taste for
Provence

A TASTE
for
PROVENCE

Helen Lefkowitz Horowitz

The University of Chicago Press

Chicago and London

Helen Lefkowitz Horowitz is the Sydenham Clark Parsons Professor of American Studies and History, emerita, at Smith College.

The University of Chicago Press, Chicago 60637
The University of Chicago Press, Ltd., London
© 2016 by Helen Lefkowitz Horowitz
All rights reserved. Published 2016.
Printed in the United States of America

25 24 23 22 21 20 19 18 17 16   1 2 3 4 5

ISBN-13: 978-0-226-32284-1 (cloth)
ISBN-13: 978-0-226-32298-8 (e-book)
DOI: 10.7208/chicago/9780226322988.001.0001

Library of Congress Cataloging-in-Publication Data

Names: Horowitz, Helen Lefkowitz, author.
Title: A taste for Provence / Helen Lefkowitz Horowitz.
Description: Chicago ; London : University of Chicago
    Press, 2016. | © 2016 | Includes bibliographical refer-
    ences and index.
Identifiers: LCCN 2015051043 | ISBN 9780226322841
    (cloth : alkaline paper) | ISBN 9780226322988 (e-book)
Subjects: LCSH: Provence (France)—Description and
    travel—History. | Americans—France—Provence—
    History. | Travel writing—United States—History. |
    Provence (France)—Foreign public opinion, American.
Classification: LCC DC611.P958 H595 2016 | DDC
    944.9—dc23 LC record available at http://lccn.loc
    .gov/2015051043

♾ This paper meets the requirements of ANSI/NISO
Z39.48–1992 (Permanence of Paper).

To Janet and David Lefkowitz III

Great cooks, generous hosts,
and enthusiastic travelers to Provence

Contents

Illustrations

ONE

Introduction

Why had I come to Provence? As I sat in a hotel in Aix, my mind
turned to a moment in the Dallas/Fort Worth airport a few years
back. In making a connection on a westbound flight, I glimpsed a
shop in the terminal. On my return flight a few days later, I knew
exactly where I wanted to spend the minutes between planes. I sped
to the distinctive storefront of mustard yellow and, in L'Occitane,
bought the Verbena liquid hand soap that I had been hankering for.

And now I was in Provence, the place of the soap's supposed
origin. But, I reasoned, there had to have been more than this
subliminal prompt to impel me across the Atlantic into southern
France. In the mid-1960s, when my husband and I took a long trip
in France, we never went south of the Loire Valley. Now, in the
second decade of the twentieth century, the hills of Provence were
the first place that came into my mind as the two of us talked about
where we wanted to travel. What made this particular part of the
earth emerge as special and call me to it? Why Provence?

With this question I began to imagine a book that set out a history
of how Provence emerged as a significant travel destination. As I set
about research in books and articles on travel, my first steps were
conventional ones, but then the story began to take an unexpected
turn. I started to venture deeply into Americans' changing relation-

ship with food. *A Taste for Provence* thus has a double meaning—
yes, "taste" as aesthetic appreciation of the region's special qualities, as for example its light and air and landscape; but also "taste" in
the literal sense as it pertains to food. The ability to enjoy Provençal
cuisine became an essential element in the desire to go there.

No one has understood this better than Patricia Wells, an American journalist, food writer, and culinary teacher based in France
who lives part of the year in Provence and writes about and offers
classes in its cooking. In addition to her celebration of Provençal
food, Wells provides another key to understanding the region's
appeal—the association of Provence with special meanings. After
she and her husband, Walter, bought and restored a house at the
edge of Vaison-la-Romaine, northeast of Avignon, she wrote, "It is
more than sunshine that draws us to Provence: We come because
life here seems more real, less modern, more slowly paced, more
personal, and more richly human than almost any other place we
know on earth."[1]

Wells was writing about the hills of Provence, not about its
southern edge on the Riviera. The Côte d'Azur had long been easy
to love. British seekers after the sun came to it as a destination as
early as the eighteenth century, and other denizens of northern
Europe followed soon after. Facing the sea and the sun, these travelers ignored the land reaching into the hills behind them. They
were on the French Riviera. In the words of one British writer,
"They never would have called it living in Provence."[2]

It took much longer for the English-speaking world to discover
the many positive aspects of the land stretching to the north.
English guidebooks of an early era took the land above St. Tropez
and Cannes seriously in only one way. Echoing the educational
purposes of the Grand Tour, their intention was to instruct visitors about the important Roman ruins, principal religious sites, and
the once papal city of Avignon. However, if the influential *Murray's
Handbook* (1873) is an appropriate bellwether, linked to these land-
marks was the wish that they be located somewhere other than in
Provence. The guide tried to disabuse its readers of any romantic

notions they may have harbored of "a region beautiful to behold, and charming to inhabit." With the exception of the "little paradise" near Cannes, it instructed, the region's "nature has altogether an arid character;—in summer a sky of copper, an atmosphere loaded with dust, the earth scorched rather than parched by the unmitigated rays of the sun, which overspread everything with a lurid glare. The hills rise above the surface in masses of bare rock, without any covering of soil, like the dry bones of a wasted skeleton." The Murray guide found the landscape of Provence to hold "a sombre, melancholy sternness" and characterized its people as often violent, loud, coarse, and rude, speaking a language unintelligible even to the French.[3]

There were travel accounts that went against this grain. In the late eighteenth century, Thomas Jefferson stood in thrall before Provence's monuments and enjoyed its sun and wine. Almost a century later, Henry James explored the important Roman sites of that part of Provence close to the Rhône and reported his guarded appreciation. He was followed in the early twentieth century by other Anglo-American travelers appreciative of Provence's unique monuments and atmosphere. Lovers of art came to view and respect both its Roman and medieval ruins and its restored churches.

The Americans who began to flock to the Riviera in the 1920s in summer as well as winter typically ignored remnants of the past. Converging around Gerald and Sara Murphy, this well-publicized gathering of American writers and European and American artists and filmmakers—as well as the merely wealthy—typically placed themselves near the beaches. Some of the Americans tried out expatriation; others stayed only for a while for work or pleasure. The fame and seeming carelessness of this "lost generation" attracted others in imitation and made the Mediterranean coast an important destination for Americans and Europeans.[4] But except to venture into the immediate hills for a quick view or a restaurant meal, Provence was essentially ignored.

Of course, because of its exceptional light and relatively low cost of living, the Provence that lay north of the sea had attracted a few

Continental artists in the nineteenth century. Paul Cézanne, born and raised in Aix, chose to return there to paint its landscape and people. Vincent van Gogh took refuge in Arles and Saint-Rémy-de-Provence, and Paul Gauguin came to visit. In the early twentieth century, modernists followed in their wake. The work of painters drew appreciative tourists to the region, but on the whole these visitors came only for a quick look at the locations of artistic endeavor.

Today's Provence of desire is neither coastal nor a place of study or art appreciation. It is inland, and life there is domestic and leisured. In the American imagination of those, such as Patricia Wells, who came into adulthood in the second half of the twentieth century, Provence exists to draw travelers to dream of the bounty of weekly produce markets savored in farm or village houses in the sun. One ideal is to own a second house in those hills, especially a farmhouse looking like it came out of a Cézanne painting (plate 1). This is the Provençal *mas* best described as one of the "massive looking, walled in farmhouses . . . made out of stone and mortar" typically "pale . . . yellow, pink, off-white," and topped with tiled roofs.[5] For most Americans, such a second home is out of reach, and the dream becomes the desire to go with close friends or family and rent one for a month or a week or two. Or, if time is of the essence, merely to have a restaurant meal and view quickly this earthly paradise. Provence as the re-creation of Eden wasn't always there. It had to be created in the mind—and, to some extent, in reality.

Exploring the evolution of Provence from Roman ruins and rough land to a destination of desire has led me research and write this book. I am a traveler *and* a cultural historian, keenly interested in the ways we are influenced by the changing culture of the places we encounter, especially those we come to love. I want to understand the many ways culture has shaped us in the past as it moves into the present, guiding us to think and feel. In the case of Provence, what interests me is how economic and social transformation in that French region and the many changes in life in the United States have affected Americans over time as they have moved through their lives and traveled. Thinking about being in Provence in the second decade of the twenty-first century led me to examine what had been written and pictured about this region, past and present. It drew me to powerful, imaginative evocations of both travel and place.

So I began what became a fascinating quest. I looked for and found messages about travel to Provence in a wide range of media, including books and magazines, guidebooks, cookbooks, goods, advertisements, paintings, films, and television. The examples I've selected involve all levels of culture and the varied ways commerce enters into the mix. For this mélange and its blend of high and low I have no apologies—only an explanation that it is the cultural stew itself, not any single element, that shapes perceptions and feelings in the United States and has engendered a taste for Provence.

I give substantial attention to the work of travel writers describing Provence. From among the wide range of those discussing the landscape, food, or other aspects of the region I've selected those writers who were particularly influential or who illustrated key aspects of the tourist experience. Let me point out just a few who exemplify the range. Peter Mayle dramatized Provence's pleasures for many in the late 1980s. Paul Zimmerman in 1971 had the broad readership of the *New York Times* of his era, but Willa Cather in 1902 had only those in the orbit of the *Nebraska State Journal*. Each of these, however, has something important to tell about traveling and lingering in Provence that I feel deserves exposition or emphasis.

I treat a wide range of informants about Provence and promoters of the region, including authors of important works of literature, a Founding Father writing a flirtatious letter, a major novelist, a future museum curator, a French studies scholar trying out anthropology, established journalists and magazine writers, celebrated but hard-up authors commissioned by travel magazines, and those in the business of selling a service or a product. In thinking about my interest in Provence, a friend said, "Keep your eye on the money." This, of course, is something not hard to do in the present age when everything and every act seem monetized. Nonetheless, these words did alert me to what I might have missed. Commercial considerations are almost always present. Even Thomas Jefferson's 1787 trip was financed by his role as United States Commissioner so that he might learn firsthand about agriculture and transport (and secretly gather foreign intelligence). The time he spent viewing Provence's Roman ruins came during recreational breaks.

The absence of a monetary motive is why I dwell on the truth-teller A. Hyatt Mayor, who in the 1920s wrote an unpublished travel journal for only himself and a few members of his family. I see the work of the academic Laurence Wylie partially in this light, even though he published a book in 1957 that was to bring him both wide attention and royalties. What is important in the words of both men is that they saw and experienced parts of Provence without trying to draw others to venture there. In doing so, they have provided important markers along the way, leading me to explore the ways Provence itself has changed over time, especially how it developed to accommodate travelers and to appeal to them in new ways.

While all who publish their writings do so for a purpose, even if in many cases this is disguised, the thrust of writing has nonetheless shifted over the years. Many of even the greatest authors did indeed depend on royalties for a living, but what emerges as increasingly important by the mid-twentieth century is the commercial impetus driving writing on Provence. The leader in travel writing, *Holiday* magazine, was launched in the late 1940s out of the discovery of a niche market for advertising—vacationers with discretionary income to spend on fun.[6] *Travel & Leisure* was from 1971 to 2013 the offspring of American Express. Agencies with clients seeking rentals in Provence and companies formed to sell products from the region have an undisguised commercial motive. With the changes in Provence and its image after World War II, marketing, promotion, and advertising increasingly have become the engine driving the printing of words about travel there.

I've sought numbers to learn how many Americans in the past have traveled to Provence and presently do so, but, as the most serious scholar to have studied tourist statistics kept by the French has found, useful numbers are hard to come by.[7] In the case of my subject, this is more difficult because data about inland Provence, the region of my specific interest, are generally blended with those of other parts of southeastern France and, at the same time, separated from areas joined by history and custom.[8] Despite the lack of hard numbers, I have been driven forward by an awareness that I care not only about real travel to the region but also about virtual travel through reading, viewing, dining in restaurants or at home, and purchasing Provençal-themed goods. Once a taste for Provence is acquired, it can be satisfied in many disparate ways.[9]

I begin this account with the understanding of Provence as a travel destination that held from the eighteenth century until the mid-twentieth century—the region is important because it contains valued Roman ruins. I then get to the heart of my story, the changes that followed World War II both in the United States and in France. Americans' long love affair with France centered around Paris.[10] As early postwar travel restrictions eased and transatlantic transportation improved, Americans flocked there in such great numbers that the French government sought to encourage them to seek out the provinces. However, for the fascinating but very poor region of Provence to emerge as a significant travel destination required more than just advertisements. It took the evolution of a complicated tourist infrastructure involving transportation and accommodations, including those that offered the possibility of longer stays in a single place. These considerations are the ground on which a critical part of my story rests—the reinvention of Provence directed at the minds and hearts of American travelers and dreamers.

Important transformative words and photographs began in the 1960s, but their true impact came in the 1970s when they were broadcast widely to a newly receptive audience. In uncovering this development, my primary sources have been works in English by writers in the United States and Britain, along with their accompanying images. These include travel pieces in books and magazines, cookbooks and descriptions of furnishings, and information about agencies that negotiated international rentals, all replete with commercial considerations. Joined with them are paintings, photographs, television, and film—the visual media that form the many ways that Provence was brought to the attention of Americans. My eye has been trained on this foreground. These portrayals of Provence evoked a cultural shift in the United States that turned Provence from a place of Roman ruins and rough living into an imagined destination that promised to fulfill the desire for the good life.

Despite my disclaimer that I'm a cultural historian, I've worried at times that I might be mistaken for the anthropologist R. J. Sheldrake, the fictional professor of tourism in David Lodge's *Paradise News*. Yes, I admit that just as he made lists of the word "Paradise" in Hawaii, it has occurred to me that I might count the number of times that lavender appears in images of Provence. But I have never lectured on tourism nor been offered champagne at a hotel I was not paying for, as was David Lodge's character. Moreover, I am no debunker of the travel experience. Sheldrake announced that he was "doing for tourism what Marx did to capitalism, what Freud did to family life. Deconstructing it." He was determined to puncture the myths that sent people to Hawaii for a holiday, in the hope they might stay home.[11] I, on the contrary, enjoy travel. And I have come to love being in Provence. What follows is inquiry and analysis, but not deconstruction in the negative way Sheldrake put it. For me, learning about how the taste for Provence developed has added to the pleasure of going and being there.

The fictional Sheldrake's field emerged in the 1960s when the impact of travel to faraway places for pleasure became too powerful to miss. A range of scholars who studied travel established the field of tourism studies. Economists got into the act early on, measuring the effects of such journeys on the economies of both hosts and guests. The subject of travel attracted sociologists and anthropologists as well, and with the revival of radicalism within the academy, political considerations moved into play in these disciplines. Tourism, especially in the Third World, was linked to the heritage of imperialism. In the 1970s, ecological concerns came to prominence in the social sciences, and new work began to emphasize damage to the hosts' environment. Voices emerging later in that decade began to look at guests no longer as negatives but as explorers seeking authenticity, evoking a wide range of interesting studies. Fresh social science scholarship appeared, exploring tourism from different facets, including human interactions, the gaze, language, image performance, and pilgrimage.[12] Some of these studies, despite their often turgid language, have opened my mind to new insights and interpretation. As a cultural historian exploring the transformation of Americans' awareness of Provence, however, I have a different cast of mind. As one way of marking this and differentiating my work from the rigors of social science and tourism studies, I tend in this book to employ the word "traveler" rather than "tourist."

In understanding the lure of Provence, one concept of particular value in this literature is the "tourist imaginary." In the eyes of its creators, the key to this concept's power is that it offers the opposite of the life lived at home. The tourist imaginary is one of those "implicit schemas of interpretation" that carry practical import, for it can lead to a real outcome—travel to the place of desire. It is a collective, not an individual, vision, blending many voices and images, and is widely shared within the broader culture. Tourist imaginaries all share the desire of escape from the imperfect life of the present to a place that offers satisfaction. Interestingly, it can be amplified and manipulated by those seeking the economic benefits of tourist dollars.[13]

Anthropologists studying this phenomenon are likely to focus on indigenous, non-Western peoples and on travel to their regions. Provence, by contrast, offers a Western world as destination. But certain of the elements of the "tourist imaginary" being pursued there are the same as those in Bali. As does the Indonesian island, Provence exists in the tourist imaginary as eternal, "unchanged." It is heaven on earth. And it offers the promise of self-realization. The way that Provence emerged in this light—became reinvented as travel destination both in the mind and on the ground—speaks for more than itself. Exploring how a taste for Provence developed allows insights into similar processes that have been at work elsewhere in the world.

In one important way it matters that Provence is Western and a part of France. American foodways were changing. Culinary tourism intensified in the 1960s and 1970s, and its search for distinctive, authentic tastes made food a central element for many travelers. This came, however, at a time when the imperialistic world order was being challenged across the globe, posing a problem for some. What did it mean to appropriate the food of others, to assume the conqueror's place at the table? At the same time, there were others, more cautious, hearing variant stories of Montezuma's revenge, who, despite their desires for new tastes, held fears about the safety of food and drink in faraway places. Provence posed no issues for worriers of either stripe. Writers appreciative of Provence's special tastes, Julia Child's impact, and cookbooks teaching Provençal cuisine prepared a new destination for culinary adventurers. Distinctive and authentic, Provençal cuisine was the product of the French republic and met modern Western standards (plate 2).[14]

The Provence that fills the imagination of food adventurers and travelers is a relatively new creation. To understand it better some background is needed, for until less than a half-century ago, the region appeared tough to love. To some Americans travelers Provence once may have seemed a French analog to Appalachia—beautiful scenery and warm sunny weather, but peopled by rough folks living in poverty. Horace Sutton, the enthusiastic guide for the first generation of tourists to France after World War II, was almost at a loss for words to describe it. This "mostly dry, scrubby, rocky, arid land" could be, he wrote, compared to Italy, and Palestine, and "no other place on earth."[15] Such a place, until the 1970s, seemed unlikely to attract many strangers to linger.

In this seeming French backwater, locals still spoke a dialect of Occitan, a separate language. Although children were taught French in the schools, for many, at least until the 1950s, the Provençal tongue in its regional variations remained the first language of home. Even today some of its sounds persist in the distinctive rhythms and word endings of natives in the region. For the Provençaux these sounds are a source of pride, marking their region as distinctive and serving as evidence to back up its claim to being one of the first civilized places in Europe.

Provence today is a state of mind as much as a region, suggestive of clear skies, bright sun, gentle breezes scented with lavender and wild herbs, scenery alternately bold and intricate, and delicious food and strong wines. As a real place, it has been during its long recorded history a colony, a kingdom, a province that was an official unit of France, and a territory splintered into *départements*. And today it is an administrative region. Across its long history Provence has taken different shapes on the map and in the modern era has yielded to subjective forms outside of official designations.

In reflecting on Provence's protean origins, the British writer Lawrence Durrell wrote of its "shifting contours" that once "seemed to encompass . . . an improbably vast territory. But over the years its outlines hovered and retraced themselves until it assumed the outlines of our modern Provence."[16] Rome left a strong imprint, beginning with its settlement in 154 BC, when the Greeks, who had founded Marseille some 450 years before, called on the Romans to help them resist invasion by the Celts. The Romans came and stayed and expanded their hold. Originally they called the territory Narbonensis, or simply Provincia, and it ultimately covered the southern swath of France from Spain to Italy. The region attracted traders and former Roman soldiers, and settlement spread up the Rhône from Marseille.

After Rome fell, Provincia remained. Colonizers stayed, and crops were harvested each year. As feudal lords gained land and power, the large region divided into Provence to the east, Languedoc and Roussillon to the west.[17] Provence had its own rulers and nobility, its own coins, its own wars. In 1486, Provence came under the French king, but in the Old Regime France was composed of many provinces, each with its own traditions, customs, even laws. In Provence, there was a provincial *parlement*, which met in Aix, its capital.

Compared to some other regions that became part of France,

Provence was home to many freeholders, living outside the feudal system and able to buy and sell property. Agriculture was oriented to the market, and farmers tended to specialize. Villages kept control over many local institutions. There emerged a strong communal culture, with public life centered around cafés and the market. In each locale were the full range of social classes, but, unlike many other parts of France, class boundaries in Provence were somewhat blurred. At the upper end, the grandees were often less grand and more willing to participate in business than their counterparts elsewhere. Landlords were often absentee, choosing to live in Marseille or Aix, and the Church held less land in its grip. At the lower end of the social scale, peasants partook of commercial life, coming with their produce to the market and buying their necessities there as well; in winter, they did artisanal work. At the same time, those living in the towns cultivated small plots. This blending prepared the ground for Provence's distinctive society.[18]

The French Revolution changed the relation of the nation's many subdivisions, including Provence, to the state. In 1790, the national government ended the provinces and their assemblies and divided France into eighty-three departments. This dissolving process, identified today as Jacobin, sought to break the hold of the earlier provinces, standardize the laws of the nation, create small governable administrative units, and strip the nobility of its power. Regional dialects were denounced. In the years that followed there were many changes in the government of France, but the state's efforts to centralize power continued apace. Only since 1972 has regional organization, however weak, returned to France and thus partially to Provence. These larger units were strengthened in the 1980s during the presidency of François Mitterrand, and today there are six departments in the southeast corner of France that make up the region now known as Provence-Alpes-Côte d'Azur or, more simply, PACA.[19] They include the historic areas identified with Provence—Bouches-du-Rhône at the southwest, Vaucluse above (including the once Papal region known as the Comtat Venaissin), the Var at the southeast, and Alpes-de-Haute-Provence to its north.

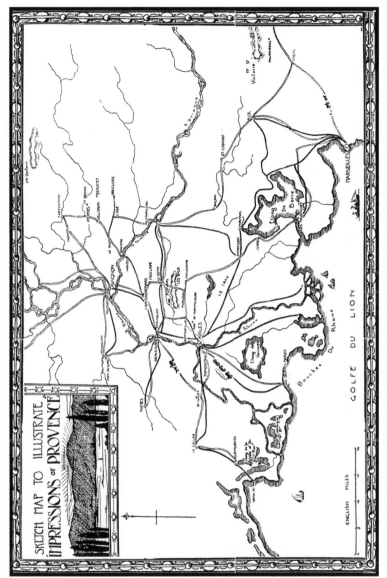

1 Historic Provence with the Rhône at its center. Percy Allen, *Impressions of Provence* (London: Francis Griffiths, 1910), 317.

Provence as it exists not in administrative units of the state but in the imagination can be a somewhat different and significantly smaller area. In the minds of many of the French, it covers an area west of the Rhône that includes Nîmes and Villeneuve-lès-Avignon. And it disregards much of the Mediterranean coast and most of the territory beyond Vaucluse and Bouches-du-Rhône. Lawrence Durrell, in his 1959 travel piece "Ripe Living in Provence," wrote of Pepe, his traveling companion, who had a tattoo on his chest that defined the "true Provence." The tattoo was an elongated diamond, bounded to the south by Marseille; to the north by Montélimar; to the west, Nîmes; and to the east, Apt. On the ground the distances between these points are relatively small, roughly 100 miles north to south by 60 miles west to east. However small this diamond-shaped Provence, it is, not unlike Tuscany or the Cotswolds, a treasured place of beauty.

While this Provence may be the imagined one of Durrell and many others, my use of the term includes it and on occasions stretches beyond to contain the area that goes to the eastern boundaries of France, for that is the Provence understood by many of my historical and contemporary sources. Just as the mid-twentieth-century writer stated that those enjoying the French Riviera "never would have called it living in Provence," so, too, do I normally exclude the Côte d'Azur from this work. My focus is on what is often called the "hills of Provence." I use this affectionate term for the large area of the region that lies inland from the sea, despite the fact that it is an imperfect descriptor. Roughly the size of Maryland, this Provence includes—along with its famous mountains and perched villages—agricultural valleys, low-lying towns, and important cities.

Government edict may be one thing, but true integration of Provence into France was another. It took a great deal of time for the Provençaux to join the French nation economically and socially. The national railroad crossed Provence in the mid-nineteenth century, as Napoleon III oversaw the building of a line from Paris to Marseille, but many inland places away from the tracks remained isolated. Without a rural road system to link villages to each other and to major population centers, the fruits of the earth remained bound to a small area. "As long as villages remained roadless, the peasants ignored general market conditions. Fruit and other produce could not be shipped for sale, so their possibilities were not worth exploring. In Var figs were fed to local pigs." Not until the 1880s could wheeled vehicles reach the trains and give local farmers access to broader markets. Once roads and railroads connected Provence to Paris and other major cities, it became economically possible for farmers to plant fruit trees, cultivate melons, and transport olive oil and wine north. Thus toward the end of the nineteenth century, rural Provence was on the way to becoming a true part of France.[20]

Yet in these same years, a counterforce began throughout much of France, a regionalism that celebrated the nation's distinctive cultures.[21] Within Provence a group emerged that sought recognition of its language and unique heritage. In 1854 seven poets, including a young Frédéric Mistral, founded the Félibrige, an association to promote Provence's literary culture. In Paris, Mistral's friend Alphonse Daudet called on the memory of his early life in Nîmes to pen images of the Provençal landscape and create an array of characters who have, since their introduction in the late 1860s, haunted literature and later film. Daudet's fiction presents a world lit by the sun and forgotten by time, where passions run deep and talk, long. In his tall tales filled with human and animal characters, pathos mixes with comedy. In the quiet of his "beautiful Provençal landscape" may come "faintly, afar, the sound of a fife, a curlew amid the lavender, the mule-bells on the highway," but wrongs fester, and violent revenge lurks.[22] In America at the turn of the century, the Félibrige found admirers in the writer Thomas A. Janvier and his wife, the artist Catharine Drinker Janvier. The two brought to literary readers in the United States an appreciation of Provençal customs and translations of the poetry of members of the Félibrige.[23]

It has been argued that part of the enthusiasm for regionalism in France came out of Paris's inability to absorb the many aspiring provincial writers who emerged from the educational reforms of the Third Republic, but this view is distorted by the intellectual imperialism of the French capital.[24] What the Félibrige did was to celebrate the culture of the land of home. In other places, such as Brittany, regionalists engaged in politics, sometimes of the left but often of the right. In Provence, Mistral held firm to apolitical cultural revival. In addition to his own poems, he transcribed those of the troubadours. Aspiring to rehabilitate Occitan as a respected language, he labored long and published its dictionary, some say inappropriately freezing as authoritative his version of the local patois. Mistral also became the guiding force behind efforts to restore Provençal dress, crafts, and folkways. When his contributions brought him the Nobel Prize for literature in 1904, he used the prize money to support their display in the Museon Arlaten in Arles. Today, Mistral is most often recalled through the many quotes or misquotes that pay tribute to his native region, such as "When the Good Lord comes to doubt about the world, he remembers that he created Provence."[25]

Mistral was the son of landed wealth, able to live well without ever practicing the law for which he trained. Yet for most Provençaux, life remained difficult. During the first half of the twentieth century, the region experienced ups and downs. It was subject to natural floods, droughts, and pests as well as to manmade war and economic depressions. Nonetheless, with their pride of family and place, French urban dwellers found Provence a good locale to be from and return to. From well back into the nineteenth century, Parisians with money had a tradition of establishing country residences, especially in their places of origin, as rural getaways for holidays and part of the summer, and this continued into the interwar period of the early twentieth century.

As their nation recovered from World War II, more and more urbanites began to long for a country home as an antidote to city life. Once they acquired automobiles, they were willing to go longer distances. The Riviera became a major site on their map. As crowding and resort-style building began to change the landscape of the Côte d'Azur, these city dwellers began to turn to the hills above. Times were especially hard in Provence. In the aftermath of World War II, national economic policy to turn France into a first-rate industrial power initially seemed to bypass the region. Ironically this held a key to its future. Sunny Provence north of the Mediterranean was cheap and remained unspoiled. Available almost for the taking were unreconstructed old stone farmhouses and village dwellings.

French urbanites seeking property in the hills of Provence were joined by those from other countries. British travelers had long sought the sun, and the Mediterranean held great allure.[26] Although they hardly constituted a trend, some trailblazers from the United Kingdom set out to buy and renovate properties in rural Provence before the Second World War. As the French Riviera became more crowded and expensive in the early 1950s, British citizens (along with Belgians, Germans, and Scandinavians) cast their eyes north, saw what the French were doing, and began to acquire inland properties in Provence. By the mid-1950s, property values in the perched villages were beginning to rise, and many seeming ghost towns were coming back to life.

This movement led to a modest literature in English appreciative of Provence. Noted British authors, such as James Pope-Hennessy and Lawrence Durrell, gave distinctive voices to describing and interpreting the region. A shared language and literary tradition lent them readership in the United States and publication in American magazines. Led by such words, beginning in the 1960s, a very small number of Americans began to trickle into Provence. They were pioneers, if you will, often brought by specific agendas. A French husband or artistic aspirations led to buying a property and making it habitable. American tourism in France was on the rise, made easier by airplane travel. Encouraged by advertising supported by the French government and specifically aimed at the US market, Americans traveled to France more than to any other destination. Although Paris was at the center of the tourist universe, France encouraged Americans to explore many of its provincial regions.

Brittany and the Loire Valley were early favorites. Provence began to beckon.

Coinciding with this were deep changes both in Provence itself and in America. The push after World War II for electrification brought a great dam that helped to control both flooding and drought over a significant part of the region, turning the land green. High speed motorways and trains made for more rapid access to southern destinations. More stars appeared on the maps of Michelin Red Guides, denoting good restaurant food to be had in Provence. Gradually, a secondary market of restored properties in the hills of Provence became available for rent by Americans looking for a summer getaway in the sun.[27]

Opportunity was met by changing desires and tastes among Americans. The 1960s and its aftermath produced profound transformations that dug deep into the psyches of many. Elements of the culture seemed to split apart. Aspects of life once accepted, including American foodways, were now challenged. The travel industry began to see that there were many more ways to roam, and some involved sitting still. Out of this, a new image of Provence emerged, and the selling of the region was on. Beginning in the 1970s, Provence—for a summer, a month, or even a week or two— became a desired destination for many Americans.

Thomas Jefferson and the Love of Antiquity

In Nîmes in the early spring of 1787, Thomas Jefferson stood enthralled. He gazed at the Maison Carrée, the great Roman temple located in this city just west of the Rhône in southern France, for "whole hours . . . like a lover at his mistress."[1] He came to Nîmes while he was serving as commissioner to France in the years after the American Revolution. He had planned a long trip south to explore agriculture, seaports, and water transport, but before setting off he injured his wrist, and his physician recommended that he seek the waters at Aix to help it heal.[2]

Jefferson's sight of the Maison Carrée was the climax of his time in Provence, but much of that period (as well as the rest of his journey of several months in Europe) was spent in more practical ways, in learning about the land, its crops, its people, and its wine. He traveled alone, taking his own carriage and hiring horses along the route. He chose not to take one of his own slaves or servants as his valet but to secure successive ones along the way, for he was in the mood for solitude. The pace was slow, and it allowed him to see the countryside and think of adapting European crops to America. In Provence, Jefferson became enamored of the olive trees he first saw near Orange and from that point on noted them throughout his passage, first to the Mediterranean coast and then up into the mountains on the back roads from France to Italy. On his return to

Paris, he promoted the cultivation of the olive in South Carolina and arranged for the importation of trees there.

Jefferson paid attention to the work in the fields, noting disparagingly the strenuous labor of women (without seeming to connect what he saw to the work of female slaves on his own plantations), and he gave special attention to "the wine called Hermitage" and its rocky vineyard.[3] It was late March, and Jefferson was bewitched by the sun and the seeming fertility of the earth. He wrote, "I am now in the land of corn, wine, oil, and sunshine. What more can one ask of heaven? If I should happen to die at Paris, I will beg of you to send me here, and have me exposed to the sun. I am sure it will bring me to life again."[4] His enthusiastic reaction to the region led to one misstep. Because Jefferson did not experience Provence's summer heat and aridity, he made assumptions about the adaptability of its agricultural products to the American South—only to be corrected when those imported olive trees failed to flourish.

It was on the way to Aix and its waters that he took the detour to Nîmes, approximately sixty-five miles away, for Jefferson was a great lover of Roman antiquity. He already knew of the Maison Carrée, the extraordinary Roman temple in Nîmes, as the empire's "most perfect and precious remain." Before to coming to France, he had learned of the building's important rediscovery following the clearing out of the surrounding medieval structures that had long obscured it. In Paris Jefferson enriched his anticipation by his association with the great antiquarian Charles-Louis Clérisseau, whose work *Monumens de Nismes* had been published a decade before. Prior to Jefferson's travel in southern France, he commissioned Clérisseau to oversee the making of a model of the Maison Carrée and had it shipped to Richmond as the prototype for the new capitol of Virginia.[5]

Jefferson lingered in Nîmes for five days. He visited the Arena, the Temple of Diana, and nearby the great Roman aqueduct Pont du Gard. This extraordinary feat of engineering and design with its three tiers of arches spanning the Gardon River was for him "sublime." Secretly during that time he was also conferring with a

2   The drawing of the Maison Carrée that inspired Thomas Jefferson. Charles-Louis Clérisseau, *Monumens de Nismes* (Paris: P. D. Pierres, 1778), plate II.

Brazilian about the prospects for revolution in his country, but in the bright light of day he reveled in the past of the Roman Empire. "Were I to attempt to give you news," he wrote Adrienne Catherine de Noailles, Countess de Tessé, "I should tell you stories one thousand years old. I should detail to you the intrigues of the courts of the Caesars, how they affect us here, the oppressions of their praetors, prefects, &c. I am immersed in antiquities from morning to night."[6]

Both before and after Nîmes, Jefferson took careful measurements of France's Roman buildings. Although at times he was angry at the way that the French had earlier disregarded their Roman heritage—as when they knocked down a section of the wall of the arena in Orange to build a road—he found much to admire in Orange, Vienne, Arles, and Aix, as well as Nîmes. He was an enthusiast. As he wrote to Noailles, his look at the Maison Carrée had been so long and ardent that, observing him, "the stocking weavers and silk spinners . . . consider me as a hypochondriac Englishman, about to write with a pistol, the last chapter of his history."[7] But rather than coming from a distressed soul contemplating suicide, Jefferson's long looks contributed to his architectural knowledge and bolstered his will to create in America classical buildings of comparable beauty. It was in those moments in Nîmes that something of the national heritage of the United States became linked to Provence.

TWO   # Roman Ruins and
                       # Rough Land

Until the later decades of the twentieth century, few Americans
took Jefferson's journey to the land above the Mediterranean in
southeastern France. When they did, it was likely that they, too,
were drawn by a desire to see the ruins of Rome's great empire.
There were, however, many reasons why this region was not on the
ordinary traveler's map. One of the primary ones is that, outside its
cities, Provence was a rough land and its people were not eager to
welcome visitors.

Those with wealth and leisure may have come to Provence as
part of completing their education or as a way of passing time, but
the ones we know about—the travelers who wrote and published
about their journeys—sought to coin their findings. It is important to remember that even revered writers, such as Henry James,
made a living from the words they wrote. And in the autumn of
1882, needing to write another book—but one that would be a break
from fiction after completing his monumental *Portrait of a Lady*—
James planned a travel book on France.

Determined to observe and offer to readers the France that was
not Paris, James journeyed throughout France expressly to write
about it for the English-speaking reading public. James found much
of his travels tedious. Most of the towns he saw were "less rich in
the picturesque" than he had anticipated, but he was determined,

as he wrote to his brother William, "to do something with them."[1]
In Provence, James perked up a bit, for its Roman ruins held for
him strong interest.

As he moved from town to town—Aigues Mortes, Les Baux,
back to Nîmes, Tarascon, Arles, Avignon, and Orange—he typically commented on the emptiness of their streets, the quiet and
the melancholy. Everywhere were evidences of past Roman grandeur, but now these were remnants resting in a poor land, largely
a backwater. He normally liked places less when they were used
for current activities of local residents, such as the arenas in Nîmes
and Arles, in his time sites of bullfights.[2] For James it was better
when the ruins were only quiet stones, allowing him, as he did once
in viewing a Roman bath, to surrender himself "to contemplation
and reverie." In that instance, James wrote, "it seemed to me that I
touched for a moment the ancient world."[3]

Long a resident in London, James organized his trip by *Murray's Handbook* and used it as one of his references for descriptive details. For example, he followed Murray's instructions and,
immediately on alighting from the train in Nîmes, hired a coach
to take him to the Pont du Gard, roughly fifteen miles away. At the
great aqueduct he took the measure of its three tiers. "Nothing,"
he wrote, "could well be more Roman. The hugeness, the solidity,
the unexpectedness, the monumental rectitude of the whole thing
leave you nothing to say . . . and make you stand gazing." Continuing to explore, James made a careful visual assessment, walking
on a road to look at it from below. He sat alone for an hour in the
waning light, and then and later distilled this experience to reflect
upon Roman culture. The monument, magnificent as it was, had
"a certain stupidity, a vague brutality," an aspect that he felt was
characteristic of Roman building, which made too much of means
in getting to the end, in this case, "to carry the water of a couple
of springs to a little provincial city." To him the Pont du Gard was
an example of "Roman rigidity" whose aesthetic weakness was "to
overshoot the mark."

Nonetheless the Pont du Gard held for James "a kind of manly beauty, that of an object constructed not to please but to serve." As he sat in the twilight and watched the shadows gather in the valley, it seemed to him "as if the mighty empire were still as erect as the supports of the aqueduct." He believed at that moment that "no people has ever been, or will ever be, as great as that, measured . . . by the push they gave to what they undertook. The Pont du Gard . . . speaks of them in a manner with which they might have been satisfied."[4]

Oddly enough, in contrast to Jefferson's appreciation, the Maison Carrée held little attraction for James. He had seen it too many times in photographs, he wrote, and now faced with its solid presence he found that "curiosity and surprise are almost completely, and perhaps deplorably, absent."[5]

Photographs in this instance may have limited his enjoyment, but they were important in another way. One can see this in his initial reaction when he arrived in Nîmes. He reflected, "It was a pleasure to feel one's self in Provence again,—the land where the silver-grey earth is impregnated with the light of the sky."[6] As he wrote about the drive to the Pont du Gard, he continued, "After I had left the town I became more intimate with that Provençal charm which I had already enjoyed from the window of the train, and which glowed in the sweet sunshine and the white rocks, and lurked in the smoke puffs of the little olives. He commented that the olive trees were "half the landscape," that their "mild colorless bloom seems the very texture of the country."[7]

The absence of color suggests that James was seeing what the photographs of his day had trained him to see. He had to rely on them, for unlike the regions of Italy to which Provence is often compared, no world-famous painters of the Renaissance captured the Provençal hills in color. As James drove back to Nîmes, he reported that the moonlight "added a more solitary whiteness to the constant sheen of the Provençal landscape."[8] As he reflected on his own observations, writing at a later time and at some remove from the scene, James noted, "It may appear that I insist too much upon the nudity of the Provençal horizon. . . . But it is an exquisite bareness; it seems to exist for the purpose of allowing one to follow the delicate lines of the hills, and touch with the eyes, as it were, the smallest inflections of the landscape. It makes the whole thing wonderfully bright and pure."[9] The many photographs of Provence that James had viewed, mentioned at various points in his descriptions, prepared him for his visit in 1882. These luminous images caught the light of the sun and its reflection on the olive trees. But they were not in color, only in varying shades of black and white and silver-gray.

Several decades later, another writer traveled to Provence in the expectation of paying her way with publication. Willa Cather was then a school teacher in Pittsburgh in her late twenties. She came to the region in 1902 with a commission from the *Nebraska State Journal* to write about her travels abroad. She had published in the paper since her college days at the University of Nebraska in Lincoln. Her preparation for the trip was less photography than literature. Since girlhood, she had treasured French literature and studied it in college. She was especially versed in the writings of Alphonse Daudet, the French writer born in Nîmes. After his death in 1897, she wrote several articles that summed up his career for the Nebraska newspaper. In 1902 she titled her travel piece on Provence "In the Country of Daudet," and that is just what it was.[10] Much of what she saw in Arles and Avignon and the surrounding region came filtered through his words.

Cather was a close observer of the landscape, and her rural childhood in Virginia and Nebraska served her in good stead when she paid attention in Provence to the crops in a September dry season. When she turned to characterize the region's people, however, little seems to have come from direct experience. In considering the area around Arles, for example, she wrote that inside the "feudal manor" of one of the "shepherd kings" or "farmer barons" typically lived three generations of the family and their servants, including their shepherds. "No farmer has a desire to be anything else, or to live in any better house than the one his father lived in, or to see a

larger city than Arles." Their aspirations were "to live honourably
and long, to marry their daughters well and to have strong sons to
succeed them, to avoid innovation and change, to drink their Mus-
cat wine and eat their boiled snails and tomatoes fried in oil to the
end."[11] In 1902 Willa Cather was an apprentice writer with a great
future as a novelist ahead of her, but in this travel piece she was rely-
ing on images from Daudet for a Nebraska audience. That words
beget words is useful to note, for it warns us that some writing on
Provence is derivative. It also tells us about the way writers' words,
as well as visual images, can both shape travel desires and give form
to experiences while on the journey.

What was Provence really like in the early twentieth century? Here
the candid statements of one who was not being paid to write can
give testimony. In the archives of Syracuse University rests the
manuscript by A. Hyatt Mayor, then a young American on a spring
break from university in 1926, making his way around Provence on
a bicycle. He documented his travels in a remarkable journal meant
only for family eyes.[12]

Mayor set off on April 11, 1926, for a one-week bicycle ride cir-
cling around Avignon. At age twenty-six Mayor had an inquisi-
tive mind and a good eye and literary gifts that would later serve
him well. He also had skill with languages, openness, education,
and great family connections, through his aunt's marriage to the
wealthy Archer Huntington. Although riches did not flow young
Mayor's way, access did.[13] After going to Princeton as a day student,
tuition free, and teaching history of art for a year at Vassar, he had
won a Rhodes scholarship to Oxford. During his two years in the
British university he was welcomed into many homes of the elite
in England and, during the long vacations, into those on the Continent, including Villa I Tatti of Bernard and Mary Berenson. His
independent streak led him to adventurous travel.[14] Other young
people were seeking ways to take to the road on a tight budget.
At this same time, Mayor's contemporary at Princeton, the future

wine writer and purveyor Frank Schoonmaker, was working on his *Through Europe on Two Dollars a Day*. Within its pages, he included tips about low-cost travel through Provence.[15]

The young Mayor spent much of his time in Provence in serious contemplation of its antique treasures. His sites seem carefully chosen, and many of them paralleled those Henry James had selected. As in the eras of Thomas Jefferson and Henry James, the principal interest in inland Provence in Mayor's time lay in its great Roman ruins. To this Mayor added his art-historical knowledge of important medieval churches, such as St. Trophime in Arles. The dramatic moments in his travel diary, however, come from his experience of the countryside. What he saw both fascinated and bewildered him.

The first day of his journey was the adventure of his life. In the morning he approached Gordes in the *département* of Vaucluse. A glamor spot today, it was then a perched village in decay. Looking across a chasm, he saw houses tumbling down "humpty dumpty, mostly ruined, so one looks into the floors of the bottom ones, mere broken shells." From there he made his way to the Abbaye de Sénanque, once a Cistercian monastery. Pushing his bicycle up a cow path, he took in the surrounding view. Comparing what he saw to the depopulated regions of Spain, he wrote, "It is the real despoblados of France, long deserted for the easier valleys." He was fascinated by what looked to him like many "igloos or kilns" made of local rocks coming off the hills. Each of them seemed to have "a hole to creep through into a beehive for sleeping in, all curled up like a dog. It was like the site of some forgotten cult." Mayor didn't know it but he was looking at what is now called the "Village des Bories," since 1976 listed as a French historic site. Around him, he continued, "the slag land made the derelict olives, long uncared for, more cindery. It was too starved for even a cricket. It was as silent as the sun. On the ridge the rocks, for there was no path, dropped into an eroded gulley, hideously deep. It was like a photograph of Arizona, all the more so as it was all gray."

Once Mayor arrived at the abbey, he found it deserted. The monks had departed twenty-two years before, and there was only a silent woman with keys to allow him entry. As he made his way through the desolate place, filled with the smell of rotting wood, this keeper observed his every move. He went up the stairs to the dormitory. The floorboards were loose and broken. As he stood there, her "head rose up the floor through the stairs, watching me, either suspicious or to make me go." The day was waning, and he needed a meal and a bed for the night before traveling on to Carpendras, his next stop, but the woman adamantly refused to provide either. He reluctantly followed her orders to go to the farmhouse down the road to seek shelter, but when he got there it was shut tight and vacant. He was in a worrisome situation, for it was nearing 6:00 p.m., and the sun of early April had already dipped over the hills.

Now really hungry, Mayor bicycled on and found a stone cabin. A dog barked, a sign that the dwelling was inhabited and he might find a meal and a bed. He went around back and rang the bell on his bicycle. "An old woman hobbled out calling 'Pardi! Pardi!' with a caved in grin." To his revulsion she was holding "a saucepan in her hand full of half-cooked greens that looked as tho the dog (at best) had licked it. She was bundled up in what seemed the scuffed-out feet of old stockings miraculously stitched together." Realizing she didn't understand his French, he pointed and asked directions to Carpendras. "She picked off the scabby incrustations from her cheek-bones to see me better & started the strangest lingua franca ever, which I could make out thickly thru Spanish & Italian." He recognized enough words to learn where the road began.

What followed his escape from the elderly woman brought him to the edge of terror. As Mayor pushed his bicycle over the crest of a hill, he found the road and began to ride. But the road turned treacherous, and he had moments of panic when, coasting down into a ravine, his brakes failed. He was going too fast to throw himself off. "The bicycle began to sail faster & faster, grip the brakes I would. It began to take stones & ruts with a mind of its own & run away with me." In the waning light, he glimpsed the rocky crags "through of the corner of my windy-weeping eyes as the bicycle swooped & lurched at stones & swerved over the dry stream below." Suddenly he found himself in a great valley, and he was able to fling himself onto the grass "& tremble in comfort." But with the dark settling in, he needed a place in a town to lay his head.

Once calm, he found Venasque on his map and continued on his journey. As it emerged he saw "a castle suspended on the airy promontory of an undercut cliff; as fantastic as a landscape of the 16th century school of Brussels." He climbed up to find in the town "a delicious tiny 'Grand Place,' irregular, & in the center a fountain of a globe of stone spouting four streams." A meal and a bed seemed at hand at last, for behind the fountain was an inn. He went to the door "& asked for a room & dinner. A sulky woman said she had no rooms & could give me nothing to eat. She said it was no use having a hotel in Venasque because tho many people came to see the place, no one ever stopped." In 1926, the area of Provence spanning from the Abbaye de Sénanque to Venasque held no provision for tourists.

There was nothing else to do but to push on in the dark. Ultimately in St. Didier Mayor saw "a light shining on round cafe tables & chairs. Inside was a deserted billiard table & forlorn electric bulbs, but they had a room, and so to bed."

Mayor was a young man, and his day became for him a memorable adventure. He wrote soon afterward that nothing else in Provence quite compared to "that glorious first day." And no published writing compares to his vivid and blunt travel account in his 1926 journal describing the hills of Provence. The Gordes he saw was a ruin, the famed bories of today were unknown, the Provençal language seemed impenetrable, Venasque sheltered no tourists, and St. Didier, while open for business, was a sad little place. The region of Provence he delineated was then merely back country.

There was a major exception in his telling. In 1926, the Pont du Gard was such a well-traveled site that Mayor had the reverse of the difficulties he had experienced on his trip from Gordes to St. Didier. He found there a "chic restaurant hidden in the trees so as not to spoil the view with a house." But, it was in fact "so chic

they would hardly serve me, all dusty & rained upon." He was ultimately able to lunch there and afterward lay on the rocks to admire
the great aqueduct anew.

Mayor also examined Roman ruins unknown in the time of Jefferson or James, those in Vaison-la-Romaine, northeast of Avignon.
As he watched workmen excavating what had been a Roman town,
Mayor was handed one of their findings to keep. It was "a little piece
of glass as iridescent as a decayed sardine." It was likely an invitation, for subsequently the workers offered to sell him four Roman
coins. Finding them "pretty clear & well struck," Mayor bought
them. Today, the Roman ruins of Vaison, one of the most significant archeological sites in France, are highly protected. In 1926,
however, nothing there was sacrosanct.

More than forty years later, following Mayor's career as a curator at New York's Metropolitan Museum of Art and an important
writer on prints and drawings, he was interviewed for the Archives
of American Art. He recalled his delight in biking in Provence:
"In the Twenties when the roads were empty it was a great way
to travel. I hired a bicycle once in Avignon in the spring . . . for
a week[,] where it was so exceptional to have a tourist that I was
arrested as a suspicious character."[16]

Actually Mayor was merely stopped for questioning after he
went up to two gendarmes in a small village to ask if he could enter
the grounds of a chateau. One of them challenged him to present
his papers. Mayor gave him his passport. "He looked very grave &
said: 'Rien que ça?'" Mayor had been traveling without the *carte
d'identité* required for a stay of more than fifteen days. Peppered
with questions, Mayor put on his best manner and explained the
nature of his trip. The gendarmes agreed that if his possessions
backed up his story, they might let him off. They looked at everything, including his journal. This "amused them both & I said that
it held most learned & valuable notes on architecture of the Midi,
which was the most beautiful in France. Or perhaps I said it was
the most beautiful in the world—at any rate, it worked." As the two
men let him go, they offered to treat him to a beer.

One additional element of Mayor's journal holds special interest. During the week, an American acquaintance also on university break unexpectedly appeared. Mayor spent a day with him and the lad's mother as they motored by auto to the Camargue, south of Arles. As Mayor looked out the car window, he found himself repeatedly exclaiming, "How like a Van Gogh!" In his journal for March 30, he expanded in this reaction: "There are his torch-flame spirals of dried grass, his gouty trees with rheumatic joints here & there. The soil is peppered in parts with snarled states of grape vines in rows to the horizon, shrinking smaller & smaller to dots. His landscapes are not fantasies. It is all there, but what a genius it took to see it."

As glorious as were the Roman ruins, much of inland Provence lay undeveloped for travel, and many of its sites undiscovered at the time of Hyatt Mayor's 1926 trip. Away from the cities and the established sites, he found a very rough land that he was young and tough enough to experience as adventure. Additionally his eyes were opened by the art becoming admired in his era. Other travelers may have focused on the work of Paul Cézanne, but for Mayor, the paintings of Vincent van Gogh helped prepare the way.[17] Both artists were to have a profound impact on Provence's unanticipated future.

That future would not come, however, until after World War II. In 1935, in the midst of the Great Depression, Provence attracted American attention in a book that both celebrated the region and delineated its less appealing features—Ford Madox Ford's *Provence: From Mistrals to the Machine*.[18] Ford brought to the work strong credentials. He had long appreciated Provence and was, in some ways, born to it as the son of Francis Hueffer, a German who made his career in Britain writing on music and the Provençal troubadours. By young manhood, Ford had experienced much travel on the Continent and become a Catholic. Following World War I, he legally changed his name from Ford Hermann Hueffer to

Ford Madox Ford, echoing the name of his mother's famous British father, the pre-Raphaelite painter Ford Madox Brown. A member of the avant-garde artistic and literary world in Paris, England, and the United States, Ford wrote and published prolifically and fostered the new work of many others. By 1935, he was coming to the end of his long and well-published writing career that spanned more than four and a half decades. His *Provence* is a strange, albeit oddly insightful, book on the region. It is difficult to know its broader influence when published because, given its author's reputation and readership, probably anything from his pen would have been touted in the press.

In interesting and unusual ways Provence had long figured in Ford's life and novels, and in this work, written near the end of his long life, he attempted to pull together his feelings and deep associations with the region. Neither a guidebook nor a memoir, his book has been characterized as a work of literary Impressionism. It is an attempt to get at "the frame of mind that is Provence," presenting Ford's subjective sense of a place, culture, and people.[19]

It is a hardly perfect work, containing sections that are tedious and indecipherable, and is, as one writer put it, among other attributes, "a completely engaging act of self-indulgence."[20] But Ford did bring important insights about southern France to an American audience. Scattered throughout are testaments to Provence as Eden, although they are Ford's own idiosyncratic version of humanity's biblical first home.

Ford saw the Provençal land offering its bounty, freely and wildly. "The olive there gives its oil; the vine lets down the grape and its juices; the hills are alive with hares, boars and, in thousands, with the *grive*, the partridge, and the ortolan. Garlic there grows wild amongst all the other potherbs."[21] He himself grew vegetables and believed in good cooking with spices as essential to civilization. But oddly enough, even with his love of garlic, Ford denigrated the cuisine of Provence. At one level, he simply did not like cooking with oil, preferring butter or goose fat. But it was more than that.

In his judgment, a traveler to the region, unlike to other parts of France, would "never . . . be able to enter an unknown town and go into any restaurant with any certainty of good food." Except along the Mediterranean shore—that in another passage Ford claimed as outside the real Provence—"Provence has no regional dishes and the true Provençal has neither the gift, nor the patience nor yet the materials that are necessary for the serious cook."[22]

Provence contains an eccentric history of the region, informed by deep knowledge but crosshatched with digressions into the author's peculiar views of London and British history, along with anecdotes of his experiences with people and places. What underlies the work is Ford's understanding of the "Great Trade Route," along which merchants brought goods and civilization from Asia to England and ultimately to the Americas via Provence. He posits that in the wake of this world-changing force came all the good and evil of past and present.[23] Although Ford's vision was eccentric, his statement of it contains passages that glow. What drew Ford to Provence was something almost mystical. In Provence he saw not the turbulence of his times but a glimpse, through the region's ancientness, of the eternal.[24]

Much of the book was thus written from memory. He wrote he did not doubt "that illusion that made my first sight of Provence the most memorable sensation of my life and makes my every renewal of contact with those hills where grows the first olive tree of the South almost as memorable. It is as if one wakened from a dream of immortality to the realization of what is earthly permanence."[25] Provence also represented an antidote to the morality that Ford scorned. A libertine by all accounts, Ford's Eden was a world in which the concept of sin, as known in the Anglo-American world, was banished. Yet Ford also saw that life in this Paradise had its risks and dangers. "Provence will always have its three flails . . . *Le Parlement, le Mistral et la Durance,* . . . the dire river that with sudden and utterly unforeseeable disaster floods the whole valley of the Rhone."[26]

But there was also history and art, which, along with government and nature, shaped the Provençal temperament. He admired painting in Provence with its proletarian as well as elite roots. He believed that, because Provence missed the Gothic period in sculpture and architecture, its ancient buildings reflected only the "jovial and the libidinous." There are no grotesques in Provence, only "traditions of beauty, discipline, frugality and artistic patience."[27]

In the region's bullfights, Ford saw a reflection of that sudden turn of fate that the Provençaux frequently experienced. He believed that bred into the people of Provence was a certain cunning. Facing all he has had to face, "the Provençal being a fatalist is by nature conservative." He plays the game of *boules* and goes to his bullfights, immune to politics and to conquerors. The true Provençal is the male peasant working his patch of land, seeing nature as his "little squares in the orange, sun-baked earth." This piece of nature is littered with the ruins of the Roman Empire, a shrine, a Venus, a "stone chest with a curious ribbon pattern that once held the ashes of a paladin who died beside Roland at Roncevaux." Ford imagined the man working his field as self-sufficient in the wine made from his own grapes, the oil from the olives he gathered, the vegetables he grew, and the cheese from the milk of his goats.[28]

Toward the end of his book, Ford wrote that, on a bus to Nîmes, in a crowd of peasants going to a bullfight, he saw "a grim, incredibly ancient *mas*—a bare, baked farm-house that seems for ever to slide off a small pinnacle of rock more bare and more baked," and he decided to inhabit it.[29] He hoped that by residing in that house, he could realize his dream of living a life of subsistence on the land. But when the mistral blew his money away, Ford found he had to return to his craft to write another book in order to survive. And thus *Provence* came to be.[30]

The book was published to acclaim. In the *New York Times*, the reviewer called it "a new and exciting interpretation. . . . a superb evocation of Provence." It was written, in Noel Sauvage's words, not only with "unbounded enthusiasm" but also "with the deep comprehension of Provence and the thorough familiarity with its people that years of residence there have given him."[31] But as appealing to the literary world as was Ford's *Provence* at the time of its publication, the region he described could hardly entice many Americans to find their way there. The sun may have been shining and the land filled with seasonal bounty, but the cuisine was unappealing; the peasants, impoverished; and the life Ford led, far too rough to be inviting.

Laurence Wylie
and the Authentic
Provence

Laurence Wylie's French friends were astounded at his decision in 1950 to live for a year with his family in Roussillon, a small village about thirty miles east of Avignon perched on ochre cliffs in that part of the Vaucluse known as the Luberon. Such an opportunity today might call for a murmur of delight from those who know Roussillon as a beautiful site and an important destination for tourists. But at the time of Wylie's sojourn, seemingly little had changed since Ford Madox Ford's era. Economic development in France after World War II went elsewhere, to the north, keeping inland Provence depressed and many of its people discouraged. Despite the favorable mention of Roussillon's houses as forming "un ensemble pittoresque" in the 1949 *Provence, Côte d'Azur* volume of the Guides Bleus, Wylie's friends wondered how he could choose to spend a year in "a small, isolated community with neither modern comforts nor cultural facilities!"[1]

Wylie was an American professor of French studies who underwent training in anthropological methods. Out of his observations during that year, Wylie produced *Village in the Vaucluse* (1957), and because of its graceful prose and insights into a traditional French world the book was the making of his distinguished career. Its many American readers, however, could only concur with Wylie's French friends, for in his book he described Roussillon as a backward place that no one would choose for a pleasurable time in France. The Provençal village he presented was no Eden.

Instead his Roussillon was "authentic." Its people were decent but rough. They lived very close to the margin in cramped houses, largely without indoor water closets, running water, or electricity. They tossed trash and sewage, including human waste, down the village's beautiful ochre cliffs. The seeming "comfort and security" of Roussillon—that could be observed even then by a casual outside visitor on a Sunday afternoon—was "achieved only by hard work, constant worry, vigilance, and ingenuity."[2]

Wylie lived in the village center as a participant observer. He volunteered in the schools. His wife and two young boys broadened his access, opening wide the world of women and children. Renaming the town Peyrane, Wylie distilled his observations and organized his material for the book to follow the life course, beginning with childhood. In contrast to permissive American parents, he saw those of Peyrane rearing their children to obey. Adults taught them to keep themselves and their clothing clean and to avoid breaking their few toys. The primary school required not only obedience but stillness. The community gave adolescents a period of freedom, even hell raising, but after this, as young men and women, they were expected to settle down and become *sérieux*, meaning that they were to work, marry, have children, and act responsibly.

Life in the village meant propinquity but not true community. Though deeply connected by place, its residents were divided by intense animosities, exacerbated by politics. With some of their neighbors, they were *brouillé*, on the outs, and had broken off social relations. With a few, they were *bien*, on friendly terms. But with others, they were neither, and these neighbors were simply ignored. Living in a small, compact setting, those in Peyrane kept within their families. Although some of the men met at noon and in the early evening to enjoy an aperitif and talk, Wylie understood that they sustained such regular amicable relations only by cultivating a social self that hid any real feelings. Women visited less in public and more in small, intimate sewing circles in their homes or gardens. Life was hard, and, as they faced it, villagers were stoic. A woman told Wylie that all, but especially those of her sex, were "born to work and suffer." Men commonly spoke of this "bitch of a life."[3]

Villagers talked of national and regional government and bureaucracy as "ils," or "they"—forces that impinged on them from the outside and were "dangerous" because they were "anonymous, intangible, and overpowering." *Ils* caused harm through red tape, restrictions, taxes, and inflation. The general sense was that once a person attained power, for example by being voted into office, he became evil. Villagers labeled officials "a pile of bandits." All this had to be accepted because, as they said, "That's the way it is." Among other *ils* were newspapers, corporations, and Americans. In this post–World War II world, distrust was rife. It took Wylie a long time to remove himself from suspicion. When he first joined the aperitif circle at the café, political talk stopped, for villagers believed he was there to plan an American invasion.[4]

The café served as a place for male patrons only. However, one night a week it turned itself into a movie house and welcomed women. Algerians who mined the ochre were also part of the film audience (otherwise they remain unmentioned in the book and seemingly invisible to Wylie). Normally the villagers watched the weekly film with little emotional reaction or conversation at its close. One exception was *Marius*, the 1932 Marcel Pagnol film—it attracted a large, animated crowd, many of whom had previously seen it as many as eight or ten times. In thinking about the movie's popularity and the reactions of the villagers, Wylie noted that César, the Marseille barkeeper at the center of the film, was a person who protected "his tender feelings by directing witty shafts at the people of whom he is most fond." Wylie judged that in César were "the humor and pathos of the southern French stereotype."[5]

Wylie believed that the moviegoers in the village saw *Marius* as reflecting their own experiences. He concluded, "It would be hard to imagine a people more realistic than the people of Peyrane. 'C'est comme ça' is the phrase that is most frequently on their

3 Laurence Wylie's authentic Roussillon. "Francis Favre at his plumber's bench." Laurence Wylie, *Village in the Vaucluse*, 1964 edition, opposite 174.

4 Laurence Wylie's authentic Roussillon. "Madame Prayal washes lettuce." Laurence Wylie, *Village in the Vaucluse*, 1964 edition, opposite 174.

lips." Throughout their lives, they faced many pressures—from the outside forces of nature and government to the personal problems posed by physical ailments, family conflicts, the difficulties of meeting the standards of the community, and the complications of getting along with others. "Although they complain about the problems of life," Wylie wrote, "from childhood they have learned to face them."[6]

Already by 1950 Roussillon housed more than year-long residents. The pride that urban French people took in their roots in the countryside led a few of them to keep a second residence in their natal place, even in one as depressed as Roussillon. But these *estivants*, as they were called, normally spent only a few summer weeks in the village. This left their second homes vacant for most of the year, helping to cause the housing shortage that forced young adults to live with their parents, even after marriage. In an example, Wylie wrote of the largest house, sitting right in the village's center, owned by an architect from Moulins, a city in central France. In the summer he went to Brittany and came to Provence only during the Easter vacation to "get away from the rainy north to camp out in the Peyrane [i.e., Roussillon] house for a few days." For the remaining part of the year, the house stood "vacant and gloomy."[7] It was a fitting symbol for much that ailed Roussillon, a village that, in 1950, Laurence Wylie believed to be "without a future."[8]

As Wylie's French friends suggested, Roussillon, his *Village in the Vaucluse*, was a backward place, one that a traveler would hardly choose for a pleasurable time in France.

THREE

France, Yes!
But Provence?

I

Ironically, when Laurence Wylie's *Village in the Vaucluse* was finding readers after garnering strong reviews, France was beginning to
actively promote American tourism in Provence, "where Louis XIV
lived like a king . . . and you can too—for $9.50 a day—complete!" A
reader flipping through *Holiday* magazine couldn't miss the advertisements attempting to lure travelers to areas of France beyond
Paris, supported by the French Government Tourist Office.[1] In May
1957, the text of an ad picturing the Riviera suggested moving from
there to Les Baux, a site in Provence known for its famous medieval
ruins and castle sitting atop a rocky outcrop, with the suggestive
words "romance . . . by moonlight."[2] At the height of this effort,
in April 1960, a two-page spread of color photographs lured vacationers to a stay in Provence in the Hostellerie de l'Abbaye de la
Celle with the enticing reference to Louis XIV and the attractive
day rate. (At the time, a small hotel room without a bath in the Left
Bank of Paris cost less than a third of that price.) The ad's large photographs caught the joy of a female model posing as a tourist acting
like a queen in her castle, triumphing on the bed (in full dress),
swimming in the antique pool fed by fresh water, and dining by can-
dlelight opposite an older man in its romantic "grand salon beamed
with olive wood." "Fortunately for the imaginative traveler," the ad
touted, "most of the French provinces are still off the beaten track."[3]

What provoked this effort by the French government was the realization that tourism in the provinces offered economic opportunity for the nation's deserted regions combined with relief from the swarms of Americans who flooded into Paris each summer. By the late 1950s, anti-Americanism was swelling in Paris. Americans brought needed dollars to France, but they also crowded out local residents and created discomfort. As one historian has said about American visitors of an earlier era, American tourists tended to act "as if Paris existed solely for their own enjoyment," a sentiment that stung proud Parisians.[4]

Americans had long had a love affair with Paris. Immediately following its liberation from the Germans after World War II, with words such as "I'd like to see Paris before I die" in their heads, they began to dream again of travel there. For many, the hiatus had been much too lengthy. First had come the Depression, severely affecting France as well as keeping many Americans at home, and then the Nazi occupation and long, brutal war. But except for those working to rebuild the ravaged nation—or report on these efforts—France had to remain off limits for a while. Much repair had to be done before prewar patterns of leisure and travel could be reestablished.

In the aftermath of the war, the French government understood that American tourism offered a major route to recovery, and the United States was more than cooperative. The Marshall Plan provided much of the means. The US government aided the French by offering relief in the present and the resources to help spur modernization for the future. Behind US generosity was the calculation that a strong France could be an ally against the Soviet Union and the spread of Communism. Within the larger American effort, tourism offered a means to three goals—economic stimulus, a model for planning, and increasing contact to ease anti-American feeling.[5]

Yet, initially, as Americans returned to normal life after the war, their attention was on the United States. Whatever their dreams for the future, both travel and travel literature in the early postwar era reflected this. When *Holiday* opened with its first real issue in 1946, it focused on domestic travel. As Richard Popp has made clear, the magazine itself was an artifact of the new field of marketing. Its parent company, Curtis, identified a group of consumers with discretionary income who could be appealed to through targeted advertising. *Holiday*, its name chosen to imply leisure and fun, was consciously built to attract ads related both to travel and to the consumer goods associated with it and other kinds of pleasures.[6] States, such as North Carolina, dominated early travel advertising, promoting their vacation destinations alongside ads from the railroads promising to take visitors there.

By 1947, with reconstruction proceeding apace, France was gearing up for American travelers. An ad placed by the French National Tourist Office in American magazines—"Dear France; Thank you for a lovely vacation"—was designed to reassure the wary. It offered testimonials by well-traveled Americans returning to the place they had known and loved. "You haven't lived until you've seen Paris" read a caption under a photograph of café-goers. Not only do the trains run and the hotels house, the "resorts are gay" and the "casinos amuse." The ad promised a France that offered "vacation *completeness* unknown elsewhere in the world."[7]

Yet reality had a way of intervening, even unintentionally. American travelers may have wanted to dress like the elegant fashion models in the handsome tailored suits portrayed in a travel piece on what to wear abroad in 1948, but cautions in the boldface headings of the article's text would have made them pause: "Transport and fuel are short"; "Europe Still Has its Queues"; and "Clothing is Still Rationed." The images illustrating the text showed a Europe no one would want to visit—citizens hovering around a coal dump to get their meager supplies, crowds jamming access to trains, and long lines out in the street for restaurant service.[8]

So it came as no surprise that in his initial foray into travel literature, *Footloose in France*, published in 1948, Horace Sutton was unsparing in his criticism of the myriad ways that postwar conditions and French customs made life miserable for American tourists. Nonetheless he had the knack of inspiring Americans to make the trip and offering them the information they wanted. The

French National Tourist Office gave Sutton its full cooperation and had its agent in North America place all its "facilities" at his "disposal," including planning his itinerary, providing him with background materials, and giving him a personal guide in each of the French regions. It is likely that service in Army Intelligence during the war didn't hurt Sutton's investigative abilities either.[9]

Once Sutton began his descriptions of Paris (to which he devoted fifty pages) and the French regions, he was generally enthusiastic. He had the touch, honed in the advertising department of the *New York Post* before the war, of making the reader feel comfortable. Not for him was high-flown guidebook language, replete with architectural detail. For Sutton, "travelers were everybody," and he consciously sought to make his writing entertaining.[10] His book proved not only enjoyable but useful, for the *Guide Michelin* allowed him to abridge its forthcoming edition of star-rated hotels and restaurants and add it to the book.

In the next few years Americans began to venture abroad again as ships and planes returned to civilian use, economic growth in the United States allowed more distant travel, and postwar reconstruction advanced in Europe. France was a typical choice, for more than any other nation, it drew visitors from outside its borders. France had long held a special place in the imaginations of Americans as the pinnacle of civilization. Knowing the French language was a mark of culture for the eastern elite of the United States, and partaking of the country's cuisine and wines afforded status along with pleasure. For generations Paris had been a mecca for American travelers seeking art and high-end goods; leading society women had been known to take an annual pilgrimage to its couture houses for the upcoming season's gowns. More ordinary Americans saw it as a beautiful city with important monuments, outdoor cafés, and great restaurants.[11]

For the French public, American admiration in the years immediately after World War II was both a mark of pride—a demonstration of *rayonnement,* or national radiance—and a source of hope for

the future.[12] Tourism emerged as a major element in restarting the
French economy. Early in the postwar years the economic returns
from tourists were "the equivalent of over four-fifths the value of all
goods that France exported."[13] In 1949, for example, Americans who
traveled to France spent $65 million, a sum in the range of $1.9 bil-
lion in today's dollars.[14] At this time cooperation between the governments of France and the United States was perceived as mutually
beneficial to the self-interest of both nations. France defined tourism as an industry, enabling it to get resources from the central economic plan. The Marshall Plan gave funds for the initial campaigns of
the European Travel Commission. The French Government Tourist Office set up shop on Fifth Avenue in New York to run its public
relations campaigns and to work with New York advertising firms.[15]
The early ads it commissioned were modest—in black and white and
taking only part of a page—looking quite like ads placed by states
such as North Carolina and Florida. But change was in the offing.

By the 1950s, American citizens were doing their full part with
little official prompting. American movies, such as *An American in
Paris* (1951) and *Sabrina* (1954), gave France a special place, as the
imagined backdrop of high romance, artistic greatness, and personal makeovers. To the elder it was "Gay Paree." To the young and
venturesome, it was the world of Sartre and free love. To families,
it was the Eiffel Tower. American travelers crossed the Atlantic as
quickly as the combination of personal finances and transportation
systems allowed. By 1950, more than 250,000 traveled to France
each year. The numbers rose to almost 800,000 a decade later.[16]

Fueling this was a major change in how Americans got to France.
New luxury ships joined existing ocean liners, and to advertise
them the French Line commissioned brightly colored full-page ads.
Their message was pleasure and indulgence, the "French flair for
living in all classes." For example, in the February 1951 issue of *Holiday* the French Line trumpeted "Your Gay Entrée to Europe" and
pictured a bottle of expensive Bordeaux, alongside a glass of wine,
cheese, crackers, apples, a wine list, a cigarette in an ashtray, and a
vase of flowers.[17]

Although the six-day passage across the Atlantic was treasured by some in the pampered upper class and by students below deck, it was air travel that transformed Americans' visits to France. Despite what the ads of ocean liners promised, those adults who endured lesser accommodations on cabin ships had reason to dread the crossing, and travel by sea was costly in time for all. The first planes were in the air by 1946, offering luxury service by 1947, but they were expensive and hardly comfortable. Initially, even the wealthy who could afford to fly preferred ocean liners because propeller planes were noisy and bumpy and required three stops for refueling. In 1952, tourist class began on planes, and the price of flying went down. Although discomforts remained, the air carriers' speed sent travel numbers upward, for planes allowed upper middle-class travelers limited to three-week vacations to get to Europe and back.[18]

In 1958 came the most important change—jet planes. An intense advertising campaign prepared the way. "What will it be like to fly in a jet?" an ad for the DC-8 asked, then answered, "You climb steadily, serenely, quietly." Up, at seven miles above the earth, traveling a half mile at every breath, "you sense a tranquility, a detached peacefulness, a freedom of spirit."[19] When *Vogue* sent its travel editor to cover the first nonstop transatlantic jet flight to Paris, she wrapped her experience in the breathless prose of travel journalism in her era. As Mary Roblee described the takeoff in her piece, "In the Jet Set, New York to Paris in a Boeing 707," she echoed and elaborated the advertising of the airlines. "The rev-up came with a furious rush of wind that seemed to speed us down the strip," she wrote, "then, with the smooth leap of a greased gazelle, the jet sprang into the sky." What impressed her most was the quiet that followed. "Floating higher, softly and unperceptively, the jet tuned to its own orchestration: an obbligato curiously reminiscent of flutes in a Debussy tone poem rather than the Wagnerian thunder of piston-engined planes."[20]

On her particular flight she experienced a disappointing stop for refueling, made necessary by the full capacity of her plane and accompanying headwinds. But, she reassured readers, no stop would be necessary next year, when passengers would see "bigger, newer jets." In addition, at Idlewild Airport (renamed JFK in 1963), there were soon to be "protected boarding ramps straight into the plane." But even with a smaller plane and the need to go outside to board, the new jet service was "fast, new, untiring." Oozing pleasure, Roblee exclaimed, "Paris and the jet are a potent mix and, admittedly, one of the more lovable ways of working."[21]

Between 1958 and 1960, the number of Americans who traveled to France rose by more than a quarter million.[22] To accommodate the growing numbers, large hotels emerged on the periphery of Paris. American travelers had long criticized the smaller hotels of France, with their cramped rooms, communal bathrooms, and quirky service. The French government supported the construction of new, American-style hotels to handle large numbers, give guests en suite bathrooms, and offer American breakfasts and rapid service lunches. Oddly enough, given international respect for French cuisine, meals were a major source of disquiet among many from the United States in the 1950s and 1960s. Although eager to view the Eiffel Tower, they desired the familiarity of home food to sustain them.[23]

Often travelers made their way to Paris as part of a larger trip that included other important capital cities in Europe. Many took advantage of the package coach tours that would move them, in some cases very quickly, from place to place. For independent travelers, Eurail passes allowed reduced fares for traveling not only within France but also to other countries, such as Switzerland, Italy, Spain, and Portugal.

Beginning sometime in the 1950s, officials in the French tourist industry began to realize that the historical emphasis on *rayonnement* and the high-end American traveler needed rethinking. Earlier generations of the wealthy had made the pilgrimage to Europe in search of culture as well as couture. Belief that one should absorb the best that was thought and said in the world—and composed and painted—shaped trip planning around museums and concerts, as well as fine restaurants and shops. Keeping this in mind when prosperity began to return, France polished up its buildings, constructed new museums and refurbished older ones. But for Americans on tour, taking in a lot in a relatively short time meant emphasis on the major sites of each place, with little chance to linger beyond snapping a photograph to jog the memory or show to family and friends. Many of those able to stay a bit longer sought amusements more to their taste—the Folies Bergère and nightclubs or boats on the Seine. In all this, where was French culture—its radiance? Unquestionably the Louvre was on the list of sites to see in Paris. But was it visited only to catch a glimpse and take a photo of the Mona Lisa?[24]

II

By the late 1950s, France was well into Les Trente Glorieuses, the thirty glorious years between 1946 to 1975 of rising economic growth. But, of course, prosperity hit unequally, leaving many regions behind. To stimulate sluggish areas, the French government began a campaign to encourage travel into France beyond Paris and in seasons other than summer. *Holiday* cooperated and devoted a special issue to France in 1957, stacking the deck with well-known French and American writers who discussed aspects of France's culture.[25] Stanford University's Albert Guérard, a prominent scholar of French civilization, contributed the piece "France and America"; the well-known French writer André Maurois offered "The Forty Immortals"; and British theater critic Kenneth Tynan wrote on "The Richest Theater." There was an article on France's many different regions that did the subject little justice, but this lack was more than made up for by the accompanying photographs. In them, all seemed to glow in summer's sunshine. *Holiday* was perfecting the art of using images to convey to the future traveler the "ultimate geographic essence" of a place, planting scenes in the reader's mind to be remembered and relived when actually there.[26] Its most resplendent picture was the full-page photograph of the produce market in the heart of Aix-en-Provence, captured from above, with dappled sunlight filtering through tall plane trees.[27]

Such attention was sorely needed. But more was called for than just a mention and photograph. What Provence required was a new definition. During the early years after the war, when Paris was at the center, Provence was not off the tourist map, but it remained stuck in its earlier mold as the place of Roman ruins.

For example, in "Europe's Still There," an illustrated 1946 article in *Holiday* magazine, Edward M. Strode attempted to counter the prevailing image of wartime destruction by discussing those parts of the continent not damaged. As he turned to the hills of Provence, he stated that the region was largely intact. As he did so, he reminded readers, in much the manner of older guidebooks, of the region's Roman ruins in "almost every town and village" and its role as the gateway to the Riviera.[28]

One piece offers insights into the general understanding of Provence beyond the ruins, but perhaps quite unintentionally. George Millar, then known for *Maquis*, his book on the French Resistance, wrote a 1947 account in *Holiday* of his honeymoon trip through inland waterways on a sailboat initially bound for the Riviera. On the way he encountered Provence and had this to say: "When we tied up we heard the crickets in the plane trees and the strange accent of the Midi from loafers who drank cloudy *pastisses* in the bars." Near Marseille, there was boat trouble. "The mistral, the northwest wind from the Rhône valley that is the scourge of the Mediterranean littoral, was blowing sharply while the sun shone. Our stern came high out of the water and our rudder split."[29] That a writer with such deep experience in the region could pen such stereotypes is interesting in itself, but, more to the point for a travel magazine article, the words would hardly lead readers to venture to areas of Provence north of the Mediterranean.

Then, in 1948, with fanfare, *Holiday* commissioned Ludwig Bemelmans to write and illustrate an extensive series of travel pieces. Bemelmans was an American writer born in Europe who was best known for his Madeleine books for children. One article was set in

Arles. In "Mademoiselle Regrets," Bemelmans, a well-known gourmet, wrote lightheartedly of his gustatory experience there. It was,
however, a story of two failures, hardly inspiring a desire to travel to
Provence. First, knowing that the "*Guide Michelin* lists no famous
restaurant in this region," he followed the recommendation of his
taxi driver to a modest establishment, where he ordered the Arles
speciality of sausage made of donkey meat. What mademoiselle
regretted was that this "vrai saucisson" was no longer available. He
had to make due with a sausage made of pork, along with service
best characterized as casual. Fortunately, his meal was balanced by
local drama. Seated outside, he watched a man tie a horse to a tree,
draw a crowd, and then offer champagne to everyone in the restaurant in honor of his new horse.[30]

The second disappointment that Bemelmans faced was the total
absence in Arles of Van Gogh. Not only were none of his paintings
to be found in the town, he was lost to memory. In the restaurant,
Bemelmans inquired after Van Gogh's house with no result, then
asked a taxi driver, who apologized that "he didn't know of whom
I spoke." When Bemelmans went to the hospital where Van Gogh
was treated after slicing off part of his ear and where he painted both
its garden and his famous self-portrait with the bandaged ear, "the
doorkeeper said he did not know anyone by that name, and asked
whether he had been a patient there recently." Working against the
text, however, was Bemelmans's drawing. His visual representation of an Arles scene offered a temptation to travel there, along
with his evocation in the text of the reality behind Van Gogh's landscapes. The words Bemelmans used to describe Van Gogh and the
sky and landscape were reminiscent of those of A. Hyatt Mayor in
the 1920s: "The brightness of the large sun over Arles explains his
brilliant palette; the tortured trees that appear in his paintings still
stand there, the water is his blue, and his yellow is smeared on fields
as if it were pressed out of a tube."[31]

If Millar gave readers negative impressions about Provence, and
Bemelmans left them ambivalent, Sutton's approach to the region
in his 1948 *Footloose in France* was typically more robust. When

he got to the South of France, he peeled Provence from the glitzy Riviera, the playground of the international rich. The Provence he described in twenty pages was "one of the most individual and little known corners of France." He likened it to Italy, Palestine, and "no other place on earth." But again, what made this "mostly dry, scrubby, rocky, arid land" important was one thing—its Roman ruins.[32]

Suggesting either Avignon or Nîmes as a base, Sutton took the reader on a verbal jaunt through the ruins, blending description, history—including its role in the late war—and easy-to-take detail. When considering the Roman aqueduct outside of Nîmes, for example, he discussed the graffiti left by visitors. "I would like to report to Fanny, Jeanne, and Alex that their notice, painted in 1936, is showing signs of weather and M. Blanc's inscription nicked right into the stone back in 1860 looks a little moth-eaten too."[33] Yet, however jovial his descriptions, all remained in the traditional vein of travel writing on Provence. The region was essentially an outdoor museum of Roman antiquity.

Most of the housing and food information lay in the back of the book, in the abridged Michelin pages. But Sutton offered a small amount of practical help in the text, giving names and a bit of information on hotels and restaurants, especially in Nîmes and Avignon. The one exception, with a photograph, was the new l'Oustau de Baumanière in Les Baux, already holding two Michelin stars and soon to be the first restaurant in Provence to gain the precious three. Sutton described it as "chic and expensive," attracting "a smart crowd who motor up from Marseille for a swim in the pool and lunch in the cactus-bordered patio. Speciality of the house: canapés of fish eggs and an oily butter mixed to a mash, and spread on bread."[34] Probably not something many of his readers were likely to try.

If much of what was written about the hills of Provence suggested a place less than inviting to most Americans, this was about to change. Waiting in the wings were writers who imagined a region capable of enticing American travelers.

FOUR   # Preparing the Way to
            # Provence for Postwar
            # Travelers

Change happens in many ways. In the case of inland Provence, changing Americans' perception of the region from the place of Roman ruins to one of complex delights took several decades and many actors. Among them were the heralds in the wilderness, travel writers eager to gain an audience. But preceding them were the artists—and more important, their work. In a sense, their paintings of Provence became a critical part of the landscape the travel writers described.

The cultured world knew that Henri Matisse chose Nice, and Pablo Picasso, Cannes; and their works conveyed the colors and the light of the South of France. But these places were on the Côte d'Azur. Paul Cézanne, however, lived much of his life in Aix-en-Provence, and Vincent van Gogh ended his days in Arles and Saint-Rémy-de-Provence. These two artists went beyond depicting light and color to capture essential aspects of the hills of Provence—the solidity of its rocks, the special look of its inhabitants, the mass of its buildings, and the impact of its mistral. As early as the 1920s, in the mind of a young A. Hyatt Mayor, Van Gogh portrayed the reality of the Provençal landscape.

Cézanne was an important inspiration to a number of American artists who chose to live in France in the interwar years, including Arthur Dove, Stanton MacDonald-Wright, and Thomas Hart Benton. Marsden Hartley even moved into Maison Maria, a house in

Aix where Cézanne painted many of his important works.[1] In the years following World War II, a larger consciousness in the United States of Cézanne's work came in the wake of important exhibitions of his paintings, especially the comprehensive showing jointly organized by the Art Institute of Chicago and the Metropolitan Museum of Art in 1952.[2]

In this exhibit as in others, critics discussed Cézanne's vision and craft and marked his artistic innovations as a precursor of modernism. As the great Columbia University art historian Meyer Schapiro wrote in a foreword to the catalogue for *Cézanne: Loan Exhibition* in 1959, Cézanne "has given an impulse directly or indirectly to almost every new movement since he died."[3] But to some viewers his paintings also sent subliminal messages about place. In many of his paintings Cézanne portrayed a rural life in the hills so deep it seemed primordial—the pale stone *mas* with its thick walls set against brightly colored vegetation and vivid sky, the rough wooden tables and chairs, pottery bowls of the region holding succulent fruit, and the stern faces of a proud people pursuing their simple pleasures. To those immersed in urban or suburban life and the conflicting demands of the 1950s, these path-breaking paintings may have promised a world outside of time and modernity.

I. THE VISITOR

As *Holiday* magazine broadened its base of writers, it often turned to authors from the United Kingdom, for travel writing held a firm place within British literature. Dreaming of traveling abroad, literate Americans easily found these authors' books, as they were typically published, promoted, and sold in the United States. Between their covers were words that helped lure tourists away from Paris—to places even as far away as Provence.

Reading British travel writers could lead to imbibing their longings. Out of England's long nights, damp and cloudy days, and tubercular coughs had emerged its dream of the South. Initially it encompassed the Mediterranean, the Italian Riviera and the Côte d'Azur on the southern edge of Provence. Queen Victoria spent winters in Nice, and her palatial accommodations still overlook the city. American expatriates Gerald and Sara Murphy followed in the 1920s, gathering on their stretch of the beach a legendary group of writers and artists, including Pablo Picasso. The draw of Nice, Cannes, Antibes, and Menton remains strong today, and the British have been joined there by Belgians, Germans, Scandinavians, and Americans. For a very long time, inland Provence was simply the place through which the French train ran as it rushed to the coast. And, if it was the famous Blue Train, from Paris to the Mediterranean, much of the region was traversed during the night.

Once the French began to experience some of the prosperity of the years following World War II, they discovered the land above the coast as a place of rural retreat; but this broad development became important to Americans only in subsequent decades. Those who brought a growing awareness of rural Provence to Americans were neither French artists nor the broader French public but rather writers from the United Kingdom or those with British connections. An important influence on some of these Brits were the laws affecting gay and bisexual men, more stringently enforced in the British Isles than in France. It was not until 1967 that homosexual acts began to be decriminalized in Britain and not until the early twenty-first century that homosexuality became fully legal there. The gay English art collector and historian Douglas Cooper may well have been speaking of more than the weather when he wrote to a friend in 1967 that his countrymen were "a grey people living in a grey country."[4]

Not all gay men from the United Kingdom were as fortunate as Cooper to have the riches to buy a grand chateau and to collect important works of modern art. Some, such as the writer James Pope-Hennessy, continued to live in England but sprinkled their lives with trips to the region. Pope-Hennessy felt such a strong pull to Provence that, as he put it, he "could never again let a year go by without travelling there for a few weeks at the least. Provence is a taste or more correctly a passion which once contracted cannot be cured. A nostalgia for it creeps over you each early springtime."[5] Pope-Hennessy distilled his notes from nine visits and his wide reading to produce in 1952 the modestly titled *Aspects of Provence*.

As Pope-Hennessy wrote about Provence's landscape and monuments, he replayed writings of earlier British and French travelers, sharing their admiration for history and Roman ruins. Following his genre's approach of organizing by place, not by period, meant that passages about the ruins pop up in almost every chapter. By turns Pope-Hennessy was a wise guide and a rueful observer who allowed readers into his many moods. Although some Americans may have been put off by the book's occasional wordiness, quotations in their original French, and obscure references, those who persisted absorbed themes that have shaped writing about Provence from the author's day forward.

For Pope-Hennessy it was the color and the light that drew him there. It was a region he felt could best be interpreted by paintings. As he ventured from place to place, he described many historic sites and the treasures to be found in museums, giving nods to the long history of the region. But he didn't labor over details. His was a mood piece that contrasted the loveliness of the landscape with some of the reality of its people, their emotionality, even their capacity for "considerable cruelty."[6] Unlike many other earlier travelers, he gloried not in the Mediterranean shore but in the rich variety of the many landscapes of the Provence hills.

He was determined to present a real place, not a prettified destination of the typical travel piece. His work is not propaganda from the French Government Tourist Office. His approach is clearest when he discussed Les Baux, the uninhabited ruins from the medieval period that lie south of Avignon. He began with giving a nineteenth-century British writer's riposte to the Murray guide. Les Baux was not, as Murray suggested, a medieval town but rather "purely ruinous, more like a decayed old cheese." Pope-Hennessy repeated this to chide the current *Guide Bleu*, which highly romanticized Les Baux and urged visitors to enjoy sundown there followed by a moonlight ramble on its rocks. Not only might such an excursion turn deadly, Pope-Hennessy warned, given the perilous nature of the ruins and the possibility of a raging mistral, the place is at night "terrifyingly lonely."[7]

This tourist site evoked for him not reverence but that nightmare moment for a historian researching the relics of the past when comes "overwhelming nausea and exhaustion. . . . At such moments the past seems oppressively dead, and history appears a charnel-house."[8] Unlike other presentations of Provence, Pope-Hennessy's book has a dark undercurrent revealing the dangers and violence of the human as well as the natural world. This is most evident when Pope-Hennessy considered Avignon. As he discussed its crime and "sordid murders," he labeled it as a city with the "character of Jekyll and Hyde. Because it is an exceptionally lovely and intelligent city, it can be an exceptionally evil one as well." More generally, travelers on their way to the Côte d'Azur in spring and summer typically think of Provence as "a smiling southern country, inhabited by a handsome and amiable race," but he found the Provençaux to be emotional and sometimes cruel. Toward the end of his book, Pope-Hennessy recounted Napoleon's fierce denunciation of the region's people, who insulted and threatened him on his way to his first exile in Elba, and judged the deposed emperor's view to be partially on the mark. Provence is, Pope-Hennessy wrote, "indeed a bitter and ferocious country, full of violence and lethargy, perfidy and good nature, full of every contradiction under its burning sun."[9]

Yet balancing this judgment on its people were the attractions of its historic places and, most of all, its countryside. What animates Pope-Hennessy's book and makes one want to travel to Provence are descriptions of the varied landscapes of the region made vivid by its unique atmosphere of air and light. He wrote that France as a whole offers to the inhabitant of England an "illusion of space," a "sense of being surrounded by a limitless horizon." And, to him, this sense is strongest in Provence. As he put it, "In the south the light, as crystal clear as the fabled light of Greece, gives brilliance to the wide variety of landscapes which compose the Provençal scene."[10]

Ultimately his memories of Provence were "colour memories,"

better captured in paintings than in words. But, as he wrote after looking down at the Durance River, along whose banks "the elms, poplars and even the fresh oak trees . . . showed dark against the startling apple-green of the water-meadows, and the faultless blue of the sky," perhaps in his own case words are enough.[11]

Pope-Hennessy understood some of the critical ways that Provence was not Tuscany. Although it had Roman ruins, it did not have the treasures of art and architecture of the Italian hill towns. No Ducal Palace of Mantua, no Fra Angelico paintings in Cortona. With the exception of churches and places of religious pilgrimage, he saw the non-Roman cultural sights as minor, part of no one's significant artistic education. The museums in the towns, he wrote, had little to offer and, in 1952, were down at the heels. Pope-Hennessy explained that as France had become centralized through its monarchy and post-Revolutionary governments, Versailles and Paris had sucked away all of Provence's great treasures. Thus to him, Provence was "a country for the amateur of travel—for those who feel a passionate interest in landscapes, towns, atmospheres, and human beings." Since such amateurs were rare, "Provence will never be as overrun with tourists as, say, Tuscany."[12]

Here, we know, Pope-Hennessy was wrong. On two counts. He assumed that life in the region would be unchanging, and the land and those who worked it, eternal. And he had no comprehension that travelers' desires could change. The kind of dedicated cultural tourism that his book simultaneously represented and denied didn't end, of course, but it was overwhelmed by new desires. And now, more than six decades after his writing, Provence has an abundance of tourists. That is because many of them may have stopped seeking the exquisite rooms of inlaid wood or the world's finest Annunciation scenes found in Italian hill towns. Some may instead have found it relaxing to go to a place without such glories. They could live and breathe the air with no guilt. They no longer had to trek all day through museums and churches in order to earn the right to a good dinner.

Pope-Hennessy actually wrote about this, what he called "the elation of escape from the tyranny of the sights we ought to see."[13] He was thinking about the secret pleasure of the conscientious culture-seeker in finding a museum or chapel closed at the end of a day of sightseeing. Since the 1970s, some travelers have carried this farther. They want the relief of no culture seeking at all.

II. THE EXPAT

In the 1950s the expatriate British novelist Lawrence Durrell came to Sommières in Gard, a department on the western side of the Rhône often accepted as part of Provence's historic area. Durrell lived most of his life away from the United Kingdom. Born in India of colonial parents, he was educated in England as a boy but failed to enter university. He became a poet and a novelist, gaining his greatest fame in the late 1950s and early 1960s as the books of his Alexandrine Quartet were published. After his first marriage (he had four) in 1932, he chose to live outside of Britain, first in Corfu and then in other places in the Mediterranean world. In 1957, very hard up, he moved to southern France. There, needing the money, he wrote occasional articles for *Holiday* magazine.

Because of his travel pieces in this period, Durrell is often cited as an important interpreter of Provence. He offered these pieces, however, in the form of vignettes. In 1958, in need of cash, he signaled his interest with a short piece in the British literary magazine *Time and Tide*. There he introduced "Old Mathieu," an older wine-growing neighbor who taught him how to trim back the vines on his own rented property.[14] Three pieces in *Holiday* followed, each similarly focused on a Provençal man. Each is a narrative involving a road trip that introduces a colorful character on a mission. In the process of telling his stories, Durrell describes the landscape, food, and many of the traditions of Provence. At this point *Holiday* was seeking great writers likely to be known by the magazine's targeted audience of readers (i.e., those with discretionary income). However, as Richard Popp has documented, fearing that "sophisticated writing would confuse readers," the magazine's editors asked those writers to "dial back their literary ambitions."[15] Because of his literary fame and contributions that seemingly didn't require much thought on the part of readers, Durrell was a sure bet.

Set as narratives, Durrell's pieces nonetheless have surprising depth. "Ripe Living in Provence," first published in *Holiday*'s November 1959 issue, set the pattern for the two to follow. It told the story of Durrell's friendship with Pepe, the owner of several fighting bulls. They met in Orange during a bullfight in the great arena after Pepe spied in Durrell's knapsack a worn volume of poems by Frédéric Mistral. With that, Durrell introduced the reader to Provence's version of the sport in which only the human fighter is endangered, for the goal is not the death of the bull but the matador's acquisition in the ring of a red cockade plucked from between the animal's horns. Once that information was conveyed, Durrell dropped in descriptions of the atmosphere and landscape over the course of the piece. Durrell explained that what drew Pepe to him was less poetry than learning of Durrell's trip by river barge from Avignon to Orange. And this allowed Durrell to write lovingly about the journey he had made.[16]

When Durrell explained to his new friend that he had come on this excursion as a way of getting himself unstuck in his writing of a novel, Pepe offered to give him a view of his private Provence. This was illustrated by the map tattooed on his chest, enabling Durrell to define the "true Provence" as including an area west of the Rhône but excluding that east of Apt. Pepe followed by inviting Durrell to travel with him across this region as his guest while Pepe conducted business and saw his bulls in play. It was a special invitation, allowing Durrell to "learn to imagine as well as to see this hallowed ground" through the eyes of Pepe, a man "both knowledgeable and completely drunk on his native country." With that device, Durrell promised an inside look.[17]

During the week-long trip, they saw, and Durrell noted, the important sites, but "always en route for some contemporary gala, be it a bullfight, or a battle of flowers, or a cattle-branding, or a carnival." Whatever they did was accompanied, of course, by eating and drinking. A view of the arena at Nîmes, for example, came on the hunt for a brandade, a dish that Pepe insisted Durrell had to taste. As Durrell offered the words of a travel writer, he admitted that these repasts so affected his memory that all "was shot through with the prismatic glitter" of the cheese and the wine he imbibed.[18] Describing himself as bewitched by the region, he wrote of its vineyards, olive groves, and cypresses, "One comes to believe that they are Platonic abstractions footed in the imagination of man. Symbols of the Mediterranean, they are always here. . . . Yes, the great wines of the south sleep softly on in the French earth like a pledge that the enchanted landscapes of the European heart will always exist, will never fade against this taut wind-haunted blue sky where the mistral rumbles and screams all winter long. Yes, even if there were no history here, no monuments, no recognizable sense of a past to indulge our 20th Century sense of self-pity, the place would still be the magnet it is."[19] Evoking the wines, the earth and its landscapes, the blue sky, and the mistral, Durrell's narrative of his travels with Pepe emerged in language that was to echo in later decades and draw readers to Provence.

Durrell followed this piece up with two more that engaged the same strategy. One was a road trip to Avignon with Raoul, a plumber, under an agreement to stand by him to meet for the first time his future wife, chosen from an ad for a husband that she placed in the newspaper. Much of the play of the piece regarded Raoul's practical nature, not only in relation to his unseen wife-to-be but also the manner in which he viewed the great historic monuments en route. To Durrell's surprise, after Raoul's denigration of Avignon as old and ugly came admiration for the Pont du Gard. Raoul insisted, however, that his praise was not because of its purported beauty but rather because it was "a Roman triumph of the plumber's science." As with the road trip with Pepe, Durrell embedded sentences of straight travel writing within the narrative, in this case playing against Raoul's practicality. As Durrell described the part of the drive over the bridge across the Rhône to Avignon, he wrote, "At the last corner before you take the plunge you can see, misty across the long flat expanse of the smooth-flowing river, the conglomeration of towers and belfries which have made Avignon one of the most beautiful of the southern French towns. . . . Less formally perfect than Venice, less symmetrical in organization than Carcassonne, it is nevertheless quite as magnificent."[20]

In his third *Holiday* piece, "In Praise of Fanatics," Durrell offered another road trip with a companion and a focus on yet another character, this time a village postman, long dead, who had lived in the northernmost section of Provence. Durrell's companion was Lejoie, a newspaper editor; and the postman, known as the "facteur Cheval," was the creator of a fantastical monument, the Ideal Palace. Between 1879 and 1912, working after his long hours of government service on foot, Cheval had built of stones and cement a structure the size of a two-story house, "a sort of giant wedding cake of styles and moods all welded together." Durrell came to laugh at it but stayed to admire. The monument was a mélange of "a thousand different things," including animals, soldiers, Crusaders along with other figures from the past, and echoes of a wide range of world-famous monuments. Nonetheless, it held together, presenting "a kind of completeness of its own, the kind of completeness which only true works of art enjoy." It was no piece by a "gimmick-artist, a Dali." It was instead the authentic "palace of the world's childhood, admirably and deftly captured."[21]

And then, of course, there was the food and drink to describe. What made the excursion to the Ideal Palace the more memorable was the cooking of the great Chef Chabert, the husband of Lejoie's mother. By allowing Durrell to dine with his friend at his establishment and stay at his small hotel, Chabert admitted Durrell to the inner sanctum of worthy eaters. The dinner itself was exceptional, "gathering its way slowly like a Bach fugue, moving through scale after scale, figure after figure, its massive counterpoint swelling." Durrell followed with the menu, uncommented upon because at the moment of writing he found himself unable to describe it. Perhaps after all that wine and all those courses, he was simply too tired to put in the effort. Lejoie ended the evening by pairing the two men whose work they had witnessed—the chef Chabert was as the facteur Cheval "another fanatic."[22]

III. THE AMERICAN HUSBAND

In 1950, the aspiring American novelist Mitchell Goodman and his wife, the poet Denise Levertov, moved to Provence with their young son. Goodman was drawn to the region as was Durrell, by the need of living as cheaply as possible. In addition, Levertov's birth and early life had been in England, and she had likely imbibed the British dream of southern France and the sun. The couple had resided in France after their 1946 marriage, but this time they chose a small village near Aix to live for a year and write. It was a very difficult time for both of them, but it left experiences that each could draw on. For Levertov, Cézanne became a lodestar and inspiration. For Goodman, it was more complicated. It took another decade for him to complete and publish his World War II novel, *The End of It*. In the interim, with money tight, he turned to travel writing and found some modest success.

Perhaps stimulated by some of the success of the British writers, Goodman took up Provence as a subject. He had already published a number of travel pieces in *House Beautiful* and in 1959 placed there "Provence—Another Name for a Traveler's Dream." In this long and detailed report, Goodman wrote in the heightened language of the genre about the range of the region's glories—history, food, museums, and inns. Urging his readers to go in the autumn and winter, he never mentioned the fierce mistral that blew in those seasons. He painted only a beautiful scene, evoking images that were later to define the region. Provence was, he wrote, "still remote from the world of mass living and standardization." It was a land that "lives by the grape, the garlic, and the olive," with its men "deeply rooted in their soil and in their rich tradition." Once "the garden spot of the Roman Empire," it is now "if anything, even more alive with trees and flowers and orchards. Its hills are lavender and myrtle and thyme."[23]

Goodman urged a long, slow journey through the hills, not the typically short stop on the road to the Côte d'Azur. Describing rural Provence as "a work of art," he wrote that only by a leisurely visit to its many places could one experience the rich composition of its numerous complex parts. He paid due attention to the Roman ruins, the festivals and fêtes, but also attended to its crafts and its beautiful objects. What stands out most are the small inns he recommended, "blessed with interesting locations and with delightful far-seeing views over hills and fields to the lavender mountains or the sea." These accommodations offered the chance to enter the interior of a large Provençal house, normally closed to the outsider. And typically the food was good—if not *grande cuisine*, then at least "the fragrant regional cooking—of bouillabaisse, of local game, of Mediterranean rockfish grilled over a hot bed of vine cuttings."[24] And, of course, he paid tribute to the inn at Les Baux with its great restaurant, by then labeled one of the ten best in France.

Finally, there was the special power of the art of Cézanne, the great influence on Levertov. "In and around Aix one comes closer to him," Goodman wrote. In the walk from Aix to Le Tholonet, there is "that turn of the road that so suddenly reveals the terrific presence of Mt. Sainte-Victoire," where one could stand just where Cézanne painted it.[25] In this early foray into travel writing, Goodman turned what had been a writer's necessity—a stay in a very cheap place until he could escape elsewhere—into a glowing report.

IV. THE IMMIGRANT DIRECTOR: *TO CATCH A THIEF*

Alfred Hitchcock moved to the United States in 1939 to work in Hollywood, bringing an enormous reputation that only grew with the production of his many heralded films. In 1955, he wowed the cinema world and viewers with Cary Grant and Grace Kelly in *To Catch a Thief.* The Riviera, presented in full color in newly created big-screen VistaVision, is an important character in the film. The classy world of Cannes—with its grand hotels, beautiful seaside villas, and the grand event of a costume ball—appears in eye-popping splendor, giving ever more publicity to this playground of the rich. The plot involves the efforts to clear the name of Cary Grant's character, John Robie, once the infamous jewelry thief known as the Cat.[26]

Peeping through the grandeur of Cannes were moments in the hills above. John lives there in a beautiful stone villa. From its loggia, one never sees the sea, but only green landscape and a village that climbs up a nearby incline. Early in the film he receives a visit from H. H. Hughson, an uptight Brit. With champagne glass in his hand, the visitor looks out to the hills and answers his host's question as to how he likes the place. "Immensely. It's a kind of travelfolder heaven where a man dreams he'll go when he retires."

The complicated plot involves a potential love interest, Frances Stevens, played by Grace Kelly. During a long, wild ride the couple takes in a convertible on the magnificent but winding and dangerous Grande Corniche, the great road above the sea, one gets glimpses of village life. Frances is driving, and twice she must stop the car, first for an old woman with a basket crossing the street and then for a chicken in the road. Both pauses serve as reminders of the slower pace of life lived there. At the end of the ride, as the two take a break for a picnic, Frances tells John of her love for the beauty of the place, including "the little pink and green buildings on the hill."

As the film closes, Frances comes to John's villa, one of those buildings on the hill, though grand rather than little. After the kiss that one presumes to be the ending of the film, she says to John, "So this is where you live? Oh, Mother will love it up here." With that, John looks at her ruefully and the credits roll. But perhaps the audience got a subliminal message not unlike those conveyed by many a Cézanne painting.

Yes, that house in the hills.

These expressions of the pleasures of Provence in the 1950s came fairly early in the game. As the French Government Tourist Office attempted to lure travelers away from Paris, they faced the challenge of Americans' fixation with Paris. But help such as Pope-Hennessy, Durrell, Goodman, and Hitchcock offered was on the way. Lush images and language appealing directly to the senses began to foster the allure of inland Provence. By the turn to the 1960s there were hints to Americans that the hills of Provence were emerging from the poverty-stricken location of Roman ruins to become a treasured place of desire.

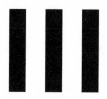

Irving Penn and the Reinvention of Provence

For Provence to emerge in a new light as a travel destination for Americans required it to be reinvented. It would never shed its Roman ruins, but they would move to the background. In the foreground emerged a region that promised pleasures of a different kind.

In 1962 *Look* magazine offered "The Eternal Appeal of Provence," an extraordinary set of photographs by Irving Penn, with affectionate commentary by Patricia Coffin, the magazine's longtime picture profile editor. Penn's photographs featured no Roman ruins or festivals. In their place, he put the new attraction, the land itself. Spread across the magazine's pages were a field of cultivated lavender, a perched village spilling down over a hill into vineyards and gardens, elegant antiques to desire, a chef pouring himself a glass of wine, a group gathered jovially around a table, and a villager straight out of a Cézanne painting sitting at a table against the background of a massive wall (plates 3–7). Offered by Penn in 1962, in the following decades these pictures were to become the iconic images of Provence.

"For centuries the unique quality of Provence has inspired painters to paint, writers to write, people to evaluate the art of living," begins the text. Penn's images and Coffin's words conveyed a Provence that was a world of beauty explicitly linked to the artist's eye. Placed to the left of a large picture of a hill and valley ran the heading, "Provence: The Light Van Gogh Loved." The accompanying text reinforced the associations: "Many of the Post-impressionists' most brilliant paintings reflect the extraordinary Provençal light. . . . Cézanne expressed it: '. . . everything stands out, delineated.'"[1]

The narrative that followed presented the contemporary re-peopling of Provence with artists. Gathering near the lavender in the early 1960s was a sociable set of individuals who came to Provence for the life, each other, the weather, and the cheap prices of real estate, most likely in ascending order. Coffin quoted the American painter Bernard Pfriem, who "bought his first ruin in Lacoste for $50 . . . has since restored three, [yet] still pays only $12-a-year local tax."[2]

One of the artists was the photographer himself. The article suggested that being hired in 1961 for this extensive photo shoot in Provence for *Look* allowed Penn to blend his professional talents with his personal needs. Married to his most famous model, Lisa Fonssagrives (then emerging as a sculptor), Penn was spending time in Provence in anticipation of possessing the property the two had bought near Lacoste—"a crumbling cluster of farmhouses in the middle of a lavender field." By then he was an international figure whose work often took him to Europe, and Fonssagrives was a star. Swedish born and once a dancer, she had been elevated by fashion photographers—and ultimately Penn—to become the leading model for *Vogue*.[3]

Pfriem emphasized not only his pioneering in the region but also the respect that painting held there and the famous artists who came in the summer. The article also quoted Douglas Cooper, the art collector who hated his native Britain, "I'm allergic to snow, fog and rain. This is the only place to live." Irving Penn was himself planning to join this convivial group. His words conclude the piece—he and his wife were buying property near Lacoste because

5 A jovial group gathered around a table in Provence. Irving Penn, "Bernard Pfriem on left, hosting company," © The Irving Penn Foundation, LOOK Magazine Photograph Collection, Library of Congress, Prints & Photographs Division.

they "found it so near everything . . . and yet so far off the beaten track."[4]

Thus, in 1962, with writing by Patricia Coffin and photographs by Irving Penn, "The Eternal Appeal of Provence" heralded the reinvention of Provence.

FIVE   # The Senses

"My first impression of Provence was smell—a mixture of orange blossoms, lavender and rosemary," wrote Olga Carlisle in *Holiday* in 1969. These scents came from the shoebox of flowers that her grandmother sent to her in Paris from Provence one winter almost forty years before. Later as a Parisian *lycée* student traveling on an outing with her school, Olga stepped into Avignon. With that began her dream to live in the sun of Provence.[1]

In the 1960s, Carlisle was one of many voices introducing Provence to American audiences. She drew on an appeal to the sense of smell, just as Irving Penn had offered images to entice the sense of sight. As travel writers sought to inform Americans about the region, they added taste to the mix.[2] These appeals to the senses hardly happened in a vacuum. They arrived at a time of new appreciations of sensual pleasure, enhanced by the growing influence of artists and writers.

I. SIGHT

In the late 1950s and 1960s, the visual arts gained new stature as many Americans came to appreciate painting in a new way. There had always been some level of respect, especially for portraits and landscapes. The Impressionists and their immediate followers were widely admired. But in this new era the works of Pablo Picasso and Henri Matisse took on a magical appeal, and the artists themselves became celebrities. *Life* magazine picked up on this and pushed the phenomenon further. During these years it repeatedly gave Picasso attention and in 1968 even produced a grand double issue devoted solely to him.[3]

Not only what such artists did but where they lived became important—and key artists chose the South of France. We have seen the early appreciation of Cézanne and Van Gogh and interest in the locales in Provence where they painted. The region's light, its promise of escape from war zones, and the relative cheapness of property there began to attract other well-known artists. By 1917 Matisse moved to a suburb above Nice, where he remained until his death. Throughout his long life in Paris, Picasso frolicked on the beaches of the Côte d'Azur. During World War II and the immediate postwar years, many French artists retreated to the South of France. In the 1950s, knowledge of these artists' whereabouts gradually filtered into consciousness. Initially it drew attention to the Riviera, but in time, especially after 1959, when Picasso took possession of the Château de Vauvenargues outside Aix, eyes began to look north to the hills of Provence.

Popular culture embraced the new interest in art and artists, and their work began to appear in Hollywood films. In 1951, movie audiences got a tease in MGM's *An American in Paris*, with Gene Kelly as the artist Jerry Mulligan attempting to paint and sell his canvases in Paris. Mulligan's visual artistry in the film was hardly memorable, but the film's music and dancing were brilliant, and its simulated views of Paris, beautiful. The motion picture was a great artistic and popular success, but it focused attention on Paris, not Provence.

With *Lust for Life* in 1956, Provence got its moment in the sun. This MGM adaptation of Irving Stone's portrayal of the life of Vincent van Gogh held key segments that captured the region. Stone based his book on the letters of the artist to his younger brother Theo, an art dealer, and the film used some of these words as narration. The drama centers on the efforts of Van Gogh, played by Kirk Douglas, to find himself as an artist. Central to the film are 200 images of Van Gogh paintings, often juxtaposed against scenes on the ground and sky. These showed viewers inland Provence.[4]

The movie assumes that the audience knows and cares about Van Gogh's work. Moving biographically through the dark places of the painter's outer and inner life, it presents him as a man beset by the mental demons that ultimately overtake him. Much of the early film, tracking Van Gogh's failures in life and love, is dark in mood. This is represented visually by locations of poverty, including his work as an evangelist minister in a coal mining village in Belgium. When Van Gogh gets to Provence, there is little change at first. He arrives in Arles by train in the evening, and corresponding dark tones and seeming poverty prevail as he settles into a dreary room at an inn. He opens the window, but the viewer sees nothing, for it is night.

It is morning, however, in the next scene, and Van Gogh wakes and opens the window to see glorious spring. A tree is in bloom, blossoms float in a stream, and as music soars there is revealed a whole arbor of flowering trees and vineyards, all set against a deep blue sky. A cut to Van Gogh's painting of the scene is bright and joyous. Suddenly the artist is painting outdoors, smiling, and rubbing his face. Moments of peace and joy.

Of course, the dark returns. There is Van Gogh's poverty, calling forth the pettiness and venality of ordinary villagers. Juxtaposed is the kindly postman, familiar from Van Gogh's famous portrait, who offers a hand. Once summer comes, the world is filled with the Provençal light—"old gold, bronze, and copper." The music is joyous again as Van Gogh walks through the landscape and paints in the open air, narrating, "The colors give me an extraordinary exaltation. The whole earth is glowing under the southern sun." As he lets himself go, he states, "No doubts, no limitations."[5] All this is reflected in his vivid paintings from that time.

These moments are followed by a downward spiral that even the pleasures of Provence could not prevent. Consumed by his art, a weary Van Gogh takes to drink, and we see a more frightening man and a seamier Arles. The mistral blows, forcing him indoors. His drinking becomes pronounced, taking place in a bar among prostitutes. His passion for painting becomes crazed—the famous painting *Starry Night* is executed by the light of candles perched on his straw hat. A failed reunion with Paul Gauguin, acted by a powerful Anthony Quinn, pushes Van Gogh over the edge. As their sharp conflict plays out and Van Gogh wounds himself by cutting off his ear, we see an even darker Arles in the meanness of its population, mocking him outside his window.

The scenes that follow—which include Van Gogh committed to institutions first in Arles and then in Saint-Rémy-de-Provence—offer the beauty of the landscape and the wonder of his paintings juxtaposed with the story, now, of the man who knows his death is near. As the sympathetic reviewer in the *New York Times* wrote, it is "the color of indoor sets and outdoor scenes, the color of beautifully reproduced Van Gogh paintings, even the colors of a man's tempestuous moods" that are the primary element in the film, offering an effective "motion picture comprehension" of the artist.[6] The movie won high esteem from the industry including one Academy Award and many nominations, but it failed to find a large audience and lost money for the studio. Nonetheless for those who watched, the film provided important early views of inland Provence.[7]

Lust for Life helped prepare a larger audience for the Irving Penn photographs in *Look*. Published in 1962, they gave the first truly satisfying look at Provence to a broad swath of Americans. "The Eternal Appeal of Provence" emphasized that Provence seemed to offer a different way of life. It was an alternative world to snow and ice and the hurly-burly of urban living. Its "people are gentle and proud. Nothing hastens them from their seat in the sun. Provence offers rewarding tranquility."[8]

In its reinvention of Provence, the *Look* piece conveyed that the region offered not only a beautiful landscape, resident artists, and cheap property but also delicious food to eat and wonderful goods to buy. Given full treatment was l'Oustau de Baumanière, the restaurant singled out by Horace Sutton in his 1948 *Footloose in France*. In 1954, Michelin crowned the establishment with its coveted three stars, putting it on the great gastro-tourism trail going south from Lyon. Three stars also meant that Baumanière offered high style, not local cuisine. Linked to the photo of Raymond Thuilier pouring himself a glass of wine, the text told an inaccurate story of the famed restaurant housed in a seventeenth-century farmhouse in Les Baux, about nineteen miles south of Avignon (plate 7). By this account, what appeared to be old and long established was actually quite new: only eight years before, according to this faulty report, Thuilier was an insurance broker in Paris, Les Baux was a ghost town, and the farmhouse was unrestored. (According to the restaurant's own history, Thuilier actually bought the property in 1945 and opened the restaurant in 1947.)[9]

Featured close behind the glamorous restaurant in the *Look* report were objects to desire, and the appeal of Provençal antiques to those who had already acquired a taste for older Americana was made explicit. One caption read, "A rustic elegance marks the furniture of the province of Provence. As in America, the earlier pieces, like the rush-bottomed chair at left, were used in humble dwellings. But the proportions are so pleasing that now they are collectors' items." The discussion then turned to the refined tastes of certain antiques found in Provence, introducing a "graceful table, influenced by the Louis XV period" corresponding to "our more elegant Queen Anne furniture." With this, the article reminded readers that members of the French aristocracy as well as farmers and bourgeoisie had peopled Provence; thus both rich and poor left objects to tempt Americans, travelers and homebodies alike. Pictured in the *Look* spread were a range of objects, "massive as a sunflower, light as a thistle," carrying with them their distinct associations (plate 6). Included as examples were both an elegant table "from the collection of Mme. Marguerite Dervieux in Arles" that usually sat at "the entrance of the old Hotel d'Europe in Avignon" and a "*pétrin* (dough box)" owned by the American painter Bernard Pfriem.[10]

Evoking the article's central theme of the good life in Provence, "so far off the beaten track," was a Penn image with this caption: "Elegant in their simplicity, two chairs wait in a narrow street for the cool of the evening, when an old couple will sit in them to watch the world go by in Lacoste . . ."[11]

Penn's gorgeous color photographs contain many of the iconic elements that came to constitute Provence's revised image (plates 3–7). One still sees them today on every kiosk holding postcards of the region. They are likely in the cameras, photo albums, and cell phones of tourists who have traveled there. Throughout the nineteenth century travelers sought out picturesque sites suggested first by landscape paintings and then by the photographs following in their wake.[12] Penn's images in *Look* did more. They drew on conceptions thought and said in the artistic world in France and gave them visual form and enduring life. They thus became essential building blocks in the reinvention of Provence.

Seeing may be the primary sense that propels travel to distant destinations. One goes to see with one's own eyes what one has seen in paintings and photographs. One takes photographs in turn to confirm having been there and to evoke the memory of the experience once home. Yet in understanding the lure of Provence, the visual cannot be separated from the other senses.

II. SMELL

Propelled by her sensual memory of flowers sent from Provence, Olga Carlisle realized her dream of Provence when she married a writer from California—"as much in love with sunshine" as she. The two bought one of the ruined houses in the hill town of Gordes and began to restore it. Although the Côte d'Azur was within a drive of an hour and a half, they chose not to go there. They centered their life and explorations in their own town and the ones nearby.[13]

For Carlisle, the scents mixed with the air, the light, and sounds to define her Provence. Its "very air . . . has a distinct density. The persistent sun casts well-defined shadows which lend solidity to all objects, even to those at great distance." Carlisle looked at the ponderous farmhouses. "When the sun is setting they turn red and so do their tiled roofs. . . . Provençal sunsets are magnificent." She also loved to see the pasture land for its sheep and the fertile valleys of "the *primeurs*, the winter-early spring vegetables for all of France." She defined and described the *garrigue*, the "special growth of junipers, live oaks, thyme and lavender" covering the plateaus that surround the rich and fertile valleys. It filled the air with its smell, "a mixture of resin, thyme and lavender," that joined the "loud, crackling song" of the *cigales*, or cicadas.[14]

Lingering in this part of Carlisle's world were the ruins. At one level they evoked the familiar stories from travel literature—the Roman baths that gave Aix its name, the troubadours, Van Gogh. But at another, such descriptions suggested something new— opportunity. Oppède-le-Vieux, high on its hill, "is made of tiers of handsome Renaissance town houses, now in ruins. Each of these houses had its vast, terraced gardens, its walled-in orchard overlooking the valley. Today these terraces, overgrown with lavender and wild oats, their retaining walls crumbing, seem to float above the valley."[15] Did the reader begin to ponder: Why not follow Olga Carlisle? Why not restore one of those houses and rebuild its garden?

III. TASTE

Often following one's nose leads to the table. Inhaling becomes tasting, perhaps first of wine and then of food. In drawing travelers to the hills of Provence, the sense of taste may be as—or possibly more—important than the sense of sight.

It took some time, however, for many Americans to develop an admiration for the food of Provence. Nonetheless, there were enthusiasts in the 1960s, including the writer Mitchell Goodman. In 1964, he returned to Provence to write a piece for the *Atlantic Monthly*. Although he had lived there in 1950 with his wife and child, in this article he created a fictional story of discovery occurring a decade and a half later, presenting himself and his wife as new travelers to the region. He and Denise Levertov became innocents, lured by a Châteauneuf-du-Pape wine to leave Route nationale 7—the highway that had taken them through Avignon, Aix, and Arles to the Riviera—to find the "real" Provence of the byways.[16]

Goodman wrote that they had imbibed the excellent wine at an outdoor café on the Cours Mirabeau in Aix and conversed with the *patron*. Enthusiastically he told them of the "back roads romantic and innumerable, of unspoiled country where no heavy traffic ever ran, of Roman ruins few travelers had seen." Then he moved on to "melons so fragrant they can perfume a whole house," of grapes and eggplants, and small châteaux with their unknown but excellent vineyards. "To taste was our object."[17] First the wines and then the food.

Taking to the road in this "least molested of Europe's prime travel grounds," Goodman found "an otherworldly scene of flowers and shepherds, olives and vines, herbs and garlic, hills of lavender, and orange-roofed villages where men play *boules* in leafy squares as if that were all they ever did." As they traveled, he and his wife drank "full-bodied and ardent" wines and ate "the spiced and herbaceous cuisine of the region." What they sought was not the food made fancy by the "important" restaurants or tamed for tourist consumption, but "good country cooking" based on local produce and regional fish.[18]

As Mitchell broadened to a more conventional travel piece, he recommended a number of different driving itineraries, all blessed in his day by the absence of other cars. He suggested staying in one of the small hotels "converted from the handsome stone houses" of pre-Revolutionary times. These establishments conveyed "the true domestic ambience" of Provence—the "vaulted rooms, huge fireplaces, and massive armoires" of aristocrats, opening onto great views of the surrounding valleys.[19]

Summing up, Goodman asserted that the Provence of his writing represented "the country of the Good Life," inspired by Cézanne and Van Gogh. This he put in contrast to "our world of mass life and standardization." Rural Provence was "earthbound and amiable, strong in its traditions and appetites."[20]

Yet one of the ironies of Goodman's report is that, despite his desire to get away from the well-traveled roads of tourists, as a travel writer he needed to have it all ways. In the midst of celebrating the authenticity of undiscovered Provence, he praised the known great restaurants and inns, celebrated for "*la grande cuisine*," including l'Oustau de Baumanière, that much-praised Michelin three-star restaurant at Les Baux. He was not lingering and savoring but always moving quickly in a rented car. And then there was his presentation of the ease and speed of getting to Provence. Air travel, he wrote, made it quick and allowed for "spur of the moment" booking. "Pan American, for instance, has about a hundred flights a day to Europe at the season's height, including one to Provence's major airport at Nice." The cost, a mere trifle: $504 round trip—a sum that translates to at least $3,650 in today's dollars.[21] Given Goodman's known money woes, belittling this cost, as well as offering his story as one of discovery, tells the twenty-first-century reader less about Goodman than about his imagined twentieth-century audience.[22]

Something important was at work here. Provence in the 1960s offered Americans the thrill of discovery. There were new sights to see, photograph, and report on—the lavender, the towns tumbling down the hill, the light that inspired artists. There were new odors to smell, especially something unique and strange called the *garrigue*. There was refreshing wine and interesting food, not totally unfamiliar but unique and made of fresh ingredients from the land and sea. And there was property, very cheap property, to buy. To Americans who imagined themselves adventurous but still wanted the security of *la belle France*, Provence as reinvented offered many temptations.

IV. A WORD OF CAUTION BEFORE PROCEEDING

Horace Sutton's travel piece in the *Saturday Review* in 1961 reminds us how much of the traditional approach to "seeing" Provence still remained in place in the 1960s.[23] On a gastronomic tour taking him from Paris to the Riviera, Sutton breezed through the region, inhaling calories and fine wines. "The road signs became wine labels, directing us off to Chateauneuf-du-Pape and to Tavel." Nonetheless, he sprinkled the piece with touristic wisdom about the region. "And through it all seethed the air of ancient Rome, which thought of this territory as its 'province.'" Sutton was clear about his preferences. After delighting in the grilled lamb at Lucullus (Michelin two stars) in Avignon, he took to the road. While "the sane world is making tracks to the sack . . . we were being driven off like waddling sows in search of whatever culture one can inhale from old stone on a full stomach and a surfeit of wine." He disliked the Palace of the Popes as much in 1961 as he had in 1947, but he loved the views of the Rhône. Then he was off to Les Baux "at a dog trot in search of new excitements."[24]

After relating its violent history in a paragraph and describing the touristic nature of the lower town, Sutton took himself to l'Oustau de Baumanière, reviewed by him fourteen years before. This time he didn't mention the food, only its outdoor terraces and inner rooms. Then he moved on to Arles in the fading light. And finally to Noves and La Petite Auberge, now another three-star Michelin attraction. All the while he threw out the usual gems of wisdom about Mistral and Van Gogh in his breezy style. And with that final dinner on the road, he went to bed "in a sea of Champagne's expensive bubbles inhaling the heady autumn air of the van Gogh country that stretched in an enormous expanse outside our second-floor window."[25]

For many Americans in 1961, Sutton's quick trip remained the preferred way to travel, even to Provence—a hurried rush to view some Roman ruins and catch the site of a Van Gogh painting on the way to the true delights of drink and the evening meal.

SIX   **Eternal Provence?**
                              Maybe Not

Provence is often written about as ancient and eternal. This is an illusion. In the 1960s the Provence that began to call lovers of the good life to the South of France was not the Provence of the late nineteenth century, or of the 1920s or even of the 1950s. Its geology—its hills and valleys—did not change, but, on the surface above, the region was undergoing a metamorphosis.

Irving Penn's photographs gave these changes visual expression in the *Look* piece that carried a title that now seems ironic—"The Eternal Appeal of Provence." This heading was part of a pattern. During the 1960s, as others gave voice to Provence's attractions— its untraveled roads and undiscovered restaurants, the region's special scents, and its run-down villages with cheap property waiting to be reclaimed—they conveyed information intended to attract those seeking the authentic, a world that in the midst of change was itself unchanged.

Laurence Wylie, however, noticed the transformation right away. He returned to Roussillon, the town he disguised as Peyrane, to prepare for the second edition of *Village in the Vaucluse*. The 1957 book had made him a famous author and brought him an appointment at Harvard. He took his second look to write a piece for the influential *In Search of France* (1963) and to add "Peyrane Ten Years

Later" to the new edition of *Village in the Vaucluse*, published in 1964.

As he approached Roussillon, Wylie saw Algerian and Spanish workers digging trenches to the familiar houses of the village. Roussillon was installing a sewage system, its first, and these workers were connecting pipes and putting toilets, sinks, and bathtubs into individual homes. He found these signs of progress curious. No industry had come to town, so what, he asked himself, was bringing about the change?

As he spoke to his village acquaintances, Wylie came to understand that 1950–51, when he had lived in Roussillon, was a particular moment in the town's life—a time of great despair. Those living there were looking to the past and what they had lost. By his return in the early 1960s, France's recovery was in progress, and residents of even this tiny agricultural village in Provence now had hope. They were living in the present and imagining a future. Wylie saw them buying tractors and television sets on credit and planting fruit and olive trees that would take many years to mature. He wrote that although the Roussillonnais were not cheerful—"despite the impression created by their southern exuberance they are not a sanguine people"—they had become more confident in their ability to face the future.[1]

With this, Wylie saw villagers now sporting a "gayer air." Beneath the bright umbrellas of the three cafés on the village's main square, younger locals mixed with summer residents and day-tripping tourists. Roussillon boasted its own one-star Michelin restaurant with a magnificent view. Already he could see that, at least for French visitors, Roussillon was on its way to becoming a resort town.[2]

What Wylie observed in Roussillon was part of a larger process that was transforming much of the French landscape, both its towns and its countryside. France was in the middle of Les Trente Glorieuses, the glorious three decades of growing prosperity between 1946 and 1975 in which France attempted to modernize its economy and build an infrastructure to support it. And this was transforming Provence.

Changes were particularly necessary because throughout its long history Provence had been plagued by recurring droughts and floods. The Murray guide of 1873 remarked on the impact of drought. In 1948 Horace Sutton echoed Murray when he described Provence as "mostly dry, scrubby, rocky, arid."[3] Henry James in 1882 fled from a flood. Ford Madox Ford in 1935 listed the Durance River, flowing from the French Alps to the Rhône at Avignon, as one of the three eternal flails of Provence.

For centuries there had been efforts to control the flow of water in the region. The Canal de Craponne that runs through Arles was begun as early as the mid-1500s to irrigate the land and provide water for the fountains. The early Provençaux also built canals to control the Durance River, and with the Enlightenment and the emerging profession of engineering came new, more powerful efforts.[4] Following disastrous floods in the mid-nineteenth century, engineers dreamed of taking a more comprehensive approach to control the Durance's waters.

In the twentieth century these efforts were linked to electric power. In the decades before World War II, a multitude of private companies supported by the national government attempted to supply France with electricity produced largely by coal-fired plants and, to a lesser degree, by harnessing moving water. A patchwork of electric power was created that served manufacturing and urban areas better than the countryside.[5] In 1946 France nationalized and consolidated the country's electrical power companies and joined the two streams of endeavor, flood control and electricity. In 1955, France began constructing the greatest earth dam in Europe, at Serre-Ponçon in the Hautes-Alpes. Its thirty-two power plants along the Durance River brought electricity to Provence. And with it came an altered landscape. The dam helped control floods and, assisted by canals old and new, brought highly controlled irrigation to 150,000 hectares (over 370,000 acres) of farmland, protecting the land from recurrent drought. An important swath of Provence turned from sunbaked brown to green, at least in the months of spring and early summer.[6]

In these same years French national policy encouraged development that drew much of its working population into the previously industrialized cities in the north. This opened up opportunities for employment in factories that attracted young workers from the farms, many in the south. Their departure also allowed the modernization of agriculture. Aggregating small plots and introducing farm machinery increased yield and fostered the profitable exportation of produce.[7]

These changes, much heralded as paths to French prosperity, ironically ran counter to a deep French longing for rural life. As Susan Carol Rogers has put it, "agriculture and rural lifeways figure in France as powerful loci of nostalgia and fantasy."[8] This French dream of rurality had powerful roots in the national culture and was strengthened by portrayals of French painters during the rise of industrialization and urbanization in the nineteenth and early twentieth centuries. Jean-François Millet injected men and women working the land into landscape painting. Working en plein air, Impressionist painters created many glamourous images of the landscape, and at their head, Camille Pissarro offered profound images of rural scenes, including ordinary peasants working in the fields.[9]

As incomes rose in the three decades following World War II, many French men and women living in cities became able to satisfy their desire for life in the countryside, at least part of the time. Work may have required residence in the city, but leisure allowed an alternate existence. As early as 1936, the French government ordained the *congés payés*, the annual vacation paid by employers for all workers, typically taken in midsummer. It began as two weeks off but became three in 1956, then four in 1968. As "les grandes vacances" of summer grew longer, more French citizens began to travel to the southern sun.[10]

For some of the more fortunate, an important opportunity arose. Population drain to the developing industrial north left much of the French countryside in the south relatively depopulated, with many of its houses and outbuildings abandoned. Although observers had noted this happening in parts of rural Provence as early as the 1930s, given the economic depression of the time and then war, empty structures occasioned only nostalgia.[11]

With the recovery after World War II and growing prosperity, more French citizens could fulfill a dream long held—possession of a second home. In centuries past the French aristocracy had begun a tradition of "résidences secondaires," and by the mid-nineteenth century the families of professionals and those in trade had made it their own. Having a retreat in the country, be it a chateau, a country house, or a tiny cottage, became part of the French version of the good life.[12] The second home offered not just prestige but the pleasure of use. First railroads, then automobiles opened broader access.

This aspiration spread to a wide swath of French society. When surveyed in the late 1960s, half of all households sampled expressed their intention to acquire a second, holiday home. Especially appealing was a home in the countryside. The ability to fulfill the dream of a second home for leisure use, however, was directly related to wealth. In contrast to those with low incomes who owned neither a primary nor a secondary property, in 1967, 60 percent of households in the top category of those with annual incomes of over 100,000 francs held a second home. Ownership, however, was not the full measure of the draw of *résidences secondaires*. Many French families had the use of country places through ties of kin or friendship, or through leasing arrangements.[13] Owners of second houses learned that, when not in use, their properties could provide a significant income stream. The outcome of all this was that the number of *résidences secondaires* grew from 500,000 in 1954 to almost a million in 1962.[14]

These French second homes were largely separate houses, not apartments, according to a 1968 census. Strikingly, unlike in most other parts of the world, the majority of them were converted farm buildings. With new structures largely limited to seaside areas, more than half of rural properties were much older buildings, originally constructed before 1914, often abandoned or long unused by their former owners.[15] They tended to be in places that sustained some of their rural character, with tilled fields or vineyards and farmers who maintained them. All of this, as one writer put it, formed in the eyes of urban dwellers an important part of "les charmes de la compagne."[16]

What happened was a change Laurence Wylie had not foreseen. In 1950, when he was still living in Roussillon, the *notaire* (the local legal official responsible in France for real estate contracts) suggested to Wylie that he buy an abandoned windmill and its hill— for $90. A few years later, one of his village acquaintances offered him his substantial house and land for $450. (Even with inflation, this figure is modest, perhaps one-fifth of an annual middle-class income at the time.) Wylie bought neither. When he reflected on this in 1964, he understood that those low prices for real estate in Roussillon and neighboring villages became the source of the transformation he witnessed. The older houses appeared desirable to members of the French urban middle class. Very inexpensive but solid, these houses turned out to be wonderfully restorable. "Gradually city people began to discover this cheap property," Wylie wrote. They could buy an older house "in the southern sun far from the cold rain and the exhaust-choked streets of Paris" and turn it into "a quaint and convenient hideaway where Parisians could satisfy the traditional French urge to play at being peasants."[17] What Wylie failed to state in 1964 was that not only Parisians but dwellers in Provençal cities such as Marseille, Avignon, and Toulon were taking advantage of their region's rural places for regular weekend getaways.

As vacations lengthened and improved transportation sped travel, many choices opened for the annual summer holiday. Provence was among the regions of France—which also included Languedoc, the Mediterranean coast, and the French Alps—to see great growth in second homes. For some seekers of the sun, the small settlements in the hills north of the Côte d'Azur—with their abandoned farmhouses—were calling. By 1968, over 30 percent of houses in the rural areas of Provence were *résidences secondaires*.[18]

The growth in the number of second homes for leisure had an important impact on the people of Provence. Pushed out of the agricultural work of their fathers, the men and women still remaining there used their skills to provide services needed by the second-home buyers. Some turned to construction, the more entrepreneurial becoming contractors. Second-home residents and their tenants, requiring all the provisions and services of daily life, became customers and clients of local business and professional persons. Those on holiday provided opportunity for restaurateurs, who refurbished existing establishments or moved to begin new ones. The famous multiplier effect went into motion, opening up new sources of income for the population on the ground. Regions, such as Provence, no longer "productive" in the old sense became productive in the new.

Wylie had noticed without comment the Algerian workers in Roussillon digging trenches alongside laborers from Spain. Algerians were more significant than he noted at the time. The renewal and reinvention of Provence happened simultaneously with the bloody war France was fighting against the forces of Algerian independence. In the nineteenth century France had colonized Algeria and had declared it to be an integral part of the nation. Many French had migrated there in search of opportunity, especially when hard times hit, as for example during the phylloxera epidemic of the 1850s-70s that killed grapevines across France. Europeans from other countries joined them and gained naturalization as French citizens. Collectively these European migrants to Algeria became known as "pieds noirs"—perhaps for the black boots of the early French soldiers or perhaps for their own darkened peasant feet. Some of the more prosperous of them began to leave Algeria in the 1950s, when Algerians' struggle for independence led to warfare, but those who remained fled in 1962 after armed resistance against independence was quashed.[19]

This reverse migration across the Mediterranean of somewhere between 800,000 and a million *pieds noirs* bought to France an economically mixed group, but it was the very poor who stood out, unwelcomed by the French and initially unaided by the government. After arriving in Marseille, many of them settled in the South of France. While a very small number were able to move to Carnoux-en-Provence, now a commune just north of Cassis, founded by *pieds noirs* from Morocco, most merely hung on. More generally, their unappreciated presence and typically conservative politics created a new dynamic in the region.[20] An American tourist considering a trip to Provence in the 1960s, however, would have no way of knowing any of this from travel or food writing, and certainly not from advertisements supported by the French Government Tourist Office.

Instead, the picture fashioned for the American public was one of harmony, bounty, and nostalgic return to a gentler life. The dominant image came from a full-color ad in the *New Yorker* in 1961, financed by the French Government Tourist Office but created by the American firm Doyle Dane Bernbach. It pictured a Frenchman bicycling down a road lined with tall trees, with two long baguettes fastened to a rack. A boy sitting behind the driver of the bike glances back at the camera (plate 8). A contemporary commentator on the ad noted, "Who can look at this tranquil country scene without longing to be there—cycling along that open road, befriended by cool green trees?" The text of the ad harmonized with the photograph, announcing in its headline, "Next time you take a vacation, uncomplicate your life." It then went on to touch all bases—easy train travel to Avignon for passengers and automobiles, the existence in Provence of Roman ruins and artists, the sun and the possibility of leisure. The copy ended with "You can shed your coat and tie, here. You can bicycle and keep your dignity. You can learn all there is to know about wine and cheese and bouillabaisse. You can fall in love here. You can even stay forever."[21]

Introduced by the French into the United States early in the 1960s, the essential message of this ad took a while to percolate and bring American travelers to seek what it called Provence's "relaxed, sunburned towns" to "uncomplicate" their lives. But when the message did strike home, they and those coming from elsewhere in the world made tourism central to Provence's emerging economy. By the time of Laurence Wylie's return visit to Roussillon in the 1960s, Provence was already becoming a destination for many travelers, heralding many future changes in the region.[22]

SEVEN

Getting Ready to Taste

I

By the early 1960s Provence was ready to receive Americans travelers, but it took a while before Americans were ready to go. A
principal barrier for many was the food of Provence. What inhib-
ited Americans' appetites for Provençal cuisine were not only old
habits and tastes but also the impact of historical developments.
Two major forces in the United States in the late nineteenth and
early twentieth centuries—industrialization and efforts to assimi-
late immigrants—put bleached bread and sanitized food on many
American tables. The rise of food manufacturing created stan-
dardized products for the kitchen. Reformers attempting to Amer-
icanize immigrants sought to banish the foodways of their natal
countries.

Counterforces always existed, however, within ethnic cultures
and even in largely Anglo middle-class kitchens. The campaign of
food reformers promoting "eating to live" rather than "living to
eat" never fully erased the desire to be delighted, comforted, and
entertained by food. Many people it seems want both the comfort
of the food they experienced as children and the playfulness of new
tastes.[1]

In the late nineteenth century, travel abroad and growing American cities with increasingly diverse populations had already begun
to widen the eating possibilities of the wealthy and middle class.

French cuisine moved into ascendency as restaurants offered fine dining to those with open pocketbooks. Among the upper elite it became a mark of distinction to hire French chefs to run household kitchens. German beer gardens and saloons served entertainment and drink along with food, appealing to businessmen and workers. For urban dwellers or visitors with more modest discretionary income, ethnic eateries, especially Chinese and Italian, brightened up taste buds. Nonetheless, in general, for many in the middle class until the 1960s, a good meal was beef and potatoes, and a great meal was glazed ham or stuffed turkey.

Even among the American elite, however, admiration for French cooking did not lead in a clear line to Provence. The journey there took a long time and held many turns. Understanding this requires a look at French gastronomy, a field with Paris at its center. As imagined by its culinary writers, France was a hexagon in which all lines led to and from Paris.[2] In the manner of an empire, the French capital took from the provinces their products, including the best of the bounty from its land, while seeking to impose its hierarchy of values on the nation. Its version of the French language was taught in schools throughout France; its critics judged art and literature; its style of recipes governed cookbooks. Of course, pushing against this was the reality that France remained a place of regions; and, despite pressures from Paris, the provinces began to reassert themselves in the nineteenth century in meaningful ways. Counter-movements such as the Félibrige inspired attention to regional cuisine, along with regional literature, folkways, costume, and crafts. With this, Provence reclaimed its distinctive history and language, and also put in print recipes for its characteristic food. Provençal cookbooks emerged, including at the end of the century Jean-Baptiste Reboul's influential *La Cuisinière Provençale* (1897). While Paris, Brittany, and Burgundy cooked with butter and cream, Provence used olive oil. Important chefs, such as the famed Auguste Escoffier, emerged from Provence and produced influential cookbooks that included Provençal recipes.

By the early twentieth century, with the advent of the automobile, culinary regionalism was opening up new possibilities. Enthusiasts formed touring clubs in France and elsewhere that promoted good roads and travel by car to distant places. This fostered interest in regional cooking, especially in France. Maurice-Edmond Sailland, known by his nom de plume Curnonsky, ate prodigiously, traveled extensively, and with Marcel Rouff wrote inexhaustibly in the 1920s about the food of the regions of France. The two searched for the "authentic" rather than the rare, and in their twenty-eight published regional guides, including *La Provence* (1922), they promoted the idea that the real glory of French cooking lay in the dishes made at home by women, not in the haute cuisine of male chefs.[3] Other travel and food writers followed suit, one even setting out seven gastronomic itineraries covering roads from Paris to Nice.[4]

Over time, the *Guide Michelin France* became an essential resource for selecting places to dine. Initiated in 1900, it began as a free handbook offering drivers assistance, especially regarding automobile tires, as they traveled throughout France. The handbook soon added information about hotels. After World War I, as more cars plied the roads, increasing numbers of restaurants as well as inns and hotels emerged to serve tourists. Beginning in 1923, Michelin Red Guides, now for purchase, included restaurants and rated them with stars. Gastronomy became the guide's most important feature, putting treasured knowledge, once known only to the elite members of France's touring clubs, into the hands of the bourgeois driving public. Drivers taking the national roads from Paris to the Riviera could be assured of a good number of three-star restaurants ("Une des meilleures tables de France . . . worth the trip.")[5] But as one got closer to the Mediterranean coast, they became fewer and fewer—in 1937, only in Châteauneuf-du-Pape did there exist even a two-star restaurant.[6] Additionally, the Red Guide made it clear that a rating in such a place was a relative one. Outside of the areas traditionally known for their fine cuisine, such as the region around Lyon, a Michelin rating under three stars was a statement that the meal was only to be judged within "establishments of the same region." Among those "fine dining" regions, Provence was not to be found.[7]

Whether or not he could afford to eat in any restaurant, Ford Madox Ford would clearly have agreed. Although this prolific British writer brought attention to the region in his 1935 book *Provence*, he did not appreciate its food. Ford's condemnation of Provençal cooking as having "no regional dishes" and no possibility of "serious" cooks helped shape assessments by sophisticates in his era.[8]

Voices countering such views gradually emerged. The most exciting to some Americans was M. F. K. Fisher. In 1937, Fisher implicitly took on Ford—and the Michelin Red Guides—when she published *Serve It Forth*, a series of essays about life and food in France. In subsequent years, after living in Aix, she focused much of her attention on meals in Provence. Fisher was a pioneer among writers, a woman who put in words the sensuous delights of eating. As Laura Shapiro has put it, Fisher created a fictional narrator who ate "hungrily, passionately," one who relished openly the "sensual, emotional, and intellectual experiences inherent in touch and taste."[9] Fisher gained a loyal following over a lifetime of writing, but she initially wrote during hard times. With the Depression and World War II, most Americans cooks had little time and few resources to indulge their more exotic appetites. More likely, what Fisher did was to create awareness and stimulate appetites whose satisfaction was only delayed.

Fisher offered vivid food memories. Writing of her childhood delight in eating dried sections of tangerine, toasted on the radiator, then chilled on the window, she asked, then answered, why this was so magical. "Perhaps it is that little shell, thin as one layer of enamel on a Chinese bowl, that crackles so tinily, so ultimately under your teeth. Or the rush of cold pulp just after it. Or the perfume."[10]

Fisher's pieces can offer the strange, dark pleasure of a Raymond Chandler mystery novel or a noir film. She wrote of the French waiter Charles, fired and then hired back for only one evening and one meal because she had requested him. She offered the vision of the perfect dinner party as an evening to kill time, a "murder of a kind." In her trope, time became a death. The dining room therefore became time's "death-chamber." So, "let it be filled with good food and good talk, and then embalmed in the perfumes of conviviality."[11] Whatever Fisher's intentions in this extended metaphor, food in such a setting took on a macabre aspect.

In her life and writing, Fisher was a woman who broke the rules—and lived to tell the tale. As César, the butcher she invited for dinner because he never included women in his own feasts, said to her husband over the meat, "She likes it, she likes good food! . . . She cannot be a real woman!"[12] Women readers who themselves liked to eat heartily must have appreciated her validation of their appetites against prevailing notions of appropriate female daintiness. Appealing to some men as well as women were both the quality of her writing and the central lesson about food she imparted. While "France eats more consciously, more intelligently, than any other nation," Fisher wrote, Americans eat "collectively, with a glum urge for food to fill us. We are ignorant of flavor. We are as a nation taste-blind."[13] American men ate a hamburger and drank a cherry Coke for lunch. Fisher was out to change that.

A new consciousness about food was gradually entering America. While many voices in the culture continued to insist in the language of food reformers that food was essentially fuel to be judged for its efficient delivery to the bodily engine, by fits and starts a different message emerged—food is one of life's central pleasures. From its first issue in 1941, *Gourmet* magazine served to organize and amplify this alternative voice. Fine dining as central to the good life was its message.

A key messenger was Samuel Chamberlain, an influential artist and author who would help guide readers to Provence. In the late 1930s, when Earle R. MacAusland got the idea of starting *Gourmet*, his first task was to gather a team to make it possible.[14] He loved good food and knew advertising and aspects of magazine publishing, but he needed an editor. On one of his early ventures he went in search of Chamberlain, a graphic artist with a strong reputation in MacAusland's Boston.

The first sight of the man was a surprise. It was in one of the old buildings of the Massachusetts Institute of Technology on Boylston Street that MacAusland found Chamberlain "pulling etchings, in a badly stained smock that made him look rather more like a genial automobile mechanic than a fine artist." When they talked about France and food and wine, however, MacAusland knew they were "on common ground."[15]

Chamberlain had spent a great deal of time in France, first as an ambulance driver in World War I, then in the 1920s with his wife, Narcissa, living abroad on fellowships, drawing, and growing a family. They settled in a house in Senlis, north of Paris, but the worsening economy in the 1930s drew them back to the United States. They moved to Marblehead, Massachusetts, and Sam worked for various publications and taught graphic arts at MIT. When confronted by MacAusland in that basement, Chamberlain had a clear sense of his own gifts—and they were abundant— and thus he declined to take on the job of editor. He preferred, instead, to be a contributor.[16] The first issue of *Gourmet* appeared with Chamberlain's "Burgundy at a Snail's Pace," adorned with the author's drawings.

The timing of the *Gourmet* launch couldn't have been worse. A glossy monthly dedicated to the art of living well, designed to signal the return of luxury dining to Americans with the end of the Great Depression, *Gourmet*'s first issue was dated January 1941. Europe was at war, cutting off most of the magazine's potential readers from the possibilities of the exquisite meals it promised. Nonetheless, the magazine survived, and in its second issue it published the first episode of "Clementine in the Kitchen," Samuel Chamberlain's fictionalized account of his French cook's experiences in America (complete with recipes), later collected in book form.

Gourmet continued during World War II amid food rationing and kept alive aspirations that could not be realized during wartime. As Americans entered the more prosperous era that followed, the magazine was poised to become an important arbiter of taste.

It also served to teach its readers new ways to think about food beyond the borders of the United States. It offered a new genre that combined travel and food writing with illustration and photography, all centered on the sense of taste.

In 1950, *Gourmet* and Chamberlain introduced the food of Provence to Americans. During World War II Chamberlain had returned to Europe to serve as a reconnaissance photographer, and after the armistice and the resumption of travel to Europe, his longing for France returned. MacAusland proposed to Chamberlain that he undertake a series on "French food, wine and travel," and Sam and Narcissa were ready to go. With that came a new direction. As Chamberlain put it more formally, "The noble art of gastronomy was creeping in, and the graphic arts were beginning to serve as accomplices to the epicurean theme." For three years during the spring and summer months, the two Chamberlains toured the French regions for *Gourmet*, creating "An Epicurean Tour of the French Provinces." They logged all the meal details, interviewed hotel owners and chefs, gathered menus and *cartes des vins*, and then wrote them up in featured articles.[17]

Gourmet's March 1950 issue held the Chamberlains' exploration of Provence, presented like all the other regions with a blend of easy travel writing, restaurant reviews, and recipes. Samuel Chamberlain was a friendly, genial, and knowledgeable guide, and he reflected the good times he and his wife had exploring all the high-end restaurants of the region.[18] Narcissa Chamberlain's services proved critical, for she translated and adapted the recipes for publication. The Provence that the Chamberlains considered in 1950, however, was the Côte d'Azur, a place they had enjoyed in the 1920s. Samuel gave only a mention of the towns looking down at it from the hills.

This was to change. In the year that followed, Chamberlain sent out questionnaires to hotel owners and restaurants across France and requested more regional recipes. Recalling this, he wrote, "Hundreds of tempting recipes rolled in," and Narcissa tested them and translated them into "basic culinary English."[19] From this came the influential *Bouquet de France* of 1952. In it, as he considered Provence, Chamberlain went beyond the coast to write about the larger region, and his tone was very different from the earlier magazine piece. The Provence of *Bouquet de France* was a "strange land of alternating poverty and plenty" with special allure. Its "barren hilly stretches are austere and melancholy. . . . Then suddenly one comes into a brilliant, lyric garden in the delta of the Rhône, a fabulously fertile area where low fields of vegetables and berries adjoin orchards heavy with cherries, peaches, pomegranates, and almonds." Chamberlain tried to describe Provence's distinctive perfume, containing "a dash of lavender, the odor of ripe melons and drying figs, the aroma of pure olive oil blended with a suspicion of fennel, thyme, and saffron, and, of course, a gentle breeze of garlic." After a tribute to the Roman ruins, the climate, and the seemingly relaxed life of the villagers, Chamberlain moved on to his real subject, the food of the region. Noting the use of olive oil rather than butter, and the importance of garlic, he particularly lauded the region's fish dishes, especially the brandade, "a thick creamy mixture made with salt cod pounded to a fine pulp in a mortar, prepared with cream, olive oil, and a few pulverized heads of garlic, and decorated with thin slices of truffle. Few dishes are subtler." Turning to wine, he extolled Châteauneuf-du-Pape, listing his choices of domaines and years. Following descriptions of the major sites of the region, he presented the recipes, prepared by Narcissa. Everything here made one want to visit Provence to see, smell, and, most of all, taste.[20]

In 1958, Chamberlain generously lent an introduction to a book that would become another beacon lighting the way to culinary Provence, *The Food of France* by Waverley Root.[21] Root, too, was a Francophile, and he shared with Chamberlain an eagerness to get American travelers away from the pretentious "international" food of the great hotels and into restaurants that offered local fare. Root had also moved to France in the 1920s, where he found work as a journalist for Chicago papers and national publications. After returning to the United States during World War II, he wrote a three-volume history of the war. He went back to France in the

1950s as a journalist, writing ultimately for the *Washington Post*. In 1958, *The Food of France* turned him into an important food writer, a calling he pursued for the rest of his life.

What made *The Food of France* distinctive were its descriptive passages of the land and its products, those special qualities of soil and climate that made the food of each region distinct, its *terroir*. Waverley Root had a particular love of Provence. He wrote in the 1958 book that it was "the most magical of all the provinces of France." There he found "nature and man . . . in closer harmony than anywhere else in France." He saw Provence as "antique" but hardly old. "You cannot live there long without becoming conscious of the vigorous pulse of the south." What called to him was not the Mediterranean Coast, then at the height of international popularity, but Provence's hills. Initially, he wrote, they might seem to be a monochromatic grayish green, "but when your eyes become accustomed to the palette of Provence-Beyond-the-Sea, you will marvel at the never-ending gradations of green." He contrasted the subtle beauty of inland Provence to the bright colors of the Côte d'Azur. The coast, he wrote, "can provoke love at first sight," but he added, it was a kind of love that "frequently leads to a quick divorce." By contrast, love of the hills of Provence was enduring.[22]

Waverley Root's informed writing attempted to get at the essence of Provençal cooking, in a manner that has proved long lasting. Consonant with French food writers, he named its three key elements as olive oil, garlic ("the truffle of Provence"), and the tomato ("which manages to get into almost everything").[23] He described many of the region's characteristic dishes made with these ingredients. Without giving recipes as such, he gave enough details of their making to render them inviting to try at home.[24] With the power of hindsight, it is possible to see that the combined work of Waverley Root and Samuel Chamberlain provided the literary template for future American celebrations of the food of Provence.

However, a major barrier to the enjoyment of the food of Provence remained—the problem of garlic. Garlic is central to the cuisine of

Provence, flavoring its most important dishes and taking center stage in its famed aïoli, its distinctive garlicky mayonnaise. Before taking pleasure in Provençal cooking in their kitchens at home or in France, Americans had somehow to get over their aversion to garlic. This was not a superficial dislike, easily avoided by pushing a hated meat or vegetable to the side of the plate. For some it was an elemental dislike.

Discussions of Provençal food in American magazines alert the reader to the obstacle garlic posed. In 1959, for example, when *Gourmet* magazine offered several Provençal recipes, this caveat accompanied them: "Well, there is at least one common factor in all these mixtures: the lavish use of garlic. That is a distinctive characteristic of all Provençal dishes, and I beg you not to be afraid of it. Garlic is what gives Provençal cooking much of its robust individuality."[25]

Avoidance of garlic carried meaning far beyond the table, for antipathy to garlic served as a key marker of middle-class propriety from the mid-nineteenth century until the late 1960s. In 1861, for example, *Mrs. Beeton's Book of Household Management*, that bellwether of Victorian mores, declared, "The smell of this plant is generally considered offensive, and it is the most acrimonious in its taste of the whole of the alliaceous tribe."[26] In the United States, the impact of immigration added fuel to an older animosity to garlic. As newcomers came to these shores, many Americans already in place sought to distance themselves. Immigrants brought with them their foodways, including the heavy use of garlic by many southern Europeans. Nativism can take odd forms. By the turn to the twentieth century and lasting at least five decades, along with hypercleanliness and the use of precise English came the banishment of the odor of garlic from the kitchen and the breath.

II

Change would come, opening the way for more Americans to enjoy the food of Provence. An initial impetus came from a surprising direction—the frightening news that assailed home cooks during the late 1950s and 1960s. They had entered their kitchens with a raft of messages about food safety from their youth—"You are protected if you shop in a bright, well-lit super market." "You can trust it if it comes in a box stamped with a good brand name." "You can be sure it's safe if it is wrapped in cellophane." All these slogans turned out to be false.[27]

The first postwar American food scares occurred in the late 1950s. There had been low-level scientific discussion and even a bill in Congress designed to help protect American consumers from the increasing use of chemicals in food production and manufacturing. But 1958 saw a screaming headline that broke through to the American public—chemicals in or on food might cause cancer. With that came a series of specific scares—cranberries, chickens, maraschino cherries. It was enough to make shoppers uneasy as they pushed their carts through the aisles. Home cooks learned to wash their food carefully and hoped for the best as they prepared their families' dinners.[28]

Following this came the shocker from the medical community that all those good meals coming from the kitchen—all that strength-giving meat and milk and eggs and butter—might be harming members of the family by clogging their arteries. In *Fear of Food*, Harvey Levenstein has written both wittily and effectively about the wide range of messages trumpeted by the media that scared many Americans both early and late. Obediently, many home cooks shifted to margarine, only to learn later about the dangers of trans fat. Some tried to substitute fish for meat in some family meals and subsequently worried about levels of mercury. As homemakers scanned the newspaper for reports, danger seemed to lurk in the most unsuspected places.[29]

In the meantime, what would later emerge as the Mediterranean diet was making its way gradually through the influence of an unlikely source of health news—*Gourmet* magazine and food writers celebrating taste, not health. In 1965, when *Gourmet* sent Chamberlain on a return trip to the French provinces, he not only waxed enthusiastically about Provence, he now emphasized the bounty of the land. Although Chamberlain admitted the aridity and barrenness of parts of Provence, he wrote, "There are also lush fields where nature's bounty is prodigious." He moved on to celebration. "The finest melons in France come from Cavaillon . . . and tomatoes, eggplant, peppers, and onions all thrive behind their protective windbreaks of closely knit cedars. Olive trees ripple on the hillsides and provide the fruit and the fundamental oil of the Provençal cuisine."[30] Chamberlain approved of good local mutton and sausages, and he liked some of the local wines from "the sun-drenched slopes of Provence," what he called "unpretentious rosés" good for a summer meal, adding that Châteauneuf-du-Pape was now a respected label. Years before, he wrote, the region had bespoke austerity, but "the horn of plenty is overflowing now."[31]

Chamberlain was an epicure writing for *Gourmet*, and as he discussed Provence and other regions of France he normally focused on the high end of refined haute cuisine. By contrast, the influential British food writer Elizabeth David turned her attention to preparations in the typical French kitchen. She became another voice reaching this side of the Atlantic. David emphasized pungent and fresh ingredients and relatively simple preparations. Similar to M. F. K. Fisher, David was a free-spirited woman who wrote vividly about food.

Her announced mission was to re-educate the British palate after the ill habits of generations and the privations of war rationing had done their work.[32] Before World War II she had spent time on the Mediterranean and enjoyed its bounty. During the conflict, while others had made do with rations and the danger of air raids, she had lived safely in Egypt and enjoyed the services of a fine Sudanese cook. She wrote that "while my own standard of living in Egypt had perhaps not been very high, my food had always had some sort of life, color, guts, stimulus; there had always been bite, flavor and inviting smells. Those elements were totally absent from English meals."[33] She could not bring Mediterranean sunshine to her homeland, but she could encourage her countrymen to eat the fruits of its land. Into the world of bland British cooking, David injected new recipes and a lively spirit. As she promoted in glorious prose Mediterranean and French food in a wide range of magazines and newspapers and in her many cookbooks, she immediately garnered readers.

David began to offer occasional vivid writing about food on these shores as early as 1957 in the American *Vogue* and its offshoot for younger women, *Mademoiselle*. It is here that many an American reader may have gotten a first chance to learn about food in Provence from a great admirer. "Once one has tasted Provençal cooking, one is addicted to it for life," David wrote. "It is the best of all cooking. If deprived for long of its savors and colors, its olives and their oil, its great ripe tomatoes, its onions, eggplants and sweet peppers, its scented melons and peaches, its spicy aromatic herbs (basil, dried fennel stalks and wild thyme) that go into the meat and fish dishes, the sauces and soups of Provence, one begins to pine."[34]

A chance encounter with Elizabeth David's words could change a life. In the mid-1960s, Ruth Reichl, later the restaurant critic of the *New York Times* and editor of *Gourmet*, but then age sixteen, found an old issue of *Vogue* in a thrift shop with a piece by Elizabeth David. Reading it was "a shock." Reflecting back recently, Reichl contrasted herself as a lonely teenager in a world of hamburgers with Elizabeth David. "She was everything I was not: unconventional, sensuous, smart and stylish. . . . I instantly knew I wanted to be just like her." And for Reichl that meant to eat like her.[35]

David wrote a number of cookbooks containing Provençal recipes, but they posed difficulties for Americans. Who could follow their recipes? They offered no separated list of ingredients, common to twentieth-century American cookbooks, and gave no numbered step-by-step instructions for preparation. Fortunately, Craig Claiborne, appointed in 1957 as food editor of the *New York Times*, stepped up to the plate. In his weekly column Claiborne came to feature home cooks as well as restaurants and to focus on a range of cuisines. In the later 1960s, as he traveled internationally, he found his way to "rustic" Provence and started planting seeds for its future discovery by his American audience. In discussing two restaurants in the region, he wondered whether the reason for their high quality, in contrast to restaurants in New York, "lies in the innate nature of the ingredients." He was convinced that "herbs have more pungence here. The fish in general have more character and so do the vegetables, tomatoes in particular." After this trip to France, Claiborne followed up a few months later with a recipe for "Boeuf en daube provencale."[36]

In 1961, Craig Claiborne's *New York Times Cookbook* appeared and in one volume offered from the columns of the newspaper many recipes for home and company. These included French ones, but Claiborne had little interest in being "authentic." He offered tasty dishes with the advantage of clear directions that were relatively easy to follow. In his regular articles and in this cookbook, as he guided cooks to enjoyable experiments in the kitchen, he emphasized the pleasures, not the dangers, of food.[37]

His book was published in the same season as *Mastering the Art of French Cooking*, the collaborative magnum opus by Julia Child, Simone Beck, and Louisette Bertholle. Claiborne was first at bat as reviewer, and he generously complimented this seeming competitor, using words like "most comprehensive," "laudable," and "monumental." He wrote, "The recipes are glorious. . . . All are painstakingly edited and written as if each were a masterpiece, and most of them are."[38] With this launch, some American home cooks began taking their first lessons from Julia Child.

Mastering the Art of French Cooking was a teaching book, intended to present clear steps so that Americans could prepare the standard dishes of French home cooks with the ingredients typically available to them in American food stores. In retrospect, the book also offers lessons in publishing and promotion. Rejected by Houghton Mifflin as too long and unwieldy, it was shepherded by Avis DeVoto and taken to Knopf, where editors William Koshland and Judith Jones championed the book.[39] Once published, Child proved an indefatigable promoter of her work, and the book was well received not only by Claiborne but by a host of reviewers. It garnered solid sales.

Then, beginning in the Boston area in 1963, public television offered Child a regular evening half-hour of cooking demonstrations as *The French Chef*, and her impact took a great leap forward. On air, Julia Child emerged as a natural guide and performer, transcending the clear steps of *Mastering the Art of French Cooking* to teach basic techniques of food preparation and offer culinary wisdom. And, magnificently, she went beyond to offer herself. Julia Child as *The French Chef* was larger than life, bursting with enthusiasm for her task and full of infectious zest. Many watched her show as entertainment, but the audience also included serious acolytes eager to follow her every direction in the kitchen.[40]

As Child cooked before the camera, she had a congenial and lusty way of talking about food, handling the ingredients, tasting as she prepared, and then sitting down with wine to savor the final dish. As she increasingly became a public figure, Julia Child emerged as a spokesperson for the joy of eating. Her "bon appetite!" became a byword signaling the new pleasure in food.[41]

Early fans of Julia Child may not have picked up the cues, but she was a great admirer of the country cooking of France. She was not out to teach her readers and viewers the haute cuisine of restaurants. She plainly stated in the very first episode of *The French Chef* that its featured preparation, *boeuf bourguignon*, was "a peasant dish" from a people who do "simple hearty cooking."[42] These words were likely ignored, however. The dish was French, it used wine and contained fresh mushrooms and pearl onions—it must be classy.

Child also admired Provençal cuisine. She included recipes from the region in the 1961 cookbook and in the ones that followed. In 1963, she and her husband had a small vacation house built on Simone Beck's property in Plascassier in the Provençal hills near Grasse. They returned each summer to "La Pitchoune," as they called their home, for rest and recreation. None of this, however,

6   Paul Child, "Julia Child cutting mushrooms," Schlesinger Library, Radcliffe Institute, Harvard University.

was initially taken in by Americans who read and watched Julia Child in the early 1960s.

These were the Kennedy years, and French high style was very much in the air. Installed in the White House was a real French chef, René Verdon, who produced well-publicized official dinners in the grand manner. Inspired by Jacqueline Kennedy's taste and Julia Child's television guidance, many ambitious American cooks in the early 1960s focused on learning recipes for food they imagined to be chic and cosmopolitan. Despite early articles in *Gourmet*, the efforts of Chamberlain and Root, the writings of Fisher and David, and Claiborne's enthusiasm, food from Provence appeared rustic, from a very old place still largely known for its Roman ruins.

Essentially, what many aspiring American cooks were searching for in these years was sophistication in the kitchen. A taste of Paris was what they were after. To those caught up in this quest, Provence was too close to "provincial," the very opposite of their aspiration to be worldly and enlightened.

EIGHT   **But Not Ready for
             Prime Time**

In the 1960s, Provence was almost ready to take off as an important
place of desire for Americans, but not quite. One can see this in the
response to two books by American women. The first was a cookbook featuring Provençal dishes; the second, a narrative of the purchase and reconstruction of a Provençal farmhouse. Neither failed
outright. Both merely fizzled from lack of interest.

    In part it was the era, one of the most turbulent in American
history. In cookbook and travel writing, most of the real world is
generally hidden. But on the streets of American cities and college
towns, conflict was there, and it was real. In the late 1960s, with the
Civil Rights Movement fractured, Black Power grabbed the head-
lines. Riots broke out in major and minor cities. Events in 1968 and
1969 were especially shocking—or eye opening. Assassins took the
lives of Martin Luther King and Robert Kennedy. Student protests
against the Vietnam War erupted on college campuses and city
streets. Brutal police violence met demonstrators at the 1968 Democratic National Convention in Chicago. Protest at the Miss America Beauty Pageant brought attention to an emerging feminism that
in more radical hands seemed to threaten the basic structures of
family and home. Open discussion of gay rights and campaigns for
change followed the Stonewall Riots. In November 1969, the Mor-
atorium March on Washington to end the war drew more than a

half million participants. Perhaps as a counter-reaction, yearning for escape led some Americans to dream of Provence, among other faraway places, but this longing did not come in time for these two books to find an audience.

I. THE COOKBOOK

When Peta Fuller saw *La Véritable Cuisine Provençale et Niçoise* in the library of a friend, she borrowed it, tried its recipes, and became its devotee. This cookbook by Jean-Noël Escudier had been published in France in 1953 but had gone relatively unnoticed in the United States. Fuller's intense pleasure in the book gave her a mission and, as she put it, she embarked on a "culinary adventure that was to lead, eventually, through the attractive pages of *Gourmet* magazine and across the Atlantic air to adorable Toulon and, at last to Monsieur Provence himself."[1] As Fuller presented him, Escudier, her "Monsieur Provence," was a major promoter of his native region and served as founder-president of the Companie des Gastronomes de Provence and publisher of the monthly *Journal d'Aix-en-Provence*. Much of this was likely fiction. As best can be determined, M. Escudier was the pseudonym of Roger Rebstock, a small-time publisher in Toulon with no such pedigrees.[2] Inspired by the cookbook, Fuller translated its recipes for what she titled *The Wonderful Food of Provence*.

Gourmet introduced the book in 1967 in three successive, handsomely illustrated articles. America's monthly purveyor of fine dining began by printing the Toulon author's introductory words, translated and amended from the 1953 book. These established the grounds for giving attention to Provençal cuisine. Escudier framed the recipes in the glamour of the history and culture of his region. In presenting his work he wrote, "*Haute cuisine* is always an indication of a high level of cultural development, and that of Provence is in the top rank of our time." In contrast to the sobriety of the Greeks and the grossness of the Romans, "the *Provençaux* feast with finesse. . . . prefer the exquisite to the copious." It was, he said, the great chefs of Provence of the nineteenth century who were responsible for bringing the lightness necessary to transform the food of northern France into modern French cuisine.[3]

In the following two issues *Gourmet* presented discussions of bouillabaisse and aïoli with recipes for each. Despite this great launch, when *The Wonderful Food of Provence* came out, it was barely noticed. The well-known cookbook writer Nika Hazelton included *The Wonderful Food of Provence* in a long list of new cookbooks she reviewed in the *New York Times* in December 1968. She praised its illustrations but stood at arm's length from its recipes. What she really did was to denigrate Provençal cooking rather than the book itself. She wrote that the cookbook "makes the most of a cuisine that basically is not too extensive or varied. The recipes are refined from the coarseness inherent in this kind of food."[4] Coarseness—that was hardly a word aspiring Americans wanted to hear about food or anything else. They were striving for sophistication, for Paris and haute cuisine.

Additionally, garlic remained a problem. Peta Fuller decided to confront this outright and inserted boldface into her translation these elitist words: "Because of immigrant labor that had floated in on a pungent wave of (mostly) Neapolitan cookery, the magic clove became associated chiefly with the lower classes."[5] Here Fuller joined a host of important food writers in the 1960s who tried to bend American food tolerances to include garlic. Writing in a more positive vein, Craig Claiborne began a 1969 column he titled "Garlic Galore" by stating, "More than one sage has noted that where people eat garlic, happiness abounds. No region is better known for its garlic specialties than that sun-filled area of France called Provence." What followed was the recipe for aïoli with all its accompaniments.[6] When, in that same year, the revered James Beard introduced his recipe for aïoli, he called it "the creamy, soft soul of garlic, the very breath of Provence." He then added that Frédéric Mistral, the Nobel-winning poet of Provence, spoke of garlic in his journal "as a symbol of the dry heat, the strength, and the soothing quality of the sun and the true essence of its home.

Those who like it not would never return to the land of the sun; those who loved it would remain one great family."[7] Ultimately such kind words, bolstered by the well-publicized health benefits of garlic, would later win over an important segment of the American population. But that time had not yet come.

II. THE FARMHOUSE

In 1969, it wasn't just desire for sophistication and the fear of garlic that kept most Americans from focusing on Provence. The cause, rather, was likely simple indifference derived from tastes not yet fully awakened. One can see this in the reaction—or, more accurately, the nonreaction—to the other major effort to draw attention to Provence.

Mary Roblee Henry had high hopes for the publication by Knopf of *A Farmhouse in Provence*, her story of the discovery, purchase, and reconstruction of a property in Séguret, a village near Vaison-la-Romaine. And well she might. She was an American already living in Paris with established credentials as a writer. And she had great connections, a good agent, an excellent editor, and an important press. She herself had been travel editor of the American *Vogue*; she was, in fact, the very one who had taken that first jet flight from New York to Paris and described it in soaring terms.

That very short trip—"two days in flight, two nights in Paris"—had changed her life. In Paris she met French diplomat Paul-Marc Henry, and, as she put it, "Nine flights across the Atlantic and three months later we were married."[8] In the years that followed the marriage she continued to write travel pieces from France.

Her book had a very strong launch. The *Atlantic* optioned the chapter on the wine harvest for its May 1969 issue.[9] *Vogue* featured Henry and her book in its "People Are Talking About" section.[10] And then, in December 1969 *Gourmet* published "Réveillon at la Sérafine," a travel and food article on the preparation and enjoyment of a traditional meatless Christmas Eve feast in the reconstructed Provençal farmhouse that she had named "La Sérafine."[11]

The *Gourmet* piece was the very first writing on Provence that I read as I began my research for this book. I was fascinated by it, and it became a kind of marker for me as I proceeded to read more. It was a good beginning, for it contains all the elements that were to become iconic representations of Provence—sumptuous descriptions of ingredients purchased at the market, local customs, carefully prepared food for the table, tradition, distinctive goods of the region, wine, and ultimately a vision of larger meaning.

First came the open-air market in Vaison. There, "a huge array of sea animals shone silver on seaweed at my fishman's. . . . The oysters and winkles looked so tempting" that Henry added them to the traditional codfish. She found cardoons at the vegetable stall, "small thistlelike blossoms that had been picked and sheltered from sun and frost and stored and saved for the holiday." When she got to the olive seller, he "dipped his pierced wooden ladle into buckets of Nyons black and green olives for me," and she found at another stand "some rough 'black pearls,' the famous truffles of Vaucluse."[12] What an enviable contrast this delightful excursion provided to pushing a cart in the chilled air of an overlit American supermarket.

An introduction to the life of the town and its customs followed. As Mary and Paul-Marc Henry shopped, his father—called "Beau-Père" in the French manner—retreated to the local bar. Once they found him, they entered and shook hands with the *patronne*. "In Provence one always shakes hands, coming and going, even if the visit lasts for only a moment." In the meantime, Beau-Père won a wild boar in a game of lotto. "Every Christmas the Provençal peasants, amid squeals and celebrations, slaughter a fattened pig, stocking their larders with sausages, pâtés, *boudins*, and hams for the coming year. A wild pig such as this great brute would add a rich dimension to any country table." But the Henrys, of a higher class, did not wish the boar and arranged an exchange with a man who had won the lesser prize of two guinea fowl. Her father-in-law dreamed of adding them to the meal, but the author resisted the addition, for "I had my heart set on having our Christmas Eve as

Provençal as the mistral and indeed, had consulted the works of the poet Frédéric Mistral for some of our thirteen desserts."[13]

Tradition remained at the center as Mary Henry set the table with the customary three cloths, topping them with an additional one of "burgundy-red-and-yellow Provençal print" complete with matching napkins.[14] After lighting the Yule log and reciting a special poem, the family, augmented by Paul-Marc's adult children and their friends, went to the church for a lengthy village pageant and returned famished for the meal that was meant to keep them awake until the midnight arrival of Christmas proper.

At the end of the great feast, described in loving detail with its accompaniments of Dom Pérignon and the house red wine, "le Clos de La Sérafine," the family opened the shutters to find snow falling. "Who could have dreamed such a dream—a white Christmas in Provence." The party went outside and leaped and danced in the snow. The author closed with an early version of what was to become the central meaning of Provence: "At last, I realized, La Sérafine had come full cycle, our sanctuary for today, for tomorrow, forever."[15] Provence offered bounty, traditions, and the opportunity for travelers—willing to stay awhile—to stop the rush of a busy and pressured life to turn a moment into eternity.

Many of these same elements are present in *A Farmhouse in Provence*, Henry's account of the acquisition and renovation of the farmhouse.[16] Here she went back to recall one of the trips with her husband and a visit to the second home of wealthy Parisian friends Roger and Régine Fabre in Vaison-la-Romaine. Roger Fabre was a native son of the region, loyal to its way of life despite his primary residency in Paris. He was respected locally for his work in helping to get the *appellation d'origine contrôlée* for the area's wines and his role in establishing the local cooperative for processing grapes. Régine Fabre, his fashionable wife, kept an elegant town establishment in Vaison. She was in the process of restoring what was to be a third residence, a farmhouse, or *mas*, where the Fabres were to have their own vineyard. They named it Chanteduc.

Once Mary Henry saw Chanteduc, she began to dream of a country house in Provence for herself and her husband. She confessed that she had not always loved Provence. Some years earlier when, "bewitched by the jeweled eyes of Italy," she traversed the region, Provence had felt "hostile, impenetrable, even sinister." She saw its "black-fingered cypresses" as "symbols of death," and "blinded to Roman France," she raced home.[17] But she had changed, and so had the region.

A comedy of errors brought her to purchase the dilapidated ruin that was to become La Sérafine. Her first encounter with the neighbor who would become the house's caretaker began facing the end of a gun. She had been brought to the property by a poacher, a Balkan painter who was not the owner he pretended to be. Her first look at the property was hardly promising. From the outside, she saw a "mournful hovel," and inside it, the rooms "seemed incredibly dank and dark." But then, it happened: "Framed in a branch of lime blossoms, it exploded before my eyes—the view. All the splendor of Provence mapped in the valley below."[18]

Her husband was at that moment on a brief side trip to Paris, but once he returned, she told him and the Fabres of her adventure. Her hosts understood instantly that the armed man who had confronted her was the truffle-hunting Monsieur Faravel, a former Paris policeman, retired on his pension in Séguret and living with his wife on the adjoining property. The next day the Fabres took Mary and Paul-Marc Henry for a proper introduction, and with that the Faravels became the "guardian angels" of the enterprise. M. Faravel first guided them to meet the real owners of the property and then introduced them to his nephew, an entrepreneurial contractor who for five years oversaw the reconstruction that brought the ruin back to life.

A Farmhouse in Provence tells the long story of creating Mary Roblee Henry's sanctuary. She perceived two major obstacles in their way. First there were the natives. "To the Provençaux we were foreigners, invaders in the guise of conquerors, in their eyes corrupters bringing a potential for change, for good or for evil. . . . We were the sun-hungry city people; they were the people born to the sun."[19] The second obstacle was her father-in-law, who came to visit them the first August, when they were staying in Chanteduc as guests of the Fabres. Beau-Père came from France's Atlantic coast and hated the dry air of Provence. He immediately declared the purchase of La Sérafine a "catastrophe" and their plans for renovation "une grande folie."[20]

The Henrys persisted nonetheless. As costs mounted, they found that Beau-Père had some wisdom on his side. Mary had harbored the fantasy that her farmhouse in Provence would be a refuge, somehow outside of market forces. Both labor and materials would be cheap in her mind. "The Vaucluse," she wrote, "symbolized the fulfillment of this illusion. Too far inland from the Riviera to attract yachting millionaires, too rural for industry, too remote and inherently French for non-French-speaking visitors, it held the *lux, calme et volupté* of faraway places, the *ordre et beauté* of uncorrupted innocence. In stumbling on to Séguret, I thought I had found an oasis bypassed by the caravans of trade."[21] But as expenses mounted, even in the 1960s, this was not to be.

In addition, she faced serious conflicts over the issue of "modern" versus "authentic" with her contractor, M. Faravel's nephew. When she told him she wanted to keep "as many of the original features as possible," she met his incomprehension. "Ironically, the restoration of La Sérafine was becoming a battle between us living in the New World wanting the old and the Provençaux of the Old World wanting the new." But it turned out that what Mary Henry wanted were only the decorative details of the past, "the old beams and tiles."[22] Equally important were the new conveniences unheard of in Provence—three water closets, a modern American kitchen filled with labor-saving devices—and speedy construction.

The plumbing and kitchen could be paid for, but speed was not available at any price. As Mary Henry arrived at the house on one holiday, she was shocked that the construction work was incomplete. "So this was my dreamy Americanized kitchen that the handsome, red-haired carpenter had taken six months to plan! The polished brown cabinets were half assembled, one Formica shelf left a gaping hole below. The wretched little stove stood far shy of the cupboards, and the refrigerator was placed alone against another wall."[23] Mary Henry's narrative of restoring a farmhouse in Provence set the pattern for the many future books on the same theme.

As did her ending, the harvesting of the wine, redeeming all the trials that preceded. She, too, caught the dream of owning a vineyard. Back in the United States, she learned of a potentially good harvest on their vines and rushed to the *vendange*, the picking and early processing of the grapes. "It was, after all, the culmination of our dream, the victory of the land, the triumph of La Sérafine." Arriving from New York, she first went to the market for vegetables and oysters and cheese, meat, and bread and then headed out to the vineyards. After a short delay caused by a storm, serious labor in the vineyard for all hands began for three long days. At the dinner to celebrate the successful harvest, "We were delirious with joy. At last we counted as true citizens of Séguret with our own *cru*. The cellars of the Clos de La Sérafine overflowed."[24]

Many elements that were to become familiar parts of the master narrative of finding and rebuilding the Provençal farmhouse can be found in Mary Roblee Henry's book, and two decades later Peter Mayle would successfully exploit this pattern. But in 1969, the audience to hear the tale did not yet exist. *A Farmhouse in Provence* did not pass unnoticed at the time, but it was hardly a best seller.

It is possible that there were other aspects to the book's tepid reception. Before it was published M. F. K. Fisher read the manuscript and advised the book's editor, Judith Jones. Once she received the published book, Fisher wrote her "honest reactions." She admitted a vicarious pleasure in the book but nonetheless "couldn't help slyly pointing out that Madame Henry never put on just a sweater; it was always a *cashmere* sweater."[25] Similarly, Laurence Wylie wrote Alfred Knopf to say that "every geographic and architectural detail was familiar to me," and he was grateful for the chance to revisit the region. "To be perfectly honest, though, Mrs. Henry is not quite my dish. There is something about her upper class gentility. . . . This didn't prevent me from enjoying the book;

it only kept me from enjoying it more."[26] The tone that both Fisher and Wylie noted clearly set off the book's reviewer in the *New York Times*. After summarizing the book's contribution in writing about "property-buying in out-of-the-way places," the reviewer turned negative. "The style of the book succeeds in elegance of a rather obtrusive sort. There is much falling back on French phrases, even in conversations supposedly being conducted in French." After giving two examples, the turned-off reviewer offered this final sentence: "This kind of swell talk, and a growing idea that most of the goings-on concern only the author and her circle, may make some readers feel rather unnecessary, *de trop*."[27]

Nonetheless, "swell talk" was the *Vogue* style in the 1960s, and *Vogue*'s copies and advertising sold well throughout the decade. Indeed, *Vogue* helped promote the book. A personal note from Diana Vreeland, the magazine's editor-in-chief, told Mary Henry that it was "delightful" and a tale "beautifully told."[28] The failure of *A Farmhouse in Provence* to find a large audience may have been less its elitism than its timing. Its fate was similar to Peta Fuller's translation of the *Wonderful Food of Provence*. Both books arrived before their time. In 1968–69, there were simply not enough American travelers and readers ready to imaginatively engage in the preparation of Provençal food or the restoration of a farmhouse in the hills of Provence.

But tastes change. Sometimes this can be hard to see, for transformation can take place with such small steps that it is imperceptible. In the case of the taste for Provence, change happened with a loud crash and a bang. All at once, with the turn to the 1970s, Provence seemed to be everywhere in the media, ready to capture the imagination of many Americans.

Julia Child and the Pleasures of Provence

In October 1970, on her popular television show *The French Chef*,
Julia Child was suddenly in color. She had a new, larger studio
kitchen and dining room, and she was no longer confined to the studio space. In sixteen episodes of the 1970–71 season, she appeared
in scenes shot in France in the previous months. For the first time
she presented French food as prepared and sold by French hands.

She and her husband, Paul Child, had taken their typical summer vacation in Provence in 1970. But, in addition, they had gone
around the region, as well as to other places in France, with members of the camera crew from WGBH, the Boston public television
station from which the program originated. As usual, the Childs
had prepared carefully in advance, determining "the sites to visit
and the people to see."[1] The crew filmed Julia at outdoor food markets and small specialty food shops or inside taking lessons from
professional cooks. She conversed with merchants and artisans,
observed demonstrations of techniques, and made the viewer want
to be there. A particular half-hour show might have one French segment or as many as four; some segments were as short as one minute, some were as long as ten.

By this time, Julia Child was already a celebrity, not merely a
cookbook writer and a demonstrator of cooking techniques. In
November 1966, she had appeared on the cover of *Time* magazine.

In 1968, she had hosted a special program on the White House kitchen as it prepared a grand banquet. In the segments filmed in France in 1970, she was a genial mistress of ceremonies to French fishwives, olive sellers, bakers, and other artisans, engaging them in conversation in French and translating as needed for American viewers.

Provence appeared in all its glory. It was magnificently beautiful as the camera focused on the flower market in Grasse or panned over the landscape nearby to reveal the Childs' second home in Plascassier. It was rough and real as the fishwives at the Old Port in Marseille shouted their wares and bantered with their customers. It was skilled and precise as a master artisan demonstrated the making of a magnificent *paté en croute* or as Simca Beck worked the dough in Julia's Plascassier kitchen (plate 9). It was mouthwatering as the maître d'hôtel of a restaurant in St. Paul-de-Vence roasted a huge leg of lamb hanging vertically in an outdoor oven and then carved it at Julia's table in the shade.

In a vivid episode, Child explores the weekly market in Grasse on her way to a *crèmerie*, a shop selling dairy products, to buy crème fraîche, a product then rarely available in US grocery stores. The camera shows her strolling around the outdoor market, admiring its abundant vegetables, and buying flowers (plate 10). She and viewers watch as the shopkeeper in the crèmerie pours out the thick crème fraîche into a cup—dramatically moving the ladle higher and higher—for Child to purchase and take away. In the studio, Child follows with instructions to the American home cook for making a simulation of crème fraîche in her kitchen, but, of course, it isn't the same. One wants to be by her side in Grasse, buying and then tasting the real thing.[2]

As the camera shifts to the Plascassier landscape, the viewer pines to be there. Child invites this. Her usually high-pitched voice softens to caress the word "Provence." As a man and a woman pick roses nearby, Child intones, "And the air is most lovely smelling country. You smell the olive blossoms and linden trees and the wild

7   Paul Child, "Julia Child buying crème fraiche," Schlesinger Library, Radcliffe Institute, Harvard University.

herbs. . . . And just look at all those flowers."[3] When the camera shows the exterior of the Marseille fish market and then moves inside, she says that she wants you to "see it and hear it."[4] As the outdoor market at Grasse comes into view, she states enthusiastically, "I'd love you to see this market."[5] These sun-filled views must have been all the more appealing to her North American audience when shown in the depths of the harsh winter of 1971. And always, there was Julia Child herself, her welcoming presence guiding throughout—commenting, translating, and praising with her indomitable enthusiasm. In the era when she emerged as an icon of Americans' new delight in food, she offered on the small screen enticing demonstrations of one of the prime pleasures of staying awhile in Provence. Julia Child might not have known it, but she was an early actor in the drama of the selling of Provence to Americans as a destination to desire.

NINE   The Sell

Although ordinary Americans watching *The French Chef* in 1970–71 were hit in the eye with the hills of Provence, the region had never been truly ignored. It had long been on the map for lovers of ancient ruins and medieval churches. At some level commerce was always present, for journeys in Provence as elsewhere require meals and a bed as well as transportation. Even in the 1920s, the adventurous A. Hyatt Mayor ultimately found a place in the Provence hills to rest his bicycle and his head. But clearly by the time Julia Child presented the region in color on television, something new had happened, something that requires attention to the money trail.

Travel in France after World War II changed when the number of intermediaries between visitors and the services necessary to sustain them grew and strengthened. In part, this evolved out of French national policy to attract dollars through tourism and its employment of American advertising agencies. In the United States, travel and food magazines, taking off after the war, embraced color photography with its remarkable power to tempt. As these publications informed and promoted places and dining, they were reliant on subscribers and advertising to keep them solvent. Novelty proved an important element in attracting readers as bait for their potentially more lucrative sources of income—advertisers for all sorts of luxury goods and services, including tourist accommodations. Thus the continuing search to discover the new—the unbeaten path—the untried destination, such as Provence.

The way to the Provence hills had been anticipated in the early 1960s, by bits and pieces, teasers really, showing a Provence beyond the Roman ruins. Nonetheless the turn to 1970 saw new drive and momentum. The reinvention of Provence, as prepared by the brilliant spread of Irving Penn photographs in *Look* magazine in 1962, was now in full swing. Commerce began to show its face in glossy pictures and writing designed to appeal as much as to inform.

Ironically, the Provence being sold was the opposite of commercialism and the glitz of the Ritz or the Côte d'Azur. The hills of Provence were presented as a place to escape from the frenzies of the present and its drives for profit, a place to live, at least for a spell, a life of ease, and perhaps of peace. Yes, the hills of Provence were there to be coined into money—by travel agents, airlines, the French government, their advertising agents, and all the restaurants, inns, renters of second homes, and provisioners of the region. But Provence was being sold in the name of getting off the beaten track and getting away from it all.

First to the plate in June 1970 was *Holiday* magazine, with a feature by Irish journalist and humorist Patrick Campbell. The article was clever, the writer, even cleverer, as the subject snuck up on the reader unawares. In the midst of a funny narrative celebrating true leisure—awakening without knowing or caring what day it was, only that it was July—the reader gradually learned that Campbell was living in a rented villa in the hills above Nice.

To any of the magazine's hard-working American readers, Campbell's day was enviable. He awoke to the strenuous tasks of examining his garden, talking with his gardener, taking a dip in the swimming pool, receiving the mail, welcoming guests, and drinking a succession of vermouth, pastis, champagne, and kir—all achieved before 10:00 a.m. The day evolved into menu planning for lunch— the *salade niçoise* "with most of the ingredients coming from our own vegetable garden,"—alongside earnest conversation with a guest about the advisability of a striped blazer as seen in *Esquire* and serious discussion about the inexpensiveness of life away from the Mediterranean coast. There was also a good deal of standing in the pool to cool off while drinking, and there were three hours of playing the popular outdoor game of boules. It was, as the title put it, a recipe for "How to Live the Sweet Life in the South of France."[1]

That issue of *Holiday* was published just at the point when Julia Child was filming scenes in France, to be aired on the *French Chef* intermittently from early October 1970 to the end of June 1971. In the midst of this television season, *Travel & Leisure* devoted its second issue, April/May 1971, to a major spread on Provence. Interestingly, although the issue included food, it featured high culture. In the lead piece, Rosamond Bernier, a renowned appreciator of contemporary art, offered the lure. Perhaps in a nod to the supposed unfamiliarity of its real location, its title, "Cote d'Azur: Artists' Choice," led with the known. But the large-print lede gave the true place: "Above Cannes and Nice on the French Riviera artists have discovered countless small hill town hideaways. As a result the whole countryside has become a living museum of modern art."[2]

Writing in words meant to reflect the growing judgment of many elite art lovers, Bernier stated that the once-favored places on the Mediterranean—Cannes, Nice, St. Tropez—were no longer desirable. Renoir's Haut-de-Cagnes, beloved by him in his late years, was being destroyed "by the relentless builders who have swarmed over the surrounding countryside," wrecking the view from his house with high-rise buildings. Once the mecca for the jet set, the Riviera was seeing "unfortunate concrete constructions" and had become "crowded." All was not lost, for in the hill towns above the Riviera, one could find "cool mountains" and many delights.[3]

Facing the opening page of Bernier's text was Marc Chagall's fanciful *Autour de Vence* (1957). This painting of reconciliation, blending Jewish and Christian imagery, shows a glimpse of Vence, the Provençal hill town, above gathered flowers and the bounty of a table. The text began with tributes to the town, the place the artist had chosen for his home following World War II. Gone were the ugly facts of German occupation, the fierce fighting in Provence with the Resistance, the deportation of Jews in France to the Nazi death camps, and the specific danger Chagall and his wife faced as Jews in France before the two were rescued in 1941 and given safe passage to the United States. Smoothing over this difficult and contested era, Bernier offered Vence as Matisse's haven when life in Nice during the war became "too difficult" for him.[4]

After a gentle description of Vence as a "center of flower culture" came a walk through the small town in language as dreamy as the Chagall painting—"dappled plane trees filtering hot sun into deep shade, worn stone, the splash of fountains. . . . A maze of steep streets winds from the square, disappearing under archways, climbing up to the cathedral, curving around ramparts, banked by crowded narrow houses with plants spilling over their sills." But Vence, Bernier insisted, was no touristic place where Parisians "have arranged a quaint holiday perch." Vence was real. Babies were howling, laundry was flapping on lines across the roads, and people were arguing near open windows.[5]

Bernier was an appropriate choice to write this piece. In 1971 she was beginning a new career as lecturer at the Metropolitan Museum of Art in New York. She had served for many years as the features editor of *Vogue* in France and had reported on the French art scene as cofounder of *L'Oeil*. Bernier let it be known that she knew France's great artists personally and offered stories from their world. In this particular piece she told of the creation of Matisse's famous Chapelle du Rosaire in Vence. In 1948, when she visited him in the hospital during his recovery from surgery, he was working from his hospital bed. There he cut out "stylized leaf shapes or geometrical elements from paper painted with gouache" to become the patterns for the chapel's stained glass windows. He told her that it was to be a church "full of gaiety—a place which will make people happy."[6]

Without missing a beat in her piece, Bernier shifted from quoting Matisse to a travel-writing mode and led the reader to the cathedral and local restaurants. Offering an insider tip, she departed from the Michelin-starred establishment to recommend her favorite, La

Farigoule, named for the thyme of the region. She liked the restaurant's "straightforward local cooking and its red cretonne décor."[7]

She then turned to St. Paul-de-Vence nearby, with its famed Colombe d'Or, a restaurant filled with great modernist art works, assembled because during hard times its owner agreed to exchange meals for pictures. Bernier had some unkind words to say about this town, seeing it as a place "so picturesque that movie stars, artists, real and pseudo, and tourists have practically taken over." But she offered its redeeming feature (in addition to the restaurant)— the admirable Maeght Foundation Museum, housing the works of contemporary masters, including Chagall, Miró, and Braque, and surrounded by a great outdoor sculpture garden.[8]

First the sense of sight, then taste. The food writer in this particular publication was Michael Field, regarded in his day as a culinary expert. Once a concert pianist, he was at the time editor of Time-Life's series of twenty-seven cookbooks, Foods of the World, setting recipes in their cultural contexts.[9] Following on the heels of Bernier's piece, Field, supported by his wife, Frances, tempted travelers away from the beaches and coastal towns with "Provencal Cuisine." As had Bernier, the couple had given up on the Riviera. "The beaches along the Côte d'Azur are hopelessly crowded," they wrote. "The roads and boulevards jammed with cars crawling bumper to bumper, and our favorite restaurants so packed that dining out is more an exercise in fortitude than a pleasure." Putting the coast behind them, they traveled to Avignon, Arles, and Aix. There they discovered the essence of Provençal cooking, the abundant use of garlic. Following in the language of Waverley Root, the Fields wrote that, unlike the Italians who treat garlic as a subordinate player, "Provençals treat it as the star. They call it the sacred herb, the truffle of Provence." They know how to cook it, keeping it unbruised for such dishes as chicken with forty cloves of garlic. And they know how to use it at its pungent best in aïoli. With this, before presenting four recipes, the Fields went beyond to state, "Whatever they touch—fish, meat, fowl, or vegetables—they invest with the touch of genius. No wonder then that those who fall in love with Provence . . . become . . . obsessed with it."[10]

Not unexpectedly, since *Travel & Leisure* was then the house organ of American Express, accompanying these two pieces was the announcement of the company's special twenty-two-day tour of France. Among the many highlights of the trip, it informed, "You will travel the countryside immortalized by Matisse, Van Gogh, Picasso, and Cezanne and explore colorful Provence, where the warmth of the hospitality is reputedly unmatched anywhere in Europe."[11]

Bon Appétit also joined the publicizing game in 1970. Although the magazine began in 1956, it had taken some years to develop into a major voice, but by the mid-1960s the publication had some heft and impact in the food world. In the fall of 1970, it offered an important feature on "The Cuisine of Provence." Given *Bon Appétit*'s interest in wine, there was a significant section on wines of the region, especially the reds of Châteauneuf-du-Pape and Hermitage and the "heady, refreshing rosés."[12]

Bon Appétit offered one sentence that resonates still today: "Provence is memorable in every way, whether you experiment with famous recipes in your own kitchen, or adventure within her special culinary and historic borders." Nonetheless, in celebrating the food of the region and its ingredients, much of the writing and the images in *Bon Appétit* seem derivative, using generic terms that could have been written by one who had mainly been to Florida. The piece, however, did quote Jean-Noël Escudier, without naming him, as saying that the Provençaux, unlike the Greeks and Romans, eat with "finesse. . . . They prefer the exquisite to the abundant." Along with a good number of recipes, the article advised that "Provence deserves time . . . it can easily consume a two to three week vacation." Next came the roll-out of Michelin-starred restaurants and a favorite place to stay. It is clear that the magazine's editors believed that garlic still posed a potential problem for its readers. More than once the author of the piece advised that, cooked in the Provence manner, garlic is not only harmless but even good tasting. It finally stated, in reference to garlic soup, that the way the Provençaux treat garlic "takes away its harsh strength and minimizes its after-effects leaving a flavor that is exquisite, aromatic and almost indefinable." The photographs were clearly shot somewhere other than in Provence. Accompanying Frogs Legs Provencale, to be eaten on a presumed picnic, was an American bicycle and a basket whose red accent proved to be not tomatoes but apples.[13]

By contrast, *Gourmet*, with its long history of illustrated writing about Provence, strove for the "authentic," now in color. Provence was featured early on in articles by Samuel Chamberlain, and the magazine presented excerpts of Peta Fuller's translation of Escudier's *The Wonderful Food of Provence* in 1967. By 1973, however, there was a new look. Now *Gourmet* offered glamorous color images of the region's food surrounded by Provençal decor. With this, the magazine conveyed important new information. Not only could Provençal food be prepared in American kitchens, but the pictured plain dark wood chairs and the distinctive, colorful Provençal tablecloths and napkins could be purchased in the United States. *Gourmet* credited the furnishings to Pierre Deux, a relatively new store in New York carrying Provençal fabrics and furnishings.[14]

By the mid-1970s *Gourmet* joined the media chorus singing for travelers the pleasures of the region. Doone Beal's piece "Auberges à la Provençale" offered the magazine's first feature on inns in Provence. "It was one of those days you dream of, a vision of late spring perfection toward the end of May. The clear dry air smelled of pine and cypress, and we inhaled it on an open terrace over deliciously iced aperitifs, while looking down on the red-tiled roofs of Old Vence." Beal went on to quote a definition of luxury and claim it for a castle-like hotel providing the magnificent view shown in a full-page color photograph and for a small, rustic cottage with seven bedrooms presided over by Madame Saucourt. Although he admitted that she "rather sidesteps some of the traditional Provençal dishes," Beal found her food praiseworthy, and everything to his liking.[15]

Beal's article began a full-court press in *Gourmet*, as one writer after another traveled through Provence, cited its beauties, lauded its restaurants, discussed garlic, and praised the local ingredients. The language in 1976 of the British food writer Elisabeth Lambert Ortiz, as she began an extended report on the region to guide future travelers, can stand in for all. "If Provence did not exist, the poets would be forced to invent it, for it is a lyrical landscape and to know it is to be its loving captive for life." She found it to combine both nature and human artifice, a rich history, and a "pure light so loved by painters, presided over by the bluest of skies." Its cooking, based "on the best that land and sea have to offer," reflects its fragrant landscape, with garlic as "not the least of its kitchen glories." With that introduction, she examined many places to visit and dine as a travel writer, and then, as a food writer, she offered recipes to try at home.[16]

The ultimate statement of the selling of Provence in the 1970s came with the May 1974 issue of *Travel & Leisure*. Its cover promised "The Flavor of Provence" with an image of two old stone buildings. Inside was a double-page spread of an *allée* of trees forming a canopy over a dirt road. In the distance through the trees could be seen an ancient structure on a slight rise. This page announced "The Good Life in Provence," by the Irish writer Sean O'Faolain.

The piece offered this opening: "It is tucked away. Meadows. Butterflies. Total silence. Good food and local wine." The page was illustrated by a photograph of the inn with a boules player sitting at a table; both Van Gogh and Cézanne were mentioned in the accompanying caption. On the next page, a beautiful woman touted as an Arlésienne stood behind a bank of vivid red roses, and below her an elderly man, "a shepherd for 60 of his 70 years," sat beside a stone wall. This caption mentioned not only Van Gogh but also Renoir, Bonnard, Gauguin, Matisse, Chagall, and Picasso.[17]

Although the accompanying box of information on Provence listed many sights to be seen, including art treasures, Roman ruins, and highly touted restaurants, O'Faolain wrote of something else completely. He came to Provence because he sought a place

unchanged since the '20s, by which he meant the 1820s: "Undeveloped. Offering slow, limpid, rustic holidays, in simple, homelike,
sympathetic inns. . . . In short, pre-touristic Europe."[18]

Looking for the authentic as well as the unhurried, he desired
cheap bottles of wine and restaurants and hotels lacking Michelin
stars and rosettes. Wondering if he could find it in the territory of
Alphonse Daudet's great subject, he fixed on Provence and selected
its western part, easily reachable by air travel to Marseille. He consulted a poet friend to find a village with a nineteenth-century inn,
one that combined "complete quiet, the sense of the past, *and* all
modern comforts." After checking that the Michelin people never
heard of the Sevanes in Mouriès, an inn that was adapted from a
sizeable *mas*, he chose it for a month's stay.[19]

His confidence was shaken when he arrived with his wife and
daughter during the rough winds of a mistral. But once amiably
greeted by the family who had adapted their home into an inn, all
doubts vanished. The inn had retained all of its "familiar character, its air of still being not 'reached' but discovered, come upon
by chance, hidden away from the world at large." There he found
an informal hospitality that allowed him to enter the inn's kitchen
to pour himself an aperitif. He loved the sense of connection to the
past, a past that could literally be smelled when walking the surrounding countryside. "The air is aromatic with . . . lavender, wild
thyme, the tall thin fennel, . . . juniper, wild asparagus, hawthorn,
mint, rosemary, any or all of which have enriched every Provençal
dinner table for centuries."[20]

In talking about food to a local man, O'Faolain learned he had
bought snails on a street corner, and they had been placed in a
glass to allow him to eat them while strolling. With that, O'Faolain
had just what he wanted. "Strolling! . . . the key word . . . for the
particular quality of the lifeway of this great triangle of countryside between the Rhone and the Durance. Strolling! And thereby
seeing everything close up." With this, he reflected on the ease of
Provence, wrought from the toil of 2,000 years of patiently working
the soil. Seeing with romantic eyes only what he wanted to see, this

Irish writer—heretofore known for his work chronicling the political and economic struggles of his countrymen—believed he had
found a world characterized by "ease of body, security of mind, a
remarkable degree of prosperity, all the reasonable refinements of
The Good Life."[21]

O'Faolain captured the dream of the past living in the present,
one of the important aspects of the authentic. Imbedded in his
report was his finding of true leisure—strolling—and its promise of
a return to the self. But his words were published (and likely commissioned) by a glossy travel magazine. Behind the periodical was
American Express and a broad field of advertisers, whose commercial intentions were quite the opposite of strolling. After such writing could O'Faolain's dream of finding the world of "pre-touristic"
Provence continue to exist? Wouldn't his words bring travelers to
follow in his footsteps to create the very world he was seeking to
avoid? Such is the irony of travel writing when it searches for and
finds the undiscovered.

TEN   **The Tomato**

"Tomatoes are so plentiful in Provence that you can't live there
very long before they are offered to you as a gift," wrote Paul Zimmerman in 1971. His was the first travel piece in the *New York Times*
to celebrate the joys of a month-long stay in the hills of Provence.
He and his wife rented an apartment in a restored building in tiny
Venasque. There they reveled in daily life, drove around the countryside, went to the weekly markets and food shops, delighted in
the fresh ingredients they brought into their kitchen, and savored
the tranquility Provence offered them. Past issues of the newspaper
had focused on historic features of the region, such as the Roman
ruins in Arles, or had announced events, such as the music festival in Aix. This piece was different, for it presented a new kind of
travel experience, a long stay in a rented place in a small Provençal
village.[1]

Zimmerman, then a young film critic for *Newsweek*, related
how he and his wife sought a new kind of vacation in Europe. A
New Yorker, he went to the office of Villas Abroad, a firm dealing
in short-term vacation rentals, to look over its offerings. He found
apartments on the Riviera well out of their price range, but a small
place in Venasque, roughly twenty miles north of Avignon, "off the
tourist circuit," would cost them far less than "an equivalent dwelling in Southampton or Cape Cod, that is, if you can find an equiv-

alent." In 1926 A. Hyatt Mayor could not locate an inn in Venasque for a single night's bed and board. Now this small village offered beautiful accommodations.

Once part of a fifteenth-century monastery, the dwelling Zimmerman rented had been "impeccably restored" in the early 1960s to have central heat, functioning plumbing, and a good working kitchen. "Done entirely in stone, great dark beams, ruddy tiles and vaulted ceilings, it perched on the edge of a 1,000-foot limestone cliff that offered us a commanding view of the Vaucluse Valley with its neat rows of cherry trees and sun-soaked apricot orchards, its scrambling vineyards, sharp cliffs and sweep of purple mountains. At sunset, we would sip aperitifs and watch the sun leave the valley."

Avoiding the Michelin three-star attractions that were "swamped by tourists and lose their character when seen in a crowd," he and his wife took to traveling by car down country roads to seek the picturesque perched villages, such as Gordes and Roussillon. Well paved and traffic free, these roads "carry you through the very center of farms among the orchards and past the sturdy old red-tiled farmhouses that are Provence."

They found good restaurants within an hour's drive, but the real gustatory pleasures were closer at hand. Zimmerman wrote of "the beauty of repairing to your own kitchen for a lunch of pate in cognac or Reblochon [a raw cow's-milk cheese from Savoy] on the heavy country bread of neighboring St. Didier." For him it offered "an improvised pleasure that cannot come from living in even the best French hotels."

At the heart of Zimmerman's piece is not just a recitation of the pleasures of the landscape, something readers of such writing had come to expect, but a celebration of daily life lived abroad, the joys of the "rhythms and rituals called the French way of life." First there was the diversion of male sociability, made possible by his fluency in French and his gender. Zimmerman told of late-night hours with the town's mayor, Julian Ruel, "a great bearish man with brilliant white hair and a heavily accented French that forces its way past a collapsed network of silver-capped teeth and a dangling corn-paper cigarette." A Socialist, farmer, and son of Venasque's previous mayor, Ruel was Zimmerman's "conduit of tradition in the town." Zimmerman also enjoyed afternoon aperitifs with a postman from Arles who told him about the town's politics over pastis, "a pernod that is the dry martini of Provence." Laurence Wylie had faced the unasked question in 1950—was he a spy? Two decades later Zimmerman was welcomed for what he was, an American traveler enjoying the many pleasures of village life.

As Wylie had himself observed in retracing his steps in Roussillon, the life Zimmerman witnessed was no longer weighed down by the loss of hope. Zimmerman and his wife visited a farming couple, who spoke about the change in the region. Monsieur Bibal was a hardworking farmer who over time had planted flourishing fruit trees. "All the while," Zimmerman wrote, "Bibal would play off his image as the rube. 'You know we're not peasants anymore,' he told me with a smile and a wink. 'Once you own a tractor, as we do, you're in *agriculture*.'"

The Zimmermans enjoyed the great town fête that gathered all ages at the village center. Its main event was a tournament where the men played *pétanque*, a form of boules. Zimmerman concluded that renting in Venasque allowed human contact with people from the town, yielding him "a pleasure that no tour of France can equal. It is, in a sense, the payoff for staying put for a month."

When Zimmerman wrote of the pleasures of food shopping in Carpendras, he began to sound like Mary Roblee Henry. First were the tomatoes—plentiful and cheap in the stores, along with other vegetables and fruits. What caught his eye was "the pure beauty of the food itself"—raspberries, strawberries, ducklings, baby chickens, pigeons, fresh vegetables, and spicy sausages. If that were not enough, "the cheese store is pure poetry—compact little discs of local goat cheese, sides of Gruyere the size of suitcases, crumbly sharp cheese from the Pyrenees and calmer, smoother rounds from Savoy."

In sum, the stay in Provence offered Zimmerman the best month he had ever spent in Europe. He had chosen the place to rent from a scrapbook, but "what we couldn't see in the snapshots of our house in Venasque was the total tranquility that soothed us the entire length of our stay."[2]

By the turn to the 1970s something new clearly was at work. Actually many new things. A restored old place in the hills of Provence was available to rent for a month. A person could go to a vacation rental agency in New York, choose a property from pictures in a scrapbook, and secure a booking. Compared to a summer residence in a familiar American spot, such as Cape Cod, the rental in France was inexpensive. These were definite attractions that pulled one to Provence.

But why the tomatoes? The tranquility? Why would a young couple travel abroad to seek a retreat from the world? Cynically, one could say that the sell was beginning to take. Zimmerman's summer month came just after Julia Child's Provence was on the TV screen. *Holiday* had just featured its comic piece "How to Live the Sweet Life in the South of France." But there have been many advertising campaigns. Remember the Edsel, that powerful symbol of failure? This car named for the Ford heir was heavily marketed and advertised by Ford Motors in the late 1950s, and when it flopped, it lost the company millions. And today, how many movie spectaculars fall short of their media campaigns? For an ad campaign to work, there needs to be some reality to support, at least in part, the claims being made, and there must be a need, however inchoately felt, that the advertised element appears to fulfill. I think of the reality as the pull, and the need as the push.

Much of the pull we have already seen: the re-creation of Provence through electrification and irrigation and the reconstruction of dwellings by French second-home owners. Change in France continued apace in the 1960s. More of those homes were available to rent for a month, and Provence became much easier to reach. Although France had long been blessed with well-engineered roads, it delayed development of high-speed motorways; but in 1970, the *autoroute du Soleil* was completed. Vacationers now had a potentially fast route from Paris via Lyon to Marseille.[3]

But just as important for American travelers was the push, including the 1950s food scares and evolving American tastes. Yet more still had to happen. It makes sense not to think of a single push but rather a variety of nudges that led some Americans to Provence. Paul Zimmerman in the summer of 1970 was an early adopter, and his experience spoke to some in his generation. When he went to Venasque, he was thirty-two. To get him to Provence—with its tomatoes and tranquility—one might look at the conditions around him, the time in the 1960s when he was a young man, just out of Amherst, trying graduate school at Berkeley and the Sorbonne, before becoming a writer.[4] This was a complicated era in which to come to maturity, a time of protest and tumult. Zimmerman would have known about or observed student protests in California and France, civil rights activism and black militancy, riots in American cities, campus strikes, and public outcries against the war in Vietnam that led to mass marches on city streets. One by one, assassins' bullets took major figures—President Kennedy, Martin Luther King, Robert Kennedy, Malcolm X. To many who lived through these days, it often seemed that the world was turning on its head.

Two environmental disasters at the end of the 1960s had the powerful impact of reminding Americans of the vulnerability of the natural world. The Santa Barbara oil spill in winter 1969 wreaked havoc on beaches and killed marine animals and birds. Then in late June 1969, the Cuyahoga River in Ohio caught fire. As with the Vietnam War, these disasters were televised. Earth Day, April 22, 1970, brought further awareness of environmental dangers and initiated a new consciousness and cause.

Then, less than two weeks later, on May 4, came the brutal shootings later named the Kent State Massacre, when members of the Ohio National Guard killed four unarmed student protestors and seriously wounded many others. This terrible event initially led to increased turmoil on campuses and city streets, but it actually marked the beginning of the end of student protest. Where did this leave those young people who had heralded the dawning of a new age? In the wake of the 1960s, many shifted gears and attempted to incorporate into their own lives what could not be won in the public sphere.

While turbulence was the public face of the late 1960s, many reactions were hidden from view, as quieter, but no less powerful, structural changes were reshaping the nation. Shifts in the nature of industry continued to feed a major population move from the rustbelts of the North and Midwest to the sunbelts of the South and Southwest. Suburbs spread, new immigrants entered, the South began to turn Republican.[5] Cities seemed to be rotting at the center, leading to ambitious, but often destructive, schemes for urban renewal. Older bonds that had connected Americans—network television, national magazines, and weekly moviegoing—were continuing their explosion into a fragmented media world that, over time, would become pitched to a thousand different tastes.

Out of these forces and the unrest of the 1960s emerged changes in the culture, one of which began to be noticeable early in the 1970s—a turning inward toward self-discovery. As Bruce Shulman has pointed out, the struggle "against alienation" had been part of the efforts to fight against "injustice, poverty, and imperialism. . . . But Sixties radicals found it easier to build new homes for themselves than to rebuild American political culture." In bequeathing "their crusade for self-liberation to the nation," they broadened "personal transformation" but also led it to be "more inwardly focused."[6]

The travel dreams that shifted for some Americans beginning in the early 1970s were one outcome of this. Going away, especially if that meant going abroad, once held the hope of acquiring culture, having a great adventure, or abandoning one's repressions to have fun. It's not that these desires disappeared, but mixed in with them was a new aspiration that time away from home could lead to self-discovery.[7] The idea emerged that one might go far away to come home to the self, to find one's center. As a writer put it at the end of the 1970s, we travel "to consider our lives, to purify and simplify our pleasures . . . to know who we are with a clarity that cannot be duplicated, on the run, at home."[8]

I think of Paul Zimmerman as a secular herald in the wilderness, calling to others to take new kinds of journeys. The path he took would grow wider, as the years went on and political disillusionment grew with events such as Watergate and the end of the war in Vietnam, along with years of stagflation. Among the new travelers who made their way to Provence were members of a new generation who moved into the world of work roughly a decade later than Zimmerman. These young professionals did not openly condemn the system but rather engaged with it, either cynically or wholeheartedly, seeking to turn it to their advantage. As they entered the ranks of lawyers and doctors or bankers and entrepreneurs they made a bargain with themselves to exchange long hours of labor for possessions and pleasures. Yet many did not fully abandon all countercultural currents of an earlier time. Instead they held on to the hope of personal freedom and sustained an environmental consciousness that sought to effect change not only in personal habits but also through local activism. When it turned to food, some of them became food adventurers, seeking exotic cuisines, while others favored the natural and organic, a blend that helped fuel the food revolution that came to America.[9]

More broadly, Americans with time and money for vacations were typically used to the relative generosity of dwellings and automobile travel. Thus many Americans after 1970 often imagined the ideal vacation as enjoying much of what they had, minus the stress. When they gave a place to their dreams in the United States, it might be a quiet home in the hills of Vermont, near the beaches of Cape Cod, beside the mesas of New Mexico, or under the open skies of Montana. But often these were missing a central part of this new dream for travel—market-fresh food, symbolized by the tomato.

The search for flavorful, unadulterated food can be traced back to Earth Day in spring 1970, for it was then that environmental consciousness met the food supply. Over time, awareness grew, and a spotlight shined on what were derisively called "Frankenfoods." While the increasing use of chemicals by farmers and food processors in the postwar period had already caused well-publicized alarms, new concerns were raised about the changes being made by food technologists. Grain had been milled into flour for about 8,000 years, but only in the years after World War II were there efforts to break "raw grains down into their basic molecular structure" and reassemble them into "foods that bore no resemblance to the raw materials out of which they were fabricated."[10]

A food revolt began, focused on the word "natural." It created what Warren Belasco, the writer who best captured these changes, has labeled "countercuisine." Its rules turned the perceived food-ways of Middle America on their head: white bread and rice were replaced by brown, and cooked food, wherever possible, by raw. Anything cooked ought be prepared from scratch and heated slowly. As these approaches percolated, even traditional home cooks began to search for unprocessed and "organic" ingredients. Belasco summarized the message: "Avoid anything complex, anything you can't pronounce, anything chemical, synthetic, or plastic."[11]

It was in this way that the environmental movement profoundly reshaped how many Americans came to think about what to eat, purchase, and recycle—and where to travel. As organized efforts in the political arena failed to do enough, private and local actions emerged as important. Although environmentally aware individuals could not make politicians at the national level pass regulations to radically reduce automobile emissions, they learned they could buy smaller, more fuel-efficient cars. Ordinary citizens might not be able to change farm policy supported by the corn lobby, but they could stop buying sodas sweetened with corn syrup. They could not get the alphabet soup of chemicals out of the processed foods in the grocery chains, but they could cook their own meals from fresh ingredients. They could work in local communities to get recycling centers and learn to separate the trash. They could organize food co-ops and encourage their towns to set up local farmers' markets where they could buy regional produce.

As these co-ops and farmers' markets came into being, many were more than stores, becoming locations of easy sociability, enjoyed for the company as well as for their fresh vegetables and fruit. Roadside stands selling summer produce in farm country had existed as part of the landscape from as far back as anyone could remember, and there were important centrally located urban markets in places like Los Angeles and Philadelphia. The establishment of regular farmers' markets in towns and cities across the United States, however, took some time, and many had yet to be created. But in Europe—and in Provence—weekly markets going back for centuries were in place. Because of its sun and warmer climate, Provence was the center for fruit and early vegetables in France, and its markets were especially appealing. Gleaming produce from Provence called. Especially the tomato, long heralded by food writers as an emblem of Provence's bounty.

These pushes and pulls combined to guarantee that the selling of Provence met with success. And once begun, it was kept alive by a place at the very heart of the food revolution. Berkeley, California, proved to hold the most dramatic example in the United States of the new appreciation for Provence. It was there that attachment might be said to have blossomed into romance.

ELEVEN

The Romance of Berkeley and Bandol

In the 1970s, Berkeley, California, perceived as a counterculture heartland, caught the attention of restaurant-goers. This hotbed of youthful energy moved from being synonymous with protest to become known as a mecca for foodies. And as it did, the cooking of Provence served as an important inspiration.

In the previous decade, Americans had been simultaneously getting ready to taste and becoming increasingly wary of what was being marketed in grocery stores. After the inauguration of Earth Day in 1970, the evolving food conversation centered more on health. In the Bay Area, however, where the counterculture remained alive, along with radicalism and a commitment to community came an adventurous food culture. A new group of food critics arrived on the scene, writing for the region's radical press. Among them were Ruth Reichl, who wrote for the *New West*, and Alice Waters, who coauthored the food column Alice's Restaurant for the alternative weekly *San Francisco Express Times*.

As Berkeley emerged as a center of the food revolution in the United States, growing interest in Provence ripened into romance. Berkeley was where Alice Waters, later dubbed by the media "the mother of new American cooking," established her famous Berkeley restaurant, Chez Panisse. Waters has often identified her restau-

rant with the cuisine of Provence and its emphasis on seasonal produce fresh from the land and sea.

Yet the region was hardly where Waters began or what initially led the restaurant to achieve its outsized reputation. Briefly,
Waters was a part of the Berkeley scene in the 1960s, after arriving
as a transfer from the Santa Barbara campus of the University of
California. Berkeley was where she began to cook seriously.[1] But
Waters had already found the writings of Elizabeth David and the
food of France. Her "aha" moment had come on a trip to Brittany, where she watched the restaurant owner catch the trout that
soon appeared on her plate, surrounded by vegetables grown in
the restaurant's garden.[2] Once in Berkeley and living with political activist and printer David Goines, she began to make her way
through Elizabeth David's *French Provincial Cooking.* The two often
cooked and ate together with friends Charles and Lindsey Shire.
Alice specialized in main courses; Lindsey focused on desserts.
Their collaboration was to be long lasting. With Goines, Waters
started writing the Alice's Restaurant column.

Thinking initially that she had found her calling as a Montessori
school teacher, Waters traveled to London for training. She followed this experience with a pleasure trip on the Continent with
Goines, and food was at its center. After the two amicably separated, she was introduced in 1970 to Tom Luddy, the manager of
the Telegraph Repertory Cinema. Waters soon moved into Luddy's tiny house, and there, creating elaborate dinner parties with
friends, she became known as a very good home cook.

This was a heady time to be young in Berkeley, a place where
much of the spirit of the 1960s remained alive. Anything seemed
possible, and in Waters's case this included opening a restaurant
without an apprenticeship in a professional kitchen or a business plan. In 1971, fed by creative energies, hope, and enthusiastic friends, Waters transformed a house on Shattuck Avenue into a
restaurant and on August 28, opened it to customers. Lindsey Shire
prepared the desserts. David Goines did the art nouveau graphics.

Tom Luddy brought in his friends from the film world, and his buddy Paul Aratow provided the initial cash investment.

The name Chez Panisse came from a movie-induced aspiration. Luddy took Waters to the Surf Theater in San Francisco to see a retrospective of the films of Marcel Pagnol that included his Marius trilogy from the 1930s. As she wrote fifteen years later, "Every one of these movies about life in the south of France fifty years ago radiated wit, love for people, and respect for the earth. Every movie made me cry."[3] When Laurence Wylie was in Roussillon in 1950–51, he noted that when *Marius*, the first of the three films, played at the village café it attracted a large crowd and aroused visible emotion. Pagnol's films are melodramatic, with many dark shadows evoking tears, but they are, of course, more. Pagnol not only created the central dramas of love and loss, of lying and truth telling, he also re-created a world that was already passing when the films were made. Moreover, his films were infused with stereotypes of the Provençaux familiar since the writings of Alphonse Daudet.

The character Honoré Panisse was one of the regular card-playing foursome who gathered many times a day at César's bar in the Old Port in Marseille.[4] Panisse was a wealthy ship outfitter who, in the words of Alice Waters, was "compassionate, placid, and slightly ridiculous." In reflecting on why she chose the name Chez Panisse for her restaurant, Waters said that she intended it "to evoke the sunny good feelings of another world that contained so much that was incomplete or missing in our own—the simple wholesome good food of Provence, the atmosphere of tolerant camaraderie and great lifelong friendships, and a respect for both the old folks and their pleasures and for the young and their passions."[5]

At its opening in 1971, Waters imagined that Chez Panisse would offer a single daily menu, as in a home, and would become a hospitable place to dine and drink for those in her social world. Word of mouth was to suffice to bring in customers. Food writers in radical publications, including the young Ruth Reichl, broadcast knowledge about Chez Panisse. Despite its name, however, the restaurant didn't initially feature the food of Provence.

In these early years, Pagnol and Elizabeth David and the commitment to community mixed with drugs, sex, and rock and roll, and it was unclear whether or not Chez Panisse would make it, practically or economically. Although the restaurant was a culinary success and friends and supporters remained loyal, financial problems threatened to bring the restaurant down. Rescued by two business allies who paid the rising debts, the restaurant was later reorganized, and the active partners formed a company that took the name Pagnol et Cie., Inc. Years after, Waters explained that they chose the name "to reaffirm our desire of recreating an ideal reality where life and work were inseparable and the daily pace left you time for the afternoon anisette or the restorative game of pétanque, and where eating together nourished the spirit as well as the body—since the food was raised, harvested, hunted, fished, and gathered by people sustaining and sustained by each other and by the earth itself."[6] Perhaps, but this recollection was likely tinctured by later experiences.

Before Provence entered into the kitchen of Chez Panisse, there was Jeremiah Tower, who answered an ad for a cook. Although he, too, was untrained, he brought daring and seeming genius into the restaurant's kitchen. His elaborate preparations generated enthusiastic reviews in the national press and drew in the larger world. Tower was fascinated—not by the desire for straightforward food simply prepared but rather by the exquisite creations of great French chefs of the past. Even from this remove it is dizzying to read through his long menus with their wine pairings. Perhaps the most extravagant was his 1975 meal accompanied by Sauternes (including a 1922 Château d'Yquem)—ham braised in Sauterne served with prunes, quenelles of salmon with crayfish butter sauce, roasted sirloin of beef, green apples filled with berries, salad, a hot deep-dish fruit pie, the almond cream dessert *blanc-manger*, and caramelized walnuts.[7]

But, beyond the restaurant's name, where was Provence in all this? It came, but only after Chez Panisse was fully established. In 1974, Richard Olney published *Simple French Food*. A gay American living in France since 1951, he was well known in literary circles as a painter, wine connoisseur, and superb cook. Waters and Tower (as well as future Chez Panisse chefs) valued his 1970 *The French Menu Cookbook*, taking it as both guide and manifesto.

This remarkable book, organized by the seasons, is filled with careful and beautifully written advice about kitchen methods and equipment and wines. Explicitly and implicitly it reinforced the message that one cooked with what was fresh in the local markets. To the chaos of the home or restaurant kitchen, Olney gave the rules behind menu planning along with the sensory reasons that made them acceptable to a new generation. A sybarite whom no one could accuse of being a disciplinarian, he wrote of a meal as if it were a prolonged sexual experience: "Each course must provide a happy contrast to the one preceding it; at the same time, the movement through the various courses should be an ascending one from light, delicate and more complex flavors through progressively richer, more full-bodied and simpler flavors. . . . Essentially the only thing to remember is that the palate should be kept fresh, teased, surprised, excited all through a meal. The moment there is danger of fatigue, it must be astonished, or soothed into greater anticipation, until the sublime moment of release when one moves away from the table to relax with coffee and an *alcool*."[8]

Beginning in 1961 Olney lived in a small house restored by his own hands in Solliès-Toucas in Var, not far from the coastal town of Toulon, and was an always-welcomed guest at the table of Lucie Peyraud, nicknamed Lulu, in nearby Plan du Castellet above Bandol. Self-described as a cook in the tradition of the "cuisine de bonne femme," inspired only by love of family and friends, Mme. Peyraud was, in fact, a key thread in the network of sources that created a taste for her region's wines and cuisine. She is central to what became the love affair between Berkeley and Provence.

Lulu married Lucien Peyraud in 1936, and, several years later, her father, a leather importer in Marseille, gave the couple Domaine

Tempier, a sizable piece of land in the hills above Bandol held by the family since the early nineteenth century.[9] In the years that followed, Lucien dedicated himself to restoring and expanding the land's vineyards and replanting the Mourvèdre vines once native to the region but lost with the disastrous outbreak of phylloxera at the end of the previous century. He worked with local vintners to get the important appellation, received in 1941, and over time labored to raise standards through the gradual increase in the proportion of Mourvèdre grapes required to call the wine a Bandol. As the family grew, the vineyards of Domaine Tempier prospered. Much of this was due to promotional work and the hospitality of petite Lulu Peyraud, a dynamo with flaming red hair.

As her many children became more independent, Mme. Peyraud put bottles of Domaine Tempier wines in her car and drove them to restaurants and stores. In an interview in June 2014, she said she was surprised one year during that time when she looked and saw that she had put 30,000 kilometers (over 18,000 miles) on her car.[10] Even more famously, she also entertained the many guests and wine purveyors who came to Domaine Tempier with the delicious food she prepared. Through this, she became the larger-than-life hostess who linked Provence to the emerging food culture of the Bay Area.

On one occasion at Domaine Tempier, Olney was present at dinner, along with Gerald Asher, the British wine writer and merchant who had relocated to San Francisco. At the time Asher was the wine purveyor for Chez Panisse and an importer of Domaine Tempier wines. When Olney came to San Francisco on his 1974 book tour in the United States, he stayed with Asher. At Olney's cooking demonstration at Williams Sonoma, Alice Waters and Jeremiah Tower introduced themselves. Filled with insider knowledge, Waters had arranged for Olney's old friend, the filmmaker Kenneth Anger, to pick him up and take him to dinner at Chez Panisse. A friendship and an alliance were born.[11]

Martine and Claude Labro, a young Berkeley couple from Vence, the Provençal hill town above Nice, had originally introduced Waters to Tom Luddy. Once they had returned to Vence they encouraged one of their good friends, Nathalie Waag, to look up Waters on a trip to San Francisco. Together the two women visited the markets, and Waag dined at Chez Panisse. She followed up by inviting Waters to be a guest at her farmhouse in Bonnieux, a village in the Luberon roughly thirty miles east of Avignon. On August 12, 1975, Waag drove Waters to Solliès-Toucas and Olney's doorstep. He immediately took her to Domaine Tempier for a tasting in the cellars, followed by dinner.

This was not the usual decorous tasting of male merchants sitting around and spitting wine into the gravel. Olney remembered the uninhibited enthusiasm Waters displayed. "After sampling all the new wines in the wood, we moved back through vintage after vintage. Alice and I danced (that is to say, we whirled with wild abandon—Alice assured me that we were dancing the tango) until we collapsed on the cellar floor. Alice fell in love with the Peyraud family."[12] Waters was to return and enjoy many times Lucien Peyraud's wine, Lulu Peyraud's cooking, and their generous hospitality. Domaine Tempier became for Waters a symbolic second home.

The romance that developed between Berkeley and Bandol went beyond Waters. In 1975, Jeremiah Tower took a break from the restaurant and went to France. When he landed at Olney's dwelling, his host pronounced him at the time as "quite mad . . . his gods are Escoffier, Ali Bab, Elizabeth David and me—but he is not so simple as all that and will certainly be a star in the food world before too many years have passed."[13]

In 1976 Tower was followed by Kermit Lynch.[14] An upstart Berkeley wine merchant with a talent for writing, Lynch approached his work with a hands-on commitment, recommending only those wines he had tasted. This led him to investigate European vineyards, better done without middlemen or the company of other importers, but for this he needed an interpreter in France. When the friend who originally planned to go with him dropped out at the last minute and suggested Olney as a substitute, the name meant nothing to Lynch. He sought Alice Waters for advice. As he later reported, "her mouth dropped open. 'Richard Olney! Don't even think about it. Pack your bags and get on the plane.'"[15]

Arriving at Olney's door in 1976, Lynch presented himself as "a recently defected hippie." Olney could not understand these words, as he had been absent from America for more than twenty years, but he took Lynch's measure as "an old-fashioned bohemian who happened to possess a remarkable nose and palate."[16] Before beginning their road trip, Olney served Lynch some wine with several mild chèvres. Lynch was amazed by the Bandol red of Domaine Tempier. He wrote, "It sounds simple, but I was astonished by that marriage of wine and cheese. . . . And by that wildly delicious red wine!" When sipped with those particular cheeses, "it became one of the most fantastically delicious wines I had ever tasted."[17]

An introduction to the Peyrauds immediately followed. Olney reflected a decade later, "The instant spark of sympathy kindled between Kermit and the ebullient family of Peyrauds could be likened to spontaneous combustion."[18] *Adventures on the Wine Route*, the book that emerged in 1988 from this and other trips, featured vineyards in many regions of France. But it gave special attention to Domaine Tempier, and the Peyrauds entered Lynch's pantheon of heroic vintners. Lynch admired everything about the production of their wine and the life they led. In the book he took the reader month-by-mouth through the year of François Peyraud, the adult son who single-handedly tended the vines with both a farmer's back-breaking labor and an expert craftsman's care. And he devoted pages to the earthy wit of Lulu Peyraud. As Olney wrote, Lynch was "absorbed into the Peyraud family . . . to Lucien he is *mon fils*."[19]

Through his book and his regular newsletter Lynch became a major national influence on wine among a certain clientele. As one writer recently stated, Lynch is the "folk hero of the funky and unfiltered, defender of honestly crafted, family-run vineyards that are sometimes called 'natural' but are more importantly just kind of inspiring and delicious."[20] One can see him as a person out of the 1960s. When he fought against the blind tastings and ratings of the

dominant wine world, he was like a parent from that era defend-
ing an interesting, individualistic, but odd child. Excellence, Lynch
argued, was not to be found in the "big" wine filling the mouth with
its power and packing "a wallop" through high alcoholic content.
A judgment of wine needed to take into consideration its balance.
"Finesse" was a word he often used for wines he valued. As Olney
taught him, wines needed to be carefully matched with food, with
their intensities building throughout the meal.[21]

Allied with Waters, Lynch emerged as a major force in drawing
attention to Provence. Some of his focus on the region was professional; some, personal. Lynch became the wine supplier to Chez
Panisse, and Domaine Tempier's rosé became the restaurant's
house wine. As Lynch continued work on his book and newsletter, he traveled again to Provence and found his life partner in Gail
Skoff, a photographer skilled at capturing the beauty of Provence
and its food and wine. In 1986, the couple bought a house outside of
Le Beausset, as Olney put it, "in Bandol vineyard country, a stone's
throw from Domaine Tempier and a half-hour drive from Solliès."[22]
There Lynch and Skoff and their offspring have spent much of
each year.

Lynch became the Domaine's major importer in the United
States, by 1994 taking one-third of its annual production. In his
writing he put a spotlight on the region. In his newsletters to customers, Lynch created a thirst not just for the wines of Domaine
Tempier but also for Provence itself. Reports of his craving for the
region began early. In 1976 he wrote that, when driving in France
south from Montélimar, the land opens into a "vast, vine-covered
plain. The effect is emotionally exhilarating, like the untying of a
mental knot, a release and a shock of open space within that mir-
rors the widening landscape without." At that point on the road
comes the sign, "'VOUS ÊTES EN PROVENCE.'"[23]

Lynch also fostered interest in the food of Provence. In 1978, in
discussing Domaine Tempier wines, he wrote characteristically
that although the red, when aged, could compare with "the great
wines of the Côte de Nuits and Bordeaux," it nonetheless "makes

good drinking" when young, "rough-edged, lively, a bit *sauvage*." What truly brings the wine out is when it is "drunk with Provençal cuisine—any dish boasting olive oil, rosemary, garlic, fennel." With that he offered a recipe for grilled marinated lamb, using rosemary skewers.[24] In 1983, when he introduced to his readers La Migoua, the wine made from the grapes growing around the house of Jean-Marie Peyraud, he wrote first of the place. "What a wild, beautiful place it is! On walks I see and breathe in the fragrance of pine, wildflowers, wild rosemary, thyme, and anise. Provence! There are cherry, olive, and apricot trees growing untended, struggling leftovers from when the ancients covered the hills with orchards. And this aromatic feast has found its way into the wine."[25] Who would not have wanted to go there and drink its wine?

And in 1987, who would not have wanted to be at the table in Bandol when the Peyrauds roasted and carved an entire lamb, barbecued "out-doors under a radiant Provençal skyscape"? About the wine, Lynch wrote, "There was an open magnum of 1984 red keeping its cool in an ice bucket. I was calmly admiring the color of that 1984 in my glass when Lucien Peyraud came back from the orchard and plopped down a big straw basket full of black cherries in front of me. The cherries were exactly the same color as the wine! And that may be as close as I will ever be to an awareness of cosmic unity and harmony."[26]

Waters and Lynch traveled to Provence, and the Peyrauds and Olney made the reverse pilgrimage. As they ventured to Berkeley, Chez Panisse came to reflect their influences both directly and indirectly. When Olney returned several times to the Bay Area, the restaurant created special menus in his honor. In 1976, Lulu and Lucien Peyraud arrived in San Francisco on an international wine excursion, and Waters hosted them. Lulu later recalled the meal, "a leg of lamb and a tart that I will remember all my life long!"[27]

The influence of the Peyrauds and Bandol was a lasting one. Chez Panisse began to feature simple preparations and emphasize local ingredients, some secured from farmers' markets, some from foraging.[28] The restaurant fully embraced garlic and came to celebrate it with an all-garlic dinner for Bastille Day in 1975. This proved to be the beginning of the restaurant's annual Garlic Festival, which developed into a weeklong event.[29] The adoption of garlic served as a declaration that the 1960s generation was now in charge. These moves prepared the way for greater appreciation of Provençal dishes, heavily identified with fresh produce and garlic.

The relationship between Chez Panisse, the Peyraud family, and Provence continued. In spring 1992, Waters held a weeklong festival of Domaine Tempier wines, and Lulu and her daughter-in-law Paule arrived for the occasion. Waters was able to laud Mme. Peyraud's gifts and welcome her into her kitchen, where together they prepared many special meals to celebrate the food of Provence.

In 2003 Chez Panisse's informal offshoot, Café Fanny, and Kermit Lynch Wine Merchant held the first Provence Day in their joint parking lot, and this continued for almost a decade. As advertised in the newsletter, "We re-create some of the tried and true pleasures of Provence. We close the parking lot to cars, set up tables under the olive trees, peel a ton of garlic, fire up the grill, and uncork a medley of delicious southern wines."[30]

Restaurant, wine store, and Provence in the parking lot were local events. But the reach of Berkeley went far wider. Waters's 1982 *Chez Panisse Menu Cookbook* conveys the growing influences of both the Peyrauds and Provençal cooking in its recipes. In this tribute to cooking with fresh ingredients, Waters thanks the family and credits Lulu as the inspiration for a particular meal of fresh herring, bouillabaisse, and lamb daube. The cookbook offers the menu for a particular Bandol Wine Dinner to celebrate the arrival of the 1971 vintage from Domaine Tempier. Beyond these instances, threading through the book are recipes specific to Provence, such as bourride, a fish stew.[31]

Alice Waters with her many Chez Panisse cookbooks and Kermit Lynch with his book and newsletter have had an important impact on American taste. As they became food and wine legends, they helped plant Provence and images of its gastronomic culture in the minds of Americans.

Perhaps the most beguiling expression of Berkeley's mission to spread appreciation of Provence far and wide came in the early 1990s with *Lulu's Provençal Table: The Exuberant Food and Wine from Domaine Tempier Vineyard*. This beautiful and informative cookbook is personal in the best sense. It is an illustrated family history, the story of a vineyard, a photographic portrait of a kitchen and its cook. And it offers a wide range of recipes spiked with personal reflection. It was a collaboration among friends. Kermit Lynch and Alice Waters dreamed up the idea, and Waters wrote the introduction. Olney did much of the heavy lifting, producing the history and recipes from his two years of twice weekly visits with Lulu Peyraud, when for three hours he would take notes as they conversed about family and food. Gail Skoff took the photographs. The Peyrauds supplied the setting and images from old family albums.

In her introduction, Alice Waters paid tribute to the Peyrauds and their influence. She wrote that, on entering their house for the first time, "I felt as if I had walked into a Marcel Pagnol film come to life. Lucien and Lulu's warmhearted enthusiasm for life, their love for the pleasures of the table, their deep connection to the beautiful earth of the South of France—these were things I had seen at the movies. But this was for real. I felt immediately as if I had come home to a second family."

In this deeply intertwined set of relationships public and private, business and pleasure have mixed indissolubly. Olney reported one such moment in the summer of 1993. Alice Waters, along with her husband and child, were staying in Bandol, a short drive from Domaine Tempier. Kermit Lynch and Gail Skoff were nearby. Tom Luddy and Eleanor Coppola were working on a documentary film about Chez Panisse and Waters. Lulu planned a lunch for twenty-eight. "Bouillabaisse at Domaine Tempier is always good theatre," Olney wrote. "Rosé flows, tapénade and anchoïde crusts circulate," a fire is built outside, and the soup is heated in a copper pot. "This day was especially dramatic as cameras clicked and turned," capturing on film the platters of fish slipping into the soup.[32]

It is in the nature of Alice Waters to blend personal and business relationships, making it hard to separate fact from fantasy. What she wrote of the Peyrauds' hospitality is what she dreamed of for her restaurant. "Always we are treated like long-lost children home for a visit, and always we are immersed in the same hospitality and the luxurious feeling of being at home." When Lucien offers a toast he "reminds us of the transcendental virtue of wine and food and friendship united."[33]

And thus, the food Lulu serves is the food Waters wants at Chez Panisse, "often earthy, always delicious, and always appropriate to the moment." Lulu chooses her daily menu from what she sees at the market. She uses the most local of ingredients, including the extra-virgin olive oil that "comes from the olives that grow at the Domaine, the herbs and fennel from the garden behind the house or growing wild on the hillsides." Similarly she takes green almonds from nearby trees, and figs and squash blossoms from a neighbor. Going to the fish market as the boats arrive, she can see the catch when "the fish are still jumping around and the crabs are trying to crawl back to the sea. . . . Lulu searches for what is alive, knowing that that is *always* what tastes best."[34]

Moving from this description to her testament to the faith, Waters wrote, "The Peyraud family's example has been helping us find our balance at Chez Panisse for years." Like the Peyrauds, "we try to live close to the earth and treat it with respect; always look first to the garden and the vineyard for inspiration; rejoice in our families and friends; and let the food and wine speak for themselves at the table."[35]

It is Olney who moves us back to Provence. He wrote, "Perhaps love and friendship can never be quite the same in the absence of the cicada's chant, of fresh sweet garlic and voluptuous olive oil, of summer-ripe tomatoes and the dense, spicy, wild fruit of the wines of Domaine Tempier, which reflect the scents of the Provençal hillsides and joyously embrace Lulu's high-spirited cuisine. For Lulu, cuisine is a language, the expression of love; for Lucien, wine is the expression of love. In Provence, cuisine and wine are as inseparable as Lulu and Lucien."[36]

Although fact cannot be separated from fancy, nonetheless beginning in the mid-to-late 1970s the deep bonds between Alice Waters, Kermit Lynch, and the Peyraud family added another dimension to the reinvention of Provence. In the United States during the 1980s and into the 1990s, the Berkeley enthusiasm for Bandol served to further stimulate the emerging taste for Provence.

1 The ideal for a second house in the hills. Paul Cézanne, *Fields at Bellevue*, 1892–95, oil on canvas, 14 1/4 × 19 3/4 in., The Phillips Collection, Washington, DC.

2 Fond food memories of Provence reproduced in an American kitchen. Mural tiles behind the stove burners in a kitchen in Charlotte, North Carolina, handmade and hand-painted by Lisette Hasbun. Photograph by author.

3 The field of cultivated lavender. Irving Penn, "Lavender field," © The Irving Penn Foundation, LOOK Magazine Photograph Collection, Library of Congress, Prints & Photographs Division.

4 The perched village. Irving Penn, "Bonnieux," © The Irving Penn Foundation, LOOK Magazine Photograph Collection, Library of Congress, Prints & Photographs Division.

5 Life in Provence as Cézanne painted it. Irving Penn, "Façade in Noves," © The Irving Penn Foundation, LOOK Magazine Photograph Collection, Library of Congress, Prints & Photographs Division.

6 Provençal objects to desire. Irving Penn, "Provence furniture," © The Irving Penn Foundation,
LOOK Magazine Photograph Collection, Library of Congress, Prints & Photographs Division.

7 The chef pouring himself a glass of wine. Irving Penn, "Raymond Thuilier, L'Oustau de Baumanière," © The Irving Penn Foundation, LOOK Magazine Photograph Collection, Library of Congress, Prints & Photographs Division.

Next time you take a vacation, uncomplicate your life.

Get out of glamorous Paris. Drive your car onto that amazing French train that beds-down cars as well as drivers and then speeds to the South. Disembark at Avignon in the heart of lazy, sunny Provence and drive a leisurely pace through provincial France, Roman France and a lot of relaxed, sunburned towns.

This is France's artists' country. Music's everywhere. And every photograph you take is an impressionist painting. You can shed your coat and tie, here. You can bicycle and keep your dignity. You can learn all there is to know about wine and cheese and bouillabaisse. You can fall in love, here. You can even stay forever.

For list of beautiful old inns and facts on Provence, write Dept. NY-1, Box #221, N. Y. 10. French Government Tourist Office, New York, Chicago, Los Angeles, San Francisco, Miami, Montreal.

8 Provence as the gentler world allowing you to "uncomplicate your life." Doyle Dane Bernbach advertisement, reproduced by permission of France Tourism Development Agency and DDB Worldwide. Photograph: Elliott Erwitt/Magnum Photos. Image scan: Duke University Library.

9 Simone Beck preparing a dish with Julia Child's assistance in Child's kitchen in Plascassier, France. Still image from Julia Child's "Spinach Twins," *The French Chef,* season 6 (1970–71), episode 203, courtesy of the WGBH Media Library and Archives, and the Julia Child Foundation.

10 Julia Child exploring the fruits and vegetables in the weekly market in Grasse, France. Still image from Julia Child's "Apple Desserts," *The French Chef,* season 6 (1970–71), episode 215, courtesy of the WGBH Media Library and Archives, and the Julia Child Foundation.

11 Food with all the furnishings—earthenware plates, dark wood tables, and tablecloths and napkins of Souleiado cloth from Provence. Photograph: *Gourmet*, March 1973, page 47. *Gourmet* © Condé Nast.

12 Lulu Peyraud's kitchen with its fabric ruffle edging the top of the kitchen hearth. Photograph by Gail Skoff, reproduced by permission of the photographer.

13 "A house transform one's life?" Robert Fréson, "Chanteduc," reproduced from Patricia Wells, *Patricia Wells at Home in Provence* (New York: Scribner, 1996), 51, by permission of Robert Fréson.

14 Robert Fréson, Patricia Wells in her dream kitchen in Chanteduc. Reproduced from *Patricia Wells at Home in Provence* (New York: Scribner, 1996), 10, by permission of Robert Fréson.

15 Tomatoes, garlic, and melons in the market at Apt, May 30, 2015. Photograph courtesy of John Steel.

16 Provence Village in Charlotte, North Carolina. Photograph by author.

TWELVE   # The Lure of Cookbooks

Cookbooks hold a special place in the larger universe of food writing. They are a world unto themselves. They are commercial products, and increasingly they have become beautiful objects in their
own right. It goes without saying that in presenting them, both
authors and publishers hope to gain money and fame for their
efforts. Words and pictures about food, accompanied by directions to make dishes in one's own kitchen, proved to be another
major lure drawing Americans to Provence, either by actual travel
or imagined trips via the table.

By the late 1980s, the association of Provence with pleasure in its
food and wine was well established. In 1988, Peta Fuller's translation of *The Wonderful Food of Provence* by Jean-Noël Escudier came
out a second time, now with an introduction by the well-known
food writer Paula Wolfert. "It is really about falling in love with a
place and its food. And who can visit Provence," Wolfert wrote,
evoking what had become its familiar symbols, "without falling in
love with it—its rocky outcroppings spotted with wild thyme, lavender, and rosemary, its cooking that is at once rustic, refined, and
lush? Provençal cooking utilizes all the good things from the earth
and sea. . . . Who can visit this land, taste this cuisine, and not say:
'I want some of this in my own life, too'?"[1]

Wolfert gave her story of the reception of the earlier edition. "I recall reading it with that same excitement and sense of discovery that I felt when I first read Elizabeth David's books in the late 1950s. The book spoke to me in the most extraordinarily poignant and insightful way of the wonderful, pure, simple basic cooking that everyone now associates with Provence." Yet, despite her own enthusiasm, Wolfert understood why the book was ignored in the late 1960s. "At that time, haute cuisine was in vogue, nouvelle cuisine did not exist, and notions of simplicity were out of fashion."[2]

This time around, rather than putting the cookbook down because of "the coarseness inherent in this kind of food," as had the 1968 *New York Times* reviewer, Florence Fabricant praised *The Wonderful Food of Provence* with these words: "Superb. . . . It explains the food of a vibrant region with honest, intelligent clarity."[3]

Timing seems to be everything when one looks at the contrasting receptions of this cookbook, first in 1968 and then in 1988. What hardly gets a hearing in one decade seems absolutely right in another. By 1988, Alice Waters was national figure, and her featuring of the food of Provence at Chez Panisse generated significant publicity. Major food magazines had taken up Provençal cuisine, and American authorities on food were celebrating it, including in their own cookbooks.[4]

In addition to offering recipes, cookbooks often have stated and implied purposes. Some authors take as their primary task to instruct and guide novices as they go about their work in the kitchen. Others serve as aspirational guides, aiding social mobility by teaching readers how to prepare the food of the economic classes above them. Almost by definition, cookbooks have offered variety, exposing readers to new possibilities for livening up mealtimes. But at some point along the historical path, a good number of them have veered in a new direction and acquired a new task—to tempt readers to venture to new places, if only in the kitchen.[5]

After World War II, as travel broadened food horizons, the mythical task of Marco Polo—bringing pasta from China to Italy—was offered to the ordinary cook in the ordinary kitchen. Travel magazines began to emphasize food tourism and, given their principal subject, placed emphasis on portraying the locations where the meals and recipes were found. This was a time when photographs permeated the popular magazines and were *Look*'s very reason for being. After *Gourmet* and *Holiday* followed suit came *Bon Appétit* and *Travel & Leisure* and, beginning in 1994, *Saveur*. With both travel and food magazines offering visual images not only of cooking methods, ingredients, and accomplished dishes but also of their places of origin and the cookware containing them, a new kind of cookbook came into being. Its size and shape were different as befit its enriched content.

Tastes were changing. In the 1960s, as Julia Child whetted the American appetite for French cuisine, teaching them the skills to achieve high-quality meals whether in Boston or Lubbock, she was joined by a host of cooks in various media preparing the food identified with other lands. Introduced via magazines, newspapers, books, radio, and television, Americans of all ethnicities began to experiment in the kitchen with a vast variety of dishes, including those from China, India, and Morocco, and in the process learned about the specialized shops that catered to immigrant communities in their area. New concerns about health entered the picture, bringing vegetarian recipes as well as foodways that traditionally relied less on meat. Emphasis turned to fresh ingredients and local sources, and some cookbooks became political statements. Mediterranean cooking became a byword. It seemed to have everything—variety, taste, health, freshness, and the promise of the sun. Coming from within the orbit of the Mediterranean world, the food of Provence took on new allure.

A cookbook featuring Provençal cuisine poses a particular problem. It exists within the world of French gastronomy, and in food as in other aspects of French culture in the past, all roads have led to Paris.[6] This has meant two things. On the one hand, the countryside was the supplier of ingredients to Parisian households and restaurants. On the other, as regions such as Provence attempted to record their culinary traditions, Paris set the terms. In Provence, as the association of regional enthusiasts known as the Félibrige moved beyond literature to folkways, cookbook writers sought to present "authentic" Provençal dishes. Just as Frédéric Mistral had to be attentive to the norms of Paris in his dictionary, so, too, did these food writers attend to the capital's expectations. And just as cookbooks in general were written for literate and typically bourgeois households, so, too, were the ones presenting the foodways of Provence. As a result, despite assurances to the contrary, it is best in such French cookbooks not to seek recipes that recall peasant customs or to search for the "authentic" or the "traditional." The form and content of these Provençal recipes have been mediated by the power of Paris.

Although earlier books had presented the food of the region, Jean-Baptiste Reboul created the foundational work in his first *La Cuisinière Provençale* of 1897, and it remains in print in revised editions today.[7] Reboul, a well-known chef, included recipes distinctive to the region of his birth and much of his career in the kitchen, nonetheless he followed the conventional Parisian-inflected practices of French cookbook writing. His book gave directions for bourgeois cuisine intended for the young housewife learning to cook or to direct servants in the kitchen. Reboul's cookbook was joined by those of Auguste Escoffier, the chef who, in the late nineteenth century brought French haute cuisine to London at the Savoy Hotel and, as a new century dawned, came to rule the kitchens at César Ritz's extensive hotel chain. Escoffier was from Provence, had apprenticed in his teens in the kitchen of an uncle's restaurant in Nice, and, even as he moved up the ladder to restaurants that served the rich and famous, never abandoned his culinary roots. In his kitchens as in his cookbook, however, he amended them to appeal to the expectations of his moneyed diners. Both Reboul's and Escoffier's recipes have continued to inform Provençal cookbooks up to the present.

The offerings of the two did differ. One way to measure this is to examine their recipes for *boeuf en daube*, the most characteristic of inland Provençal main courses.[8] It is a braised dish, meaning that the ingredients are cooked in a liquid kept at a simmer in a covered pot. By legend, its origin is lost in time, but because it involves substantial pieces of beef in a region without much grazing land for cattle, it was clearly not on the table of those living by subsistence farming. Beef was a food for special occasions in middle-class households in nineteenth- and early twentieth-century Provence, often remembered as gracing a holyday or Sunday table. Later explanations add that this meat came from the bulls from the Camargue, some after service in Provence's nonlethal version of the bullfight, but this may be only myth. Folklore would set the early daube's slow preparation on the hearth, begun with the hot fire of evening and extended overnight to cook slowly as the fire waned and ultimately went out, but the dish was more likely made on a potager, an early wood or coal burning stovetop, and later on a range.[9]

Boeuf en daube often calls for a special pot called a *daubière*. There are many different varieties of this pot, made of either metal or earthenware. An intriguing one is essentially a fat, low-bellied ceramic pot with a narrowing waist, above which is a cylindrical extension, making it almost as high as it is wide. This shape allows for a large amount of food to be cooked, while at the same time reducing the amount of food surface exposed to the air. The *daubière* often carries a concave top, the purpose of which is variously explained. It is either a place to hold burning coals, allowing the interior to receive heat from above as well as from below, or it is a place to fill with water to aid condensation on the inside and keep the cooking food moist. Recipes generally call for the top to be hermetically sealed with a long thin rope of dough between the lid and the pot.

For his preparation, Reboul suggested either a *daubière* or an earthenware pot. He specified that the meat should be stringy ("un peu neuveuse") and fatty ("grasse"), consistent with the notion that it came from a tough Camargue bull. The recipe is lengthy but simple: cut the beef into 20 pieces and place for 5 or 6 hours in a marinade composed of a bottle of wine, a cup of vinegar, 2 onions and 2 or 3

8 A contemporary rendition of a *daubière* by Philippe Beltrando (Aubagne, France) in the collection of Paula Wolfert. Todd Oppenheimer, "The Clay Mystique," *Craftsmanship*, Spring 2015, photograph by Claire Bloomberg, www.bloombergphotography.com, reproduced by permission of the photographer.

carrots, salt, pepper, a bouquet garni, and (unspecified) spices. Then, at the appointed time for cooking, render the equivalent of a scant half-pound of pork fat in the *daubière* or other pot, remove the solid pork residue with a skimmer, and set a quartered onion to brown. Following this, add the beef pieces and other solids drained from the marinade, stirring from time to time. After reduction to half, add the marinade to the pot along with 4 to 5 cloves of garlic, a bouquet garni, a piece of dried orange peel, and roughly a pint of warmed water. Seal the pot and place on low heat for 4 to 5 hours. Skim and serve.[10]

Escoffier, in *Le guide culinaire: Aide-memoire de cuisine prac-tique*, upped the ante set by Reboul. For the marinade, Escoffier used white wine and cognac, rather than red wine and vinegar. He suggested inserting strips of pork fat, sprinkled with chopped parsley, into the beef. Carrots were to be cut into rounds, mushrooms and onions chopped, tomatoes ground. Into the earthenware pot went these ingredients, along with crushed garlic, thyme, laurel, black pitted olives, and squares of blanched pork rind. Rather than merely placed, these ingredients were to be layered. After adding a bouquet of parsley and dried orange peel and pouring the marinade and meat juices over all, the pot was to be sealed and set to cook for six to seven hours.[11]

The recipes of Reboul and Escoffier for *boeuf en daube*—one plain, the other fancy—set the templates for the future. Following their trails into later cookbooks featuring Provençal food provides a way of seeing something of the intentions of the books' authors and their publishers' expectations about the market for cookbooks at a time when much was brewing to bring the cuisine of Provence to the broader public.

In France itself there was an outpouring of cookbooks in the 1950s and 1960s, designed for French city dwellers establishing second homes in what was becoming an increasingly desired location, rural Provence. Some of these books were small paperbacks meant to be serviceable in the kitchen, such as the original Escudier book of 1953, *La véritable cuisine provençale et niçoise*. Others were art books, such as René Jouveau's 1963 *La cuisine provençale de tra-dition populaire*, a large-size tome, printed on heavy fine paper, filled with brightly colored modernist prints and meant for the coffee table.[12] These books kept the recipe for *boeuf en daube* simple, essentially following the directions of Reboul.

Writing for the English-speaking world, Elizabeth David did the same. As part of her broader mission to change the dull British foodways of the postwar years, David sought to make Provençal cuisine desirable and accessible in her important books on Mediterranean and French cooking. When she presented her *boeuf en daube* in 1960 in her influential *French Provincial Cooking*, she noted that the recipe carried "all the rich savour of these slowly-cooked wine-flavoured stews" but was "easy." What she offered was a pared down version of Reboul's recipe.[13]

By contrast, Richard Olney, the American expatriate living in Provence, sought the attention of those in Britain and the United States with high aspirations in the kitchen. To put it directly, where David simplified, Olney made things more complicated. In his landmark *The French Menu Cookbook* of 1970—named by the *Observer* of London as the "best cookbook of all time"—Olney relied on the Escoffier preparation for *boeuf en daube*, and then ramped up the difficulty. In addition to being a perfectionist, Olney seemingly believed he needed to spell out all the steps that an experienced French cook would normally take, steps that he could not assume American or British readers knew. The result took up three pages, with text so complicated as to be intimidating. To give just one example, Olney, following Escoffier, larded the meat pieces, inserting into them strips of pork fat. But, writing for the uninitiated, Olney offered precise, detailed instructions: remove the rind (reserved to be simmered and desalted) and cut the fat into 2/3-inch rectangular solids, 1 to 1.5 inches long. Escoffier had sprinkled parsley over the lard strips. Olney covered the strips with a paste of peeled garlic cloves and chopped parsley, combined in a mortar. With such detailed instructions, the essence of the conventional daube—a simple preparation before a long, slow cooking—was lost.[14] Nonetheless, Olney's 1970 book has proved enduring.

Peta Fuller had a head start with her translation of Escudier's *The Wonderful Food of Provence* in 1968, but it took a while for other US cookbooks focused on Provence to emerge. The selling of Provence in major food and travel magazines began in earnest in 1970, but cookbooks take time to prepare, write, and make their way into print. And before they do, publishers and writers first have to perceive a market. Gradually, as the desire for the virtual tastes and aromas of the Provençal kitchen came into being, cookbooks appeared, some with a significant impact.[15]

In 1976 Mireille Johnston published *The Cuisine of the Sun*. She was an excellent guide. Living and teaching in the United States, but a native of France educated in its universities, Johnston was well prepared to respond to the new interest in Provence's food. She worked ten years to adapt the cuisine of Nice and Provence to the American kitchen. Her book joined others urging American cooks to not be seduced by convenience foods filled with additives. M. F. K. Fisher called *The Cuisine of the Sun* "a delight." The book garnered high praise from Mimi Sheraton in a review in the *New York Times* as offering "wonderfully clear, complete and authentic recipes." The taste for its subject was definitely growing in the 1970s. As Sheraton stated at the outset of her review, "If I were forced by some unimaginable set of circumstances to confine my eating to one corner of the world, that corner would be Provence . . . where French restraint and balance blends with the sensuous, robust flavors of Italy."[16] Although Johnston's book was ready by 1976, the creation of other cookbooks featuring Provence by American authors took more time. It wasn't until the 1980s and 1990s that these books came in profusion.

Beginning in the 1970s, there were important changes in format and content in cookbooks. Likely inspired by the growing number of food and travel magazines, color photography began to play an important role. Cookbooks got glossier, and some of them appeared in large sizes, seeming more appropriate for leisure reading than for actual use in the kitchen. During this time, nonfiction writing was becoming more personal, memoirs flourished, and a number of English-language cookbooks featuring the food of Provence followed in this path.

One book, published in the United Kingdom and the United States in 1988, that pulls together these changes is *A Taste of Provence: The Food and People of Southern France with 40 Delicious Recipes*. Written by Julian More, a well-known British actor and songwriter, it was filled with his and his family's experiences since moving to Provence. Carey More, his daughter, brought lyrical color photographs to grace the book's pages. *A Taste of Provence* begins with her wedding feast, giving a glamorous description of its foods and wines. It then turns to other important meals, such as the Grand Aïoli at the neighboring village's wine festival that featured the dish of that name in which the famed garlic mayonnaise accompanies a range of fish, seafood, eggs, and vegetables. As Julian wrote, "The creation of this book is inspired by those Provençal family binges; for its creators are a Provençal family—albeit adoptive." He then announced that he intended his book for home cooks to be "a taster rather than any attempt at a definitive work. Over the years, Escoffier, Reboul, and Elizabeth David have already done that."[17]

In fact, much of the book was travel writing focusing on food, including mushroom hunting, food and drink at nearby restaurants, and even a visit to a monastery. But some was a celebration of home cooking, introduced by such words as "there is no French perfume more exotic than the smoke of a fire of vine stocks, mingling with the aroma of wine, garlic, olive, herbs, and orange peel, which wafts from the *daube* in one's own oven." More's daube recipe followed Reboul quite closely, but he adapted it to use bacon rather than lardons and specified the spices, including crushed juniper berries.[18]

Another approach authors took to appeal to the English-reading public was the cookbook offered in the homey arts-and-crafts style. Leslie Forbes, a Canadian living in London, wrote *A Taste of Provence: Classic Recipes from the South of France.* Published in the United States and Australia, recipes in the book appeared in simulated handwriting, bolstering the author's suggestion that it was a conduit of word-of-mouth information from the ground. For example, Forbes attributed her "Provençal Daube" to her neighbor, who followed the recipe of her grandmother. The recipe itself was conventional and minimal, following the pattern of most French cookbooks influenced by Reboul. It was, however, unique in that it contained no wine in the marinade or cooking, only vinegar. It delivered its guidance in an intimate, chatty voice, conveying the essence of this kind of cookbook's effort to appeal. As she gave the French word *mijoter*, meaning "to simmer," Forbes told the reader that it also signifies "to cook lovingly; which is closer to the spirit of Provençal cooking."[19]

By the 1990s several serious cookbooks on Provence offered specialized knowledge to American audiences. In 1994, Martha Rose Shulman, a cook known from her previous books for vegetarian food, offered *Provençal Light*. An American with many years in France and much time in Provence, Shulman filled this cookbook with excellent and nutritious recipes focusing on the fresh vegetables and fruits of the markets. For her daube, she substituted rabbit, a lighter meat than beef.[20] Published the following year, Louisa Jones's *The New Provençal Cuisine* gave attention to innovation. Her glamorous book presented the recipes offered by chefs of famous restaurants in the region along with tantalizing photographs. Emphasizing as it did the new, there was no mention of *boeuf en daube*.[21]

Patricia Wells at Home in Provence successfully linked personal memoir, informative recipes, and beautiful photography. In 1979, Patricia and Walter Wells left their positions at the *New York Times* when an opportunity arose for Walter at the Paris office of the *International Herald Tribune*. Cast into the world of freelance writers, Patricia began her breakthrough book, *The Food Lover's Guide to Paris*. She worked as a restaurant critic, ultimately on staff at *L'Express*, becoming the first female and the first American to hold that post in a major French paper.[22] She started writing cookbooks based on French recipes in the late 1980s; life in a second home in Vaison-la-Romaine prompted this one in 1996.

A handsome book, filled with full-page images of the dishes and their ingredients, it exuded its author's zest for life. It offered the home itself as a subject, along with the food, and focused on its Vaison location by introducing readers to local creators and purveyors of Provençal provisions. Wells's recipe for *boeuf en daube*, for example, carried the advice of her butcher and is named for him:

"Monsieur Henny's Three-Beef Daube." Explaining the title, Wells wrote that Roland Henny recommended "using at least three cuts of beef from different parts of the animal." One contains bones to enhance flavor, another offers purer meat, and the third lends its tougher muscle to add texture.[23]

The 1990s also saw lavish presentation as the seemingly sole purpose of several cookbooks. This was perhaps best exemplified by *Provence the Beautiful*, published in 1993 with Richard Olney listed as the author. An immense book, more than 14 inches tall and 10.5 inches wide, containing 256 glossy pages, it was so heavy and bulky that it is impossible to think of putting it on a counter and using it as a guide to actual cooking. The result was at one level a dreamy book, filled with glorious color photographs of the region, spanning a whole page or even an open two-page spread. It contained significant recipes, including the one for *boeuf en daube* presented in Olney's *The French Menu Cookbook* of 1970. Reading it today, however, it is hard not to laugh at the photograph for Daube à la Provençale. This dish, best when served warm from the oven, is shown placed in an open *daubière* on a rock ledge offering a view of the village of Gordes.

Quite different in its presentation and feel was a book that Olney helped plan and then prepared with great care, *Lulu's Provençal Table* (see chapter 11). Its instructions for Daube à la Provençal confirm that this was Lulu Peyraud's recipe, not Olney's. All was simple and conventional—marinade, braising, slow cooking. One distinctive note was striking. The wine for the recipe was specified as a "young, deeply colored, tannic, red wine," something important to a family in the wine business. This daube recipe also carried one note, new to the presentations: "In Provence, it is considered essential while a daube is cooking to keep the *daubière* covered with a soup plate containing red wine, which is regularly replenished as it evaporates." While Lulu Peyraud understood that it is the condensation on the bottom of the plate that actually keeps the dish moist, she nonetheless retained this practice.[24] Perhaps one element of its hold was that the evaporating wine enhanced the aromas coming from the kitchen.

Cookbooks such as these aimed to sate a hunger, but they also created one. They called to the reader to come to Provence to try out these recipes in the place where they originated and use its local ingredients, perhaps adding to the plate Provence's special tomatoes.

Such cookbooks also may have had an important influence in getting Americans to desire the goods of Provence. As the French know, the look of a dish can be as important as the taste, and that look became increasingly atmospheric in the 1990s. In the large-size cookbooks offering Provençal food published in this decade, landscape, décor, and furnishings were as important as cuisine. Along with dishes placed on rocks in view of perched villages were glamorous shots of dining rooms and kitchens. These conveyed a treasured way of life lived among Provençal objects, old and new. Unintentionally, or perhaps with purpose, these images enhanced what began in the 1970s—a growing taste for the things of Provence.

THIRTEEN

Buying It Here, Bringing It Home

Travel, whether real or virtual, takes one away from home. Many media assist in stimulating travel desires. The British sociologist John Urry has emphasized the importance of paintings and photographs, and more recently a range of authors have considered the broad array of senses and potential experiences that engage the attention of travelers as they seek new places to visit.[1] For many Americans in the late twentieth and early twenty-first centuries, objects have come to assume an increasingly important role in taking them literally and imaginatively to faraway places. If to some degree we have come to see that we are what we eat, we have also become aware that we are what we possess and display. Messages all around us announce that the furnishings we live around help define who we are. And they, too, have led to Provence.

Appealing goods from the region, as featured in travel and food magazines, cookbooks, shops, and periodicals devoted to house and home, have emerged as an important force in developing a taste for Provence. In creating that appeal commerce has had a heavy hand. *Provence the Beautiful*, the large-size cookbook, tells us a great deal about how the business of selling goods was working to burnish Provence's image by 1993. Richard Olney's posthumous memoir offers a record of how the book got made. *Provence the Beautiful* was a corporate product. Olney was paid a fee to provide the recipes for the book; another writer was hired to describe the landscape. Similarly, a special photographer took the scenic photographs of Provence, but a different photographer shot the food dishes in a studio far away in Sydney, Australia. The book was produced in conjunction with Williams-Sonoma's Provence Festival. Put together by Weldon Owen, "an Australian publisher-packager," as part of a Beautiful Cookbook series, it intermixed recipes and pictures of the prepared dishes with crossover elements suggestive of a travel book.[2] The images of food came in two ways—one presented dishes on tables or ledges in Provence in clearly marked locations; the other involved interior shots, simple close-ups of the prepared food in the photographer's studio.

The food staged in specific settings carries not only surrounding images of place but also great attention to the serving dishes. For example, in one shot with the caption "On a Terrace in Lourmarin, Provençal Vegetable and Basil Soup," most readers likely noticed the food, but perhaps more prominent in the photograph are the yellow pottery plates holding deep brown pottery bowls. It is only barely possible to see the announced soup in the large earthenware container that holds it. And toward the back of the image is a large stone mortar holding something unnamed, perhaps a salad. All of this is set on a vivid blue Souleiado tablecloth partially covering a stone table. The shot that brings it all together is that of the *boeuf en daube* on the ledge with the town of Gordes looming behind. The hearty stew sits in a tall earthenware *daubière*, with handles on both sides, accompanied by other pottery pieces—a gratin dish, a pitcher, and a small plate.[3]

Although the interior photographs of food were shot in Australia, care was taken to picture them with things suggestive of Provence—Souleiado cloth, rustic woods, pottery, and stone. The explicit message may have been cuisine, but the subliminal one was objects, many available from Williams-Sonoma.

Provençal furnishings and objects linked to the region's landscape and food appeared at the very onset of Provence's reinvention in the

1960s. Irving Penn's 1962 photographs in *Look* magazine not only captured Provençal scenery, evoked iconic paintings of the region, and celebrated its cuisine, they also displayed its antiques as objects of desire (plate 6). In that issue, the pages of "The Eternal Appeal of Provence" were immediately followed by a bright spread on redoing a home kitchen to give it a country look, courtesy of Sears Roebuck. Was this kitchen in the Provençal style? The piece didn't say so, but its placement suggested it. Provence was definitely in sight as one turned the page to "Sophisticated Peasant Dresses," showing them in full color on models cavorting in the landscape. The outfits were made with the distinctive cotton prints that became famous as Souleiado cloth.[4]

In the 1962 *Look* piece, mentioned among a host of celebrities was "New York painter-designer Van Day Truex," who had "just bought a house in Gordes."[5] Truex proved to be a key player in bringing consciousness of Provence and its goods to an American audience. His experience of Provence went back to the 1930s. As a young man he was an instructor in the Paris branch of New York School of Fine and Applied Arts (later renamed the Parsons School). He knew how to court the rich, and during that time Alice and John Garrett of the Baltimore and Ohio Railroad fortune, friends and supporters of the school, took him to Provence. After serving as head of the school for a decade beginning in 1942, Truex returned to New York to design beautiful objects and ended up as Tiffany's design director. When an admirer gave him a large gift of money to use for housing, his earlier pleasurable experience in Provence prompted him to put it to use there. In 1962, he bought a house in the perched village of Gordes. After its renovations and upkeep proved to be an economic misstep, in 1964 he chose a place far more modest, an abandoned farmhouse with extensive grounds outside Gargas, near Apt. Once rebuilt and decorated, the Gargas house received great publicity, including a 1969 article in the *New York Times* celebrating its interiors in Truex's signature beige. Nonetheless, Truex decided he needed to relocate once again. He chose the hilltop village Ménerbes, and there he designed his new house with the help of a local Provençal architect. He persuaded Rory Cameron, a wealthy aesthete and author, to move nearby and had a hand in the design of Cameron's well-publicized Ménerbes property, Les Quatre Sources. These two houses were published in *House and Garden* in 1974.[6]

What Truex and Cameron conveyed was that one could live in grand style in the hills of Provence. However, neither of them— nor many other artists and aesthetes who chose the region in these years—selected furnishings that reflected their locale's history and traditions. The push for that came from other sources.

In the late 1960s and early 1970s, with the reinvention of Provence for American travelers, something later called the Provençal style began to appear in magazine articles. The force here was Pierre Deux, an antique store that opened in 1967 in New York's Greenwich Village and started carrying Souleiado fabrics in 1970. Quickly, the shop's goods were pictured in magazine images, such as in the 1973 *Gourmet* feature on Provençal food. What stood out in the photographic spread were earthenware plates placed on dark wood tables set with tablecloths and napkins of Souleiado cloth. All these items were explicitly attributed to Pierre Deux and presumably available for purchase at the store (plate 11).

Souleiado fabric goes back to the eighteenth century when designs based on Asian Indian cloth became wildly popular in France. Founded in Tarascon, the firm making it initially specialized in large scarves. When the fad for such scarves evaporated and industrialization overtook the making of cloth, the firm's competitors died out, but it remained and kept the old dyeing techniques. Eventually, though, old patterns were carefully transferred from wood blocks to copper plates, synthetic dyes replaced the vegetable ones, and the fabric was produced in larger lengths and widths. In the post–World War II era, one could find the bright cotton cloth used for tablecloths and napkins, quilts and other bedcoverings, and throw pillows and cushions, as well as for the women's clothing pictured in *Look*.[7]

Pierre Deux was a relatively new shop when it began to sell

Souleiado fabrics. It was the realized dream of two men named Pierre—Pierre Moulin, a Frenchman, and Pierre LeVec, a native of St. Louis. The pair had met in France in 1949 when both were working for the Marshall Plan, and when LeVec returned to work for the government in Washington, they both moved to the United States. With LeVec's retirement, the two opened the store in New York, and, with the immediate popularity of the vivid Souleiado prints, sales took off. In addition to the fabric, the business offered a wide range of Provençal antiques and furnishings. In discussing the Provençal décor the store fostered, an important contemporary decorator recently reflected back on the store's impact in the 1970s and '80s: "The original Pierre Deux store in the Village was charming and seemed so 'fresh' at the time!"[8]

Ultimately the Pierre Deux chain grew to twenty-two stores across the country. Its glossy 1984 book *Pierre Deux's French Country: A Style and Source Book* widened the appeal of Provençal goods. It served as a kind of primer, offering a valuable record of the region's riches in interiors and furnishings. It demonstrated the beauty, variety, and high degree of Provençal craftsmanship over many centuries. It first presented the objects in broad categories— fabrics, pottery, furniture, and accents. It then followed with a range of interiors, including those of great estates, such as the Château de Barbentane, urban dwellings of the haute bourgeois, and rural and rustic farmhouses. In its third section, the book explored adaptations in American homes. At the time, it offered useful sources to aid future buyers. Readers in 1984 learned where to purchase in both the United States and France not only fabrics but pottery, fittings, and furniture—everything from iron doorknobs to tall armoires. Viewed decades later, this assemblage helps one understand the larger impact of Moulin and LeVec in the broad diffusion of goods associated with Provence. The two Pierres were primary forces behind the Provençal look that took off in the 1970s.[9]

Of course, shelter magazines also did their part. In a variety of articles, they pictured Provençal objects. The periodicals portrayed these pieces in glamorous views of dwellings both in and outside of the region. Features on farmhouse restorations in Provence went beyond construction to describe and picture alluring interiors.

Magazines such as *Architectural Digest* did more. These publications, along with those dedicated to travel, offered guidance to Americans traveling in Provence for finding goods distinctive to the region. For example, in 1990, *Architectural Digest* followed the New York designer Kevin McNamara as he searched out sources in the Luberon for the houses and apartments he was decorating in the United States. His trip in the mountainous region stretching east of Avignon included not just shops for ceramics and old fabrics but also those selling immense pieces of French limestone from quarries or old salvaged remnants from dealers. He went to stores specializing in antique furniture and outside Bonnieux visited a fabricator of decorative tiles produced to the customer's specifications. "The best places are off the beaten track," McNamara insisted, suggesting the pleasures of discovery.[10]

Interest in the Provençal look led to a range of goods—or their simulations—making their way into American retail in a variety of ways. To give just one example, April Cornell, a store focused on furnishings and on women's and children's clothing, opened in Montreal in 1975 and ultimately expanded to 107 stores in Canada and the United States. It offered many Provence-styled goods, especially tablecloths and napkins. Authenticity was never emphasized, but colors and patterns similar to those in Souleiado cloth were visible and made all the more desirable by the softened aesthetic of the shops.

Lavender as color, decorative motive, and scent was often associated with these goods, and, early on, it became a central link to Provence. Its flowers provide a fragrance long treasured in cosmetic oils and perfumes in the English-speaking world. In its opening spread the 1962 *Look* piece showed "a field of cultivated lavender," in all its eponymous color. In 1969, Olga Carlisle wrote of the "orange blossoms, lavender and rosemary," remembered from her childhood, that drew her to want a house in Provence.[11] Since the early 1970s, because of Olivier Bassan, such scents with origins in Provence have been distilled and sold in shops as shampoos and other cosmetic products.

The company that emerged to offer the ultimate in Provençal style, L'Occitane, began simply. Its history remains hard to track, and the mystique that surrounds its founder and his enterprise was hardly dispelled by *The Essence of Provence*, a lavender-colored book by the mystery writer Pierre Magnan promising to be Olivier Bassan's biography. What emerges as clear from it and other sources, however, is that Bassan, as a young Frenchman in the 1960s, was similar to those Americans who were impelled into business by a vision of pure food or clothing. Able to capture the zeitgeist, he became the founder of a successful enterprise.[12]

While Bassan was studying at the University of Aix and attempting to support himself, his partner, and their child—and to pay for his psychoanalysis—he found his calling through his concern with ecology. With an old copper still, he began to distill rosemary into an oil, first for a bubble bath and then a shampoo, and, in 1976, began to peddle it to local merchants. He found a graphic artist to make labels and seized on the name L'Occitane. Aided by friends and family, he was able to set up operations in an abandoned factory in Volx, a small village in Alpes-de-Haute-Provence, and establish outlets in France selling his soaps and creams. Other cosmetic products and scents, such as lavender and verbena, followed, with Provence providing its distinctive initial ingredients. As L'Occitane grew, it became another of the pulls drawing travelers to the region.[13]

As is clear from *Provence the Beautiful*, Williams-Sonoma featured the region in important ways as Chuck Williams built his business. A child of the depression, Williams worked many jobs before World War II, including high-end retail, where he learned the selling power of personal service and design. After war service he moved to Sonoma, California, and became a contractor, renovating houses. He and his friends enjoyed cooking and had a regular rotating dinner party. On a two-week trip to France in 1953, he dined in small restaurants and marveled at what was available to home cooks in the shops—"heavy sauté pans, huge stockpots, fish poachers, and an endless array of bakeware." These were in marked contrast to flimsy American pots and pans made out of tin or thin aluminum. Seeing opportunity, Williams decided to bring French cookware home.[14]

His first shop opened in 1956 in Sonoma. At the outset it was a do-it-yourself job. Unlike department stores that basically stacked kitchen goods, he displayed them. To show off what were his unfamiliar wares, he put his goods "up on a shelf in size order, with all the handles facing the same way." Beyond the decorative value, Williams liked this display because it forced the customer to ask him to get the item, "thus creating conversation" and ensuring his personal attention. And this gave him a chance to "talk up French cooking."

Out of this came Williams-Sonoma. Williams moved the business to San Francisco in 1958, in time to catch the growing enthusiasm for French food in the city, and it was immediately profitable. Growth came from the store's relation with the new food environment. Julia Child helped, too. "As her show began to find an audience," Williams elaborated, "we found more customers. One night she showed how to make a soufflé, and the next day people came in asking about soufflé dishes." Mail order began in 1971, on a very small scale at first. Advised by an important customer—Edward Marcus, responsible for the Neiman-Marcus catalog—it grew, increasing the reach of the enterprise. Williams-Sonoma's success generated competition as early as 1972, when Sur La Table opened in Seattle.

Provence may have come earlier, but it was certainly present at Williams-Sonoma by 1974 when Richard Olney came for a demonstration to publicize his book *Simple French Food*. This was the important occasion when Olney met Alice Waters and later dined at Chez Panisse. The link between Olney, Williams-Sonoma, and Provence proved long lasting.

Some books mingled Provençal possessions with food in unexpected ways. *At Home in France*, a huge and lavish book, portrayed a variety of French houses. In each house the author, Christopher Petkanas, was served a meal, which he described in an individual chapter, giving its menu and a recipe for one of the dishes. Glamorous photographs made every possession exquisite and desirable. The book featured two houses in Provence: Le Vieux Mas, owned by Simone Beck, Julia Child's collaborator, and a small "cabane" owned by Dorothée d'Orgeval.[15]

While the houses of both Frenchwomen were filled with beautiful possessions, Beck's treasured antiques did not derive from Provence. What emerged from the text and the photographs was a vision of an elite woman living unapologetically among beautiful things and dining on fine French, but not necessarily Provençal-inspired, food.[16] The second home, a small structure in the hills above Roussillon owned by a Parisian art dealer, Dorothée d'Orgeval, offered something quite different to the reader. Its appeal came from the furnishings it held, gathered from the surrounding area. All its objects were lovingly portrayed—the stone slab that served as a dining table, once part of the Roman way that passed through the region; glazed tiles behind new stainless stovetop; shelves and aperitif table crowded with pottery; old bottles waiting to be filled with Gigondas wine bought in bulk, cushions made from old quilts of the region.[17]

Also featured, of course, was the meal d'Orgeval served to the author. Following aperitifs and appetizers came the Grand Aïoli, then a course of seven kinds of goat cheese, and finally peeled peaches as dessert. D'Orgeval downplayed everything, dismissing any notion that she was serving Provençal cuisine. This is merely local food, she said, "very rustic, ordinary poor cuisine you eat every day. . . . It is not very considered and not very refined." Nonetheless, the author presented here, as in the other chapters of the book, both the menu for the meal she served him and the recipes for the aïoli. With all that is pictured and described, this chapter captured the tastes of the meal and the look of the objects in the house and garden. Everything presented was meant to make one desire this food, these goods, this life.[18]

Other books centering on food didn't require an explicit connection. In the high-time for cookbooks featuring Provence, the 1980s and '90s, when publishers and writers clearly perceived an English-speaking market eager for the virtual tastes and aromas of the region's kitchens, cookbooks were as important for Provençal furnishings as for cuisine. Along with dishes placed on rocks in view of perched villages, there were glamorous shots of dining rooms and kitchens that conveyed a desirable way of life lived among Provençal objects, old and new. *Patricia Wells at Home in Provence* provides a handsome example. The usefulness of this book was matched by the allure of Wells's kitchen, her bread ovens in the living room and out of doors, and the beautiful food set on pottery bowls, baskets, and platters made of twigs, typically placed on old wood, tiles, or stones. Occasionally a bit of Souleiado cloth peeked through. The atmosphere of Vaison-la-Romaine was thick, with photographs portraying shopkeepers and artisans in their cheese, produce, and butcher shops.[19]

A thread linking a number of books on decoration as well as on cooking is the kitchen—and house—of Lulu Peyraud. Leafing through these works, the fabric ruffle that edges the top of Peyraud's kitchen hearth becomes a familiar signpost. It appears twice in *Pierre Deux's French Country*, opposite a look at the handsome foyer of the house with its tall grandfather clock. It shows up once again in Julian and Carey More's 1988 cookbook, this time near a photograph of Lucien Peyraud seated in the traditional dining room of Domaine Tempier. It is glimpsed behind a fruit-laden table in *Provence the Beautiful*.[20]

And finally, it is featured in *Lulu's Provençal Table* (plate 12). It is particularly the color photographs by Gail Skoff in this 1994 book that give Peyraud's kitchen a dramatic presentation. Beautiful ingredients and prepared dishes sit on a work table in the foreground, while in the background at the great hearth hangs meat roasting at table height. On its mantle is a collection of black wrought-iron grills for holding fish, meat, and vegetables over a fire. And hanging below is again that distinctive Provençal border print helping to keep the smoke away from the kitchen.[21]

What here is not to love? A warm and spontaneous woman who markets daily and cooks divinely, a loving extended family gathered around meals, a story of the development of a great wine, and then the images of the food, their ingredients, and the utensils used to cook them. There is the great copper cauldron of bouillabaisse over a wood fire, surrounded by bowls of pottery. On another page *soupe au pistou* in a large white tureen rests on Souleiado cloth, with an open bottle of Domaine Tempier rosé nearby. Portrayed are whole fish wrapped in vine leaves being cooked over coals, enclosed by a metal grill, perhaps the very one pictured above the kitchen fireplace. In a group portrait, earthenware gratin dishes, a *pot-au-feu*, and a *daubière*, along with stone mortars, are gathered outdoors on old stone steps.[22]

One of the most handsome photographs in the book gives a glimpse into the elegant Peyraud dining room with its beautiful wood mantle, handsome antiques, and formal table set for dinner— all polished and gleaming. The image is in black and white, and this choice conveys the room's timelessness. This book of reverence is more than a cookbook. Along with food and wine and tributes to a superb cook and her family, *Lulu's Provençal Table* offers a vision of a house and its furnishings that might themselves serve as a pathway to the good life.[23]

Images of the goods of Provence have appeared in many places since the 1970s. They have illustrated magazines devoted to travel and food. They have turned up in the increasingly glossy photographs of the new style cookbooks designed more for the coffee table than the kitchen. Some of the products themselves have arrived in shop windows and store displays. Publications devoted to home furnishings have contained not only Provençal goods themselves but also directions about where to find them in situ.

Once unknown, Provençal pottery, cookware, fabrics, furniture, herbs, and lavender scents and skin care products caught the public eye. Provence soon became known as a place offering special goods, some holding an almost sacred quality associated with the land. Desire for the products of Provence—drawn from the place of their origin—became an important part of the pull bringing American travelers and sojourners to the region or filling the imagination of those remaining at home. Not all longings can be fulfilled; some remain only as a dream. But the yearning for Provence was real—to see firsthand the fields of lavender, to inhabit those hills, to buy its bounty at its markets, and to search for its special objects to treasure.

Patricia Wells and the Joys of Staying in Place

"A house transform one's life? I wouldn't have believed it, but almost from the day we first saw Chanteduc our life was altered forever."[1] Written in 1996, these are the words of Patricia Wells. In 1981, she and her husband, Walter, spent a two-week sojourn at Chanteduc, a house on the edge of Vaison-la-Romaine. In 1984, they were able to acquire it (plate 13).

Patricia and Walter Wells found they were able to realize the good life in Chanteduc because much had happened in the hills of Provence to make it possible. This particular Provençal *mas*, or farmhouse, could appeal because it had been restored by a prior French owner, Régine Fabre. Mary Roblee Henry gave her sly rendition of Régine's acquisition embedded within her own tale of house hunting. Mary was in Vaison-la-Romaine as Régine's guest. Years before, their husbands had become friends when both were posted as diplomats in Lebanon and remained so during their Paris years. Roger and Régine Fabre had a second home in Vaison, his natal place, and invited the Henrys to visit. Régine had secured a third home, Chanteduc, for she desired a vineyard and found that the property suited her.

Patricia Wells learned from past sales agreements that Chanteduc had been the subsistence farm of the Reynaud family for many generations. It once produced a minor cash crop of olives, but when the

trees were harmed by severely cold weather in the 1950s, the Rey-
nauds replaced them with grenache vines.² For Régine Fabre the
property would serve another purpose. As Mary Roblee Henry put
it, "Chanteduc was her *petit Hameau*, her very own plaything. . . .
There she was Marie Antoinette with a toy house and a yielding
vineyard."³

By the 1970s, Chanteduc had another use—income. In the 1970s
Régine put an ad in the *Saturday Review*: "Provençal farmhouse furnished in antiques with swimming pool," and Rita and Yale Kramer
from New York answered it. For a number of years they returned to
Chanteduc for summer stays and in 1981 invited their good friends
Patricia and Walter Wells, by then living in Paris, to join them for
a two-week stay.⁴ Enchanted by Provence and Chanteduc, Patricia
and Walter began to inquire about buying the property. Widowed
twice, Régine was now Régine Boissarie, and it seemed possible
that she would sell. After long and difficult negotiations lasting over
two years, Patricia and Walter purchased the property and began
their own renovations.

The two described the process in *We've Always Had Paris . . . and
Provence* in 2008. Patricia wrote that "as we formed the character
of the house, it formed ours." She summed up the essence—"it was
difficult to be unhappy at Chanteduc."⁵ As she put in her cookbook,
At Home in Provence, this house and its setting "symbolized all the
essential elements of happiness" she and her husband had sought
from life. "Was it just the sun," she wrote, "or did this place have a
magic way of magnifying ordinary pleasures?"⁶

In years following the purchase of Chanteduc, through food writing, cookbooks, and culinary teaching, Patricia Wells has brought
Provence and its cuisine into many American homes. Her work,
her kitchen, and her experiences with Walter in Vaison have made
palpable the dream of the good life that Provence represents and
have added to the appetite of some Americans to buy second homes
there—or simply come for a stay in houses rented from others. In
her work and life, Patricia Wells has come to epitomize Americans'
taste for Provence.⁷

FOURTEEN

Résidences
Secondaires

I

At one level the story of Chanteduc and Patricia and Walter Wells is unique. But moving away from its particulars, it can be seen as part of a broader development that Laurence Wylie chronicled for the third edition of *Village in the Vaucluse*.

When he returned to Roussillon for another visit in the mid-1970s, Wylie found the village completely transformed. In this microcosm, he saw changes in Provence stimulated by the French government during the previous quarter century, many of which felt to him as loss. The lunchtime bar group no longer met. All the older craftsmen, including blacksmith, harness maker, and tinsmith, had left their trades, for their services were no longer needed in the age of automobiles and plastic. Suppliers of bottled gas took the place of the earlier transporters of firewood. And there were no more farmers.

He was also aware of seemingly positive developments. The village attracted visitors for a day's excursion. "The possibility of a family exploration in the ochre cliffs followed by an extraordinarily good meal in the village," he wrote, meant crowds each Sunday. The starred restaurant boasted a "substantial building" able to serve guests throughout the year.[1] Roussillon was now a place of leisure, and of businesses that catered to the leisured.

In the 1970s American curiosity about Provence was strong, and this gave Wylie opportunities to write about Roussillon beyond anniversary reflections. In a piece commissioned by the *New York Times* in 1973, he considered the larger changes affecting the village. He saw that when France focused on industrializing after the war, the government stopped protecting small farmers. There had been some efforts to make family farming viable, but this had not happened around Roussillon, and many of its farmers gave up.[2]

The village's real change came from an unforeseen direction. Roussillon and its surround, similar to other favorably placed areas, became an adjunct to France's cities, serving to provide second (or even third or fourth) homes to urban dwellers. Roussillon "with the sun of the Midi and its startling ochre cliffs, has a sophisticated city population. The house we rented the year we lived there was bought and modernized several years ago by an Italian sculptor." In place of the equipment shed that Wylie had known in 1950, there was now a swimming pool with "a magnificent view of the valley." Recently the house sold to "one of the best known journalists in Paris."[3]

Although Wylie didn't elaborate in print, in an unpublished draft of this piece he wrote about what he had known as "the dirtiest house in town." After it was bought and remodeled by a well-known violinist, it changed hands again "and now belongs to the headmaster of a New England school." The town, he wrote, had been taken over by "*estivants,* the city people with their vacation village homes."[4] Not only French *estivants*, but Americans as well.

In the face of this, the merchants and artisans who fared best were flexible enough to adjust to the changing needs of those living or visiting in Roussillon. Wylie saw that "the walls of all the restaurants are covered with paintings, for the particular lurid beauty of Peyrane attracts many artists. In the summer there is even an art gallery in the remodeled shed that used to house Monsieur Prayal's buzz saw. At the top of the hill, where Madame Bon lived as the last survivor of the 'old village,' a stylish young couple have an arts-and-crafts shop. Now every house at the top of the hill is owned by city people."[5]

The warmth of the sun had transformed the village's population. "With the increasing number of retired people, the atmosphere is not unlike that of a Florida retirement community. . . . The game of boules is played all day now because so many people are not working." Viewing Roussillon's male pastime reminded Wylie of its Florida equivalent, "shuffleboard in St. Petersburg."[6]

Wylie was a good witness, and a good analyst. By the early 1970s something truly extraordinary had happened not only to his village in Vaucluse but more generally in the French countryside, Provence included. During the preceding two decades, population throughout continental Europe had moved from south to north, fed by the greater opportunities for work in industry. During Les Trente Glorieuses, newly abandoned houses joined those left vacant in earlier times to appear desirable to those seeking second homes in the sun.

These properties offered new opportunities for work and income to those remaining. The houses needed renovation; their new owners needed all the necessities of life. A wealthier population sought amenities. Visitors required accommodations and places to eat. Second home owners, such as Régine Boissarie, could find well-paying renters, and those renters had to have shops for food. And although Patricia and Walter Wells did not hire a contractor to renovate Chanteduc, they needed a great deal of help. In the discarded shells of the old, new life began in Provence.

II

Following on the heels of the French came the British, whose experiences helped inform Americans and shape their desires. In the 1970s, Brits were embarking on a course of second-home buying abroad, especially in sunny Spain and France. Most of the studies of international migration focus on the pushes and pulls of production, for in the past in peace time the search for remunerative work has been the major spur to immigration. But growing wealth in Britain and its aging population led to significant emigration for consumption.

Winifred Fortescue had captured the British imagination in an earlier era with her 1935 *Perfume from Provence*. Although this book failed to find an audience in the United States, it was a best seller in the United Kingdom, for Fortescue was a national celebrity who had immigrated to Provence and renovated a grand house there. Important writers, including Ford Madox Ford, Lawrence Durrell, and Stephen Spender, brought Provence to British and American attention as a place to linger.

As England became increasingly urban after World War II, the beautiful rural regions of France appeared more and more desirable to visit. British guidebooks to Provence told their countrymen where to go in the hills, what to see, and where to stay.[7] Having tasted, some wanted more—to buy a dwelling. The key investigators of British home owning in France, Henry Buller and Keith Hoggart, summed it up succinctly: "The depopulation of rural France generated a stock of dwellings that are ideally suited to meeting the imagined rural idyll of the British middle classes." What happened next was equally important. It turned out that the "idealized image" of France actually met the "experience of living in France," leading to reports of satisfied home buyers.[8]

But in addition, the British found other reasons to leave their island. There was, of course, its wet climate and gray skies that had led generations of sun worshippers to spend holidays on the Continent. Added to this were new factors that came in the 1970s, such as the energy crisis, spiraling inflation, and rising real estate prices in the United Kingdom. These led some in the British Isles to look elsewhere, especially to the familiar sunny regions of Spain and France. The abandoned farmhouses of France, sought as *résidences secondaires* by French urbanites, proved equally appealing to the British.

Those facing retirement also found that, with the cost of living cheaper in France and the value of British property rising, they could purchase a more desirable house in France. It is difficult to obtain accurate numbers, given the ways that census records undercount this kind of migration, but by 1991, more than 62,000 citizens of the British Isles were known to be residing in France.[9]

While many French regions held allure, important among them was Provence, known to travelers for its Roman ruins and by readers of Elizabeth David for its enticing flavors. One of the *départements* of Provence—Vaucluse, east of Avignon, with its perched villages and dramatic mountainous scenery—was closely examined by Buller and Hoggart. They found that a particular swath of British society chose to reconstruct run-down farmhouses there. Unlike many Brits venturing to other French regions who arrived on their newly acquired property sight unseen, these home buyers tended to be familiar with the area. A greater percentage than those going elsewhere had lived outside the United Kingdom for much of their lives. They were wealthier and more likely to speak French. They were therefore seemingly less concerned with seeking a property at a bargain price and more desirous of the amenities of French rural and communal life.[10]

What British home buyers encountered in France was complex, whether in Vaucluse or in other areas. They definitely got the rural beauty they were seeking. During its drive to increase industrialization and modernize agriculture, France had largely protected its rural heritage while improving the land through hydroelectrification projects. Brits found their French neighbors to be satisfactory, reporting that, on the whole, they received civility and cooperation. And well they should. To regions bypassed by the economic development of the north, the British settlers brought new life. They gave an economic stimulus to rural regions that had seemed to be dying from depopulation.

In the process, the British newcomers made contact with the locals, sometimes, as in the case of reconstruction projects, lasting seasons, even years. They established continuing relationships with food providers and restaurant owners. Yet they also came to understand that the neighbors in their new French world, despite their cordiality and good manners, were bound by personal ties defined largely by family and long association. They learned they had entered a world that played by its own rules, not theirs. Hunting was an established practice, for example, as was the eating of horsemeat.

They also found that they were not alone among Northern Europeans seeking the good life in France, as others sought the pleasures of French rural life and cuisine. In the 1980s Belgians actually held the lead in numbers of second home buyers, and the British were closely followed by Germans and Scandinavians. France had attracted an international community of sojourners, including some Americans.

III

By the end of the 1960s, a few Americans, such as Van Day Truex, had purchased second homes in Provence, but with the selling of the region in the 1970s and 1980s, the trickle became a stream. Moving along in it were those coming from a wide range of economic circumstances, and each house buyer was impelled by a different impulse. A wise and witty friend wrote this to me about her and others' choice to buy a house in Provence, "We are all nuts, but each is a nut in his or her own particular way."[11]

Behind some Americans who acquired a second home in Provence were associations and memories. Recollection of the scent of her grandmother's flowers from Provence drew Olga Carlisle there. Looking at the golden walls in many of Cézanne's paintings and then seeing them in their three-dimensional solidity on the land impelled others. Many of those who went on study abroad to France came to have an enduring love of all things French.[12] In some cases, the love attained in college could lead to Provence and writing about it. Mary Ann Caws, for example, after finding French literature at Bryn Mawr, took her junior year abroad in Paris on the college's program, an early step along the path to her distinguished career as a scholar and writer on French culture. For Caws in the early 1970s, the choice of a second home in Provence felt natural.

She and her then husband, Peter Caws, both professors, were able to spend sabbatical years there, putting their children in French schools. For them, the lure of simplicity was not only appealing but literal. With property cheap in Provence in the 1960s and early 1970s, it didn't require riches to buy in Provence. And as for great expenses in restoration, for some they were not necessary. Mary Ann and Peter Caws, with "faith in Provence and in its skies," responded to an ad for a small farmhouse in the "valley of the Ventoux" and found a small abandoned dwelling with no stairs between the two floors, the majority of its roof tiles missing, and some of its existing ceiling and floors constructed from grape crates. They learned there was also no electricity and that water came only from a spring. They chose to buy the property because they loved its setting, and gradually, over many summers, they reconstructed it themselves.[13]

In the background was the poet René Clar, who lived not far away in L'Isle-sur-la-Sorge. Mary Ann Caws was early in her long career as a professor of French literature at Hunter College and on the graduate faculty of City University of New York. Prior to finding a place of her own in Provence, she and her family often visited Clar. In time she translated many of his poems and wrote on his work. He was a beloved figure, not only to her personally but also to his French neighbors. He was a hero during the Resistance, "*un pur,*" a man "purely himself, authentic." Behind the couple's decision to purchase the house near Mont Ventoux was a desire "at least unconsciously . . . to have our children grow up near Clar."[14]

Mary Ann Caws also sought a different life. Coming from a North Carolina childhood, she had once aspired to a "rapid way of living." Work life at her desk in New York had given her this. But in time she needed something else, the "simplicity" that Provence offered. Thirty-five years later, she wrote of her sense of belonging in that part of France, "in the land of simple pleasures, inhabited by '*les purs.*'" For Caws, it was important to take on the accent of Provence. "I will keep working at [it] and let my desk, and whatever is on it, go. This life feels real."[15]

In stark contrast to Mary Ann Caws, some Americans finding Provence were wealthy, even exceedingly wealthy, able to choose the region for one of their many houses. It was a major moment in the region when the Atlanta billionaire Anne Cox Chambers acquired property in Provence. In 1981, at the end of her service as ambassador to Belgium during the presidency of Jimmy Carter, she felt, according to *Southern Accents*, that she "wanted a place of her own in Europe." Her business interests were extensive. She was the chairwoman of Atlanta Newspapers, part of Cox Enterprises founded by her father, the former governor of Ohio and 1920 Democratic Party candidate for the US presidency. Chambers could afford whatever property she chose, and to the surprise of agents, that turned out to be a farmhouse, not a chateau. What Cox found was a property "in a state of disrepair. Tractors and farm implements stood about, and weeds had overtaken the grounds."[16]

Her agent recommended Bruno Lafourcade for restoration. He had been written up in *Le Figaro* after he won the grand prize in France's National Restoration Competition. Self-taught, in the 1960s he began working with an experienced mason to restore old properties being reclaimed for new uses. As the quality of his work was noticed, "real estate brokers, eager to market the possibilities represented in a medieval ruin or dilapidated mansion, began referring their clients to him." Initially they were French, followed by British. After his commission for Chambers, Lafourcade's clients began to be Americans. "They see Provence differently from the French," Lafourcade said about the Americans, "For them, it is a far more romantic place than it is for the people who were born here."[17] One can see this in some of the interiors of Chambers's house. She largely furnished it with antiques purchased in European capitals, but according to one report, some pieces "came from French antiques shops and help foster a sense of regional warmth." Specific nods to Provence came in floral prints "characteristic of Provençal design" and "regional pottery" placed on the dining room table.[18]

Chambers proved to be an important force drawing other Americans, especially those from southern states, to Provence. Owning a house there became a mark of prestige. As one article put it with some exaggeration, in her wake "every millionaire in Atlanta had to have a restored château or villa in Provence." Lafourcade, aided by his son, Alexandre, and his wife, Dominique, took on some of their commissions. As a *New York Times* article stated, Lafourcade "has attracted a high-flying international clientele with imaginative metamorphoses of Cinderella structures into princely estates."[19]

Among the Americans were Craig and Ginny Magher—he, a financier; she, an interior decorator. In 1996, they hired Lafourcade to reconstruct their property outside Saint-Rémy. The size of the house was immense, fourteen rooms and well over 8,000 square feet. When the work was complete, Le Mas de Baraquet, as it was named, was, like the Maghers' lavish Atlanta home, publicized in a large spread in the US shelter magazine *Veranda*. And, in at least one future Lafourcade reconstruction, it was Ginny Magher, not a French firm, who was hired as the interior designer.

Her high style certainly fit the romantic mode. One piece described Magher and her work in designer-speak: "Well known for her knowledge of Provencal materials she has created an extremely light and elegant interior, timeless but contemporary." In this Cinderella world, French elegance ruled, with fine antiques at every turn. A few country touches lent links to the region. The dining room's crystal chandelier hung from rough-hewn beams, and there was a quilt peeking out from underneath the linen table cloth. But only in the service areas—the kitchen and an upstairs bathroom—were tiles, fabrics, and furniture clearly marked as Provençal on view.[20]

At the same time that Chambers was rebuilding her farmhouse on a grand scale, Patricia and Walter Wells found themselves drawn to Provence and specifically to Chanteduc (plate 13). As Walter put it, "we were not the first humans to be preternaturally drawn to the sunshine and the dramatic landscapes—hillsides dotted with vineyards, olive groves, sunflowers, and smears of lavender even more brilliant than Cézanne has rendered them." Chanteduc had been built room by room, and it "spilled up and down with entrances on different levels." It wasn't a large house, at least by Walter's standards, but as he put it, its "hillside site is grander than a château's.

Surrounded by vineyards and woodland . . . it's hidden, like an enchanted clearing in the forest." It had mature trees, including an oak likely three centuries old, and magnificent views.[21]

The pleasures of Chanteduc were manifold, and many involved the land Patricia Wells came to know well. "When the half-dozen gnarled old cherry trees in the orchard began to bear fruit, we dropped everything to pick the shiny, purple-red fruits" and turn them into desserts and liqueurs. "The unfurling of every leaf—lettuce, grapes, figs, and irises—became the object of our weekly attention." Some encounters were harsh, however. Patricia learned of the poor soil of the vegetable garden, the wild animals that roamed, the passersby who cleaned the olives off the trees. But more than tipping the balance was the wonderful sense of village life, the enthusiasm of the butcher, the dedication of their plumber. She even accepted the poacher who gathered truffles on their land. Finally, there was the history of their property. "As time went on," Patricia wrote, "I realized that this farm had existed for centuries before us and would thrive for centuries after our deaths. That meant we would affect its existence for thirty, maybe forty years at most." With that came a feeling of obligation, to "maintain its integrity, carry on its strong, life-enhancing qualities."[22]

Walter took responsibility for carrying out much of Chanteduc's makeover and maintenance. And his telling conveys a sense of how arduous his tasks have been. Water began as and remained the most pressing and unreliable element for this house on a hill. Getting adequate water to the house required two pumps, and small radiators were used for heating it; but that arrangement presumed electric power, which proved vulnerable to storms in summer and winter. Patricia and Walter moved slowly, step by step, planning each project with local plumbers and masons.

The result of all this labor was the making of a beautiful second home in Provence. Along with its comfortable spaces and splendid views is its dream kitchen (plate 14). Patricia chose what had been a spare bedroom for the kitchen because it had a window facing west, allowing her to look at Mont Théos throughout the day and in the brilliant moments of sunset. As she wrote, "I was determined that someday I would peel carrots at that window." The creation of this room led to additional work on top of her career as a food writer. She has become a teacher of Provençal cooking, offering in the warmer months courses in this kitchen.[23]

Patricia and Walter Wells join with Mary Ann Caws and Ann Cox Chambers in exemplifying the different possibilities Provence held for Americans seeking second homes. Caws desired and found a place for a simple pleasures and a life that felt authentic. Chambers set the pattern for those of great wealth—a lavish reconstruction planned and carried out by a contractor and master builder and an interior decorator. Patricia and Walter Wells chose a farmhouse already made habitable by a previous owner and gradually modified it to accommodate their needs, tastes, and desire to extend hospitality to others. Writings by and about these three and their houses have sent—and continue to send—a spectrum of messages to a broad and diverse American public about the good life to be lived in Provence.

FIFTEEN   **Renting**

For most Americans contemplating the good life in Provence, buy-   199
ing a house or an apartment there has been out of the question. But
renting someone else's for a month or a week? To some in the middle class, that can sound just right. Renting, however, is a relatively
recent possibility, part of the change that has transformed many
vacations abroad, including those in Provence.

It was once both difficult and iffy to rent a house or an apartment
abroad. Think of it: no Internet, no pictures. An article by Joseph
Wechsberg gets us back to an earlier time. Beginning in the late
1940s and throughout the 1950s Wechsberg and his family lived in
rented houses in northern Italy, on the Riviera, in West Berlin, the
Austrian Alps, and Vienna. In 1957, he wrote of his experiences.
Though clothed in his robust humor, some of the rental situations
he described were pretty dicey. Lodged in a grand house in the
Tyrol, "one Christmas Eve the central heating broke down during
a blizzard and there was a leak in the roof. We worked all night to
get the place dry again." In an apartment in a castle near Strasbourg
with "practically no plumbing . . . the water faucets acted whimsi-
cally and the stove was on the verge of an explosion." On a particularly cold night after he lit a fire in the library hearth, a fire brigade
came to douse the flames that were coming out of the chimney,
causing Wechsberg to be hit by a steep fine. "It was a happy day

when we moved into our castle and a happier one when we moved out of it."[1]

What Wechsberg presented was both an invitation and a caution. Yes, it could be delightful to rent in Europe. It tended to be cheaper for a family, and renting made it possible to enter into the life of a neighborhood. But, in 1957, it was usually not possible to find anything to meet American standards of comfort. Lacking were good mattresses, workable kitchens, and reliable heating in winter. "Metternich or Lola Montez may have slept in your room, but it's damp and the windows rattle." He described one house in Vienna with an unheated basement kitchen so cold that the hired cooks tended to quit. "When the cook was off, my wife had to put on her fur coat to go down and make a cup of coffee." As Wechsberg made clear, there were seemingly no reliable ways to locate a good place by long distance.[2]

Wechsberg relied on his own experience to advise readers about how to proceed. Armed with international contacts, he wrote in advance to a recommended real-estate firm. He had the confidence to get in touch with the American Consulate and the languages to write to the offices of the local chamber of commerce or automobile club. For the more typical traveler he suggested an approach he used where he had no connections. He and his wife would arrive in the place, take a hotel room, and speak to the concierge about possible agents. Then on the scene, in broad daylight, the two would go around with the agent to inspect a property from top to bottom. They relied on all their bad experiences to tell them what to check and test: bathroom plumbing, hot water, location of the kitchen as well as its equipment and possible extra charges for telephone, water, heating, and electricity. Then, after that, they would look carefully at the contract, for it carried its own dangers. Wechsberg recommended that if the contract was an involved one, it was good to "check with the nearest American Consulate to avoid fine-print traps."[3]

Wechsberg came to this conclusion: A true advantage to renting a house on the Continent is that "you get homesick for America and its well-run, easy-to-manage houses. That alone is worth the money you've spent."[4] In 1957 Wechsberg's clever writing may have been amusing to readers, but renting a place abroad, with all its potential dangers, seemed risky and even dangerous.

Contrast this to what accompanied the piece by Irish journalist and humorist Patrick Campbell in the June 1970 issue of *Holiday*, presenting those carefree days in the hills above Nice.[5] If Campbell had indeed found a recipe for "How to Live the Sweet Life in the South of France," even sweeter to American readers were the pages that followed that gave specific information on how to rent "A Place in Provence." After a preliminary note touting the advantages of staying in one place and getting to know it intimately, followed by a little advice, came the payoff—a listing of agencies located in New York, London, and France ready to serve travelers wanting to rent in Provence.[6]

This was welcome news. In the years between Wechsberg in 1957 and Campbell in 1970, something had happened to make possible relatively worry-free rentals. For a house such as the one Campbell described in the hills of Provence to be available to Americans for a vacation stay, someone had to acquire and restore a derelict structure and oversee its restoration, as had Régine Fabre in the 1960s. Initially, some French families likely offered their *résidences secondaires* to persons they knew. If kin and friends did not take full advantage of the house or if the promise of income proved a temptation, certain homeowners may have gone to a local agent to arrange a rental to strangers, or may have placed an ad in a publication, perhaps in the American *Saturday Review*. From an American traveler's perspective, this could portend highly problematic experiences, such as the ones Wechsberg narrated in 1957.

In France a movement had begun that promised to solve some of the difficulties. In 1951, the senator of Alpes-de-Haute-Provence, facing the return of once fertile land of his *département* to desert-like conditions after the destruction of the war and depopulation, had an idea. He understood two facts. Postwar economic growth failed to reach much of his region, with the result that farm properties were abandoned. Ironically, as prosperity returned to cities, its dwellers were seeking to experience the countryside during their holidays. His plan: link the two together. Thus, in the small hamlet of Chaudol in the mountains high above the Côte d'Azur, there came into being the first *gîte,* the name given to private self-catering residences let commercially for vacation use, typically by the week or month. The time was right; the idea was brilliant. Within a year the plan was officially adopted, and by 1955 there were 150 *gîtes* in six *départements*. The snowball turned into an avalanche. Within two years there were 600 *gîtes* in thirty *départements*. Beginning in 1970 there was a reservation service.[7]

But for a long time, what happened in France stayed in France — or, at least did not enter into the consciousness of the typical American traveler.[8] What seemed to be required to get Americans to rent houses in France were trustworthy English-speaking intermediaries, preferably American agents, who could offer clients a guarantee that the property they were about to live in for a month or a week met their dreams and their standards.[9]

Immediately following the 1970 article in *Holiday,* "How to Live the Sweet Life in the South of France," the supplement listed three agencies in New York offering villas in Provence. Among them was At Home Abroad.[10] The story of this small company offers a good case study. Because this agency began almost a decade before 1970, its history gives needed background for understanding how Provence emerged out of the shadows into the "sell" of the region that Patrick Campbell so robustly enjoyed.

The idea for At Home Abroad began in 1960, after Lee Naiman and her husband, Robert, a New York psychiatrist, "had tried and failed to rent a house in Europe for a summer vacation with their children." A former advertising copywriter, Lee saw in this failure an opportunity to start an agency to broker such rentals. She teamed up with an associate to scout properties in areas deemed desirable at that time by American travelers—the French Côte d'Azur, the Italian Riviera, and the Costa Brava in Spain. The firm's initial concerns reflected Naiman's own desire for a safe and secure environment for her children—the availability of safe water and pasteurized milk, the existence of a local pediatrician, fencing for the yard. To find out about such matters she and her business partner developed a questionnaire to be filled in by the owner before each property was personally examined. Responses to this questionnaire became the "backbone of the company's files."[11]

A 1961 report in the *New York Times* gives the scenario. A prospective client would make an appointment to come to the firm's office on Central Park West to view photographs, a map, and specifics on the listed properties, each available for a month's minimum stay in the summer. The nascent company promised from the outset that each property had been visited in person to verify the information from the completed owner questionnaires. "We were unable to get adequate information working through national tourist bureaus," Lee Naiman stated. She made it possible for her client to learn many important specifics of the potential rental—traffic, neighbors, telephone usage, room sizes, number of beds, medical and other assistance available, and even details on maid service. After coming to an agreement with the client, the agency would then make all the arrangements for the rental.[12] Joseph Wechsberg would have been pleased.

At its launch and in its initial years At Home Abroad garnered great publicity, helped no doubt by Naiman's advertising experience. This was bolstered in 1963, when Claire Packman, who had worked for more than a decade in communications and public relations, joined the firm. Still active today, she agreed to speak with me and to share her scrapbook of brochures and articles. The information and records she provided have made it possible to piece together at least part of the story of how Americans got to Provence.[13]

In 2012 her own enthusiasm was still apparent as she looked back over her career of almost fifty years. Packman conveyed by word and intonation her relish of the work in its many facets. An avid traveler, she had been enamored of France from her Atlantic City childhood, and summer school in Montreal during her college years enabled her to polish her French language skills. She recalled that while scanning the *New York Times* ads at a time when she was looking for a job, she saw one that read "travel related," jumped at the chance, and went for the interview. Given her abilities and her interest, the position as office manager of At Home Abroad was a perfect fit. Deeply impressed by her boss, Packman recalled that Naiman "always had ideas; she was very, very bright."

In the early years, the agency charged no initial fee to use its service but added a charge to the rental deposit. Because of this, soon after Packman began work, the agency got a mention in a section of *Parade* magazine listing "freebies" available to readers, and life in the tiny office immediately changed. "The mailman was coming in the door with sacks of mail," she remembered. "I called [the two owners]. . . . It was summer, they were all out enjoying their swim in the Hamptons or wherever they went, and I said you must get in here immediately, I can't deal with it." With the mention in *Parade*, the firm was launched into a different galaxy (and began to charge an initial fee). By 1967, when Naiman was ready to move on, Packman bought the agency.

As owner, Claire Packman enhanced both the offerings of the company and its publicity stream. In 1968, a newspaper article reported that she had gathered more than 1,200 properties and secured 250 to 300 rentals each year for clients. She continued the established practice of the firm, preceding each site visit with a questionnaire to European owners seeking tenants. In going personally to check out each property, she or one of her associates looked for possible negatives, such as train tracks nearby. Reports from the field were candid, with comments such as "House has a swimming pool but it's about the size of a goldfish bowl."[14] By 1973 Packman herself was taking four such trips a year.

Article after article about the firm began to appear in national magazines, such as *Cosmopolitan, House Beautiful, Playboy*, and *Holiday*. In addition, there were pieces placed in publications targeting specific audiences—for example, *Show, Medical Economics*, and *Travel Agent*. The agency got free publicity in newspapers not only in New York and Los Angeles but also in places like Phoenix and Dallas. The high end of the market typically served as an article's opening gambit, playing on Americans' fascination with royalty and the rich. It can be yours for the month!—the palazzo on the Grand Canal in Venice, York Castle in Tangier, overlooking the Straits of Gibraltar, a villa in Cap Ferrat built into a cliff rising from the Mediterranean. But after such a come-on, each article typically grew more down to earth, and the reader learned that it was cheaper and more convenient to rent a place abroad than to stay in a hotel. And available for rent were ordinary villas, cottages, and apartments, as well as castles.

Some pieces were intended only for the high rollers. Frank Hiteshew began his article in the 1965 fall issue of *Carte Blanche* with "Every romantic has had fancies of living in a castle or equally exotic surroundings, attended by servants, transplanted right out of his prosaic day-to-day existence. If you have such an urge, don't resist it. You can make it all come true." Hiteshew gave examples of At Home Abroad's listings, with particular attention to the grand ones, such as a chateau in the Loire, an estate in Majorca, and York Castle above Tangiers. Hiteshew discussed the desired clientele: "In addition to being well-heeled, a basic requirement, the renters run to the arts and professions. Many are painters, writers and composers looking for a special spot to commune with their Muses; honeymooners, retired couples, doctors and professors." Details about the firm itself and its ways of working were sparse but well chosen. The staff was small "but well-traveled," making annual trips to inspect properties. Once a client settled on a place, all transactions, including linens and servants, came through the agency. The prices listed were, with one exception, very high. The basic message was exclusive luxury. "This is a special, limited kind of vacation obviously for the privileged and romantic few."[15] By her own account, Packman did indeed have wealthy clients, such as Governor Nelson Rockefeller and Huntington Hartford, heir to the A&P supermarket fortune. She also attracted creative spirits, such as playwright Neil Simon, writer Frank Gilroy, actress Clare Bloom, and singer Bobby Darin.

The darkly comic writer Bruce Jay Friedman, one of those creative types, was an early adopter. He and his wife had read a feature story mentioning At Home Abroad in a Sunday newspaper supplement, perhaps the *Parade* notice. They went to the agency and "were given massive scrapbooks filled with pictures of sumptuous villas in Italy and France, the kind that couldn't possibly be as good once you got there." Nonetheless the couple went ahead, taking their three children, a helper, and a cat to a large house that more than met their expectations.[16]

In the midst of comic bluster, Friedman gave more than enough information to make the reader want to follow his path. The total rental was $2,800 for two months, the price he usually paid "to rent a dozen or so nailed together planks and a refrigerator at unglamourous Fire Island." He prepaid a third of the sum to the rental agency, then, after arriving and viewing the place, paid the balance to the owner. At Home Abroad let the Friedmans know important details, such as what to bring and arrangements about housekeepers, whose services typically came as part of the package. Friedman concluded that the experience had been "remarkably smooth and comfortable for us, frighteningly uncomplicated and unless I am forgetting something, quite the most delightful experience I can recall."[17]

As the agency grew, Packman, supported by two assistants, received clients in its office, first on Fifth Avenue, then on the nineteenth floor at 136 East Fifty-Seventh Street, bordering Sutton Place. For an initial fee, prospective travelers were given a small group of appropriate catalogs and pictures to examine, the selection based on interests they had expressed. These few were culled from what became several thousand properties listed by the firm.[18] After clients looked at the materials, Packman spoke personally with them, answering questions and ultimately making arrangements.

The firm was notable for the detail it gathered. Not only did Packman or a staff member photograph properties inside and out, an on-the-scene representative of At Home Abroad scoped out possibilities for outdoor activities such as tennis, golf, and lying on beaches. Packman continued the agency's practice of gather-

ᴀT ʜoᴍᴇ
ᴀBʀoᴀD, ɪɴC.

invites you

to select your villa or apartment abroad

for the coming season

9 Brochure for At Home Abroad.
Photograph by author.

ing information about the practical side of life abroad, including medical facilities, laundry service, and pool maintenance, all specifics that might loom large during a month-long stay. Packman also came to offer special treatment to elite clients, such as stocking the rental's refrigerator and wine cellar with favorites and seeing that there were flowers on the table upon arrival. She was also willing to give her clients a great deal of hand holding when necessary, including daily calls before departure.[19]

All this suggested the wealthy renter. Nonetheless, from fairly early on, publicity went out to a broad swath of the American public. While promotional pieces for rentals continued in high-end venues, such as *Town and Country*, *Signature* (the magazine of the Diners Club), *Market Air Newsletter*, and *Medical Economics*, there were also pitches to a less affluent public in *Family Circle*, *Elks* magazine, and the Lubbock, Texas, *Avalanche-Journal*.

With this broader reach came efforts to demystify renting abroad. An article geared particularly to women explained that a "villa" wasn't a lordly mansion but simply a British term for any dwelling, even a hut that was surrounded by a patch of grass. The length of time for stays narrowed to two weeks and ultimately to a single week. Even Horace Sutton, the travel writer who reintroduced Americans to France after World War II, got into the act. In a 1970 article featuring At Home Abroad in the *Los Angeles Times*, he also described how entrepreneurial Europeans were now building clusters of villas as second homes in places like Spain's Costa del Sol that, when unoccupied, were then rented for vacation weeks to those overseas. And Sutton being Sutton, he stressed that renting abroad was not just for the wealthy or for families. "Bachelors band together and rent, too, preferring places where the Swedish girls go (France)."[20]

The success of At Home Abroad quickly led to competition. Already, in 1966, an article in *House and Garden* discussing Packman's agency also reported on World Wide Living on the West Coast, catering to those wanting "the poshest of private living quarters" across the globe; and IVY, for International Villas and Yachts, the American representative of an established British firm. It noted that At Home Abroad was listing approximately 1,000 properties, and IVY, about 800 yachts along with its land properties. To meet the growing demand, both World Wide Living and IVY were going beyond the role of intermediary to purchase or lease properties.[21] Nonetheless, At Home Abroad gained special attention, as witnessed by its many write-ups and by Claire Packman's appearance on *The Merv Griffin Show* in 1979, in a segment devoted to "Dream Houses."[22]

Although At Home Abroad's rental properties ranged from the Caribbean to Tunisia, Claire Packman's engagement with France made accommodations there a specialty, with more than 200 listings. Although Provence was not initially a featured destination, by 1967 it was on At Home Abroad's list. In that year, in a piece spotlighting the agency, TWA's *MarketAir Newsletter*, directed at traveling businessmen, offered this lure: "For the executive seeking more spacious and comfortable quarters. . . . An 18th century modernized farmhouse with swimming pool and guest house, set on 10 acres in Provence . . . where the festivals are marvelous and the food sublime."[23]

When the language of some travel writing in the 1970s changed to emphasize the vacation as a place of therapy to counter the stress of ordinary life, words about renting abroad took on a different tone. Rather than glamour or practicality, renting allowed the pleasures of the leisured life in one place, such as Patrick Campbell enjoyed. A 1973 piece in the "Diners Club International News" section of *Signature* magazine gave the basic narrative. There were two Europes offered to American travelers. One was the Europe of airports, railway stations, hotels, waiters, and bellhops—a hectic merry-go-round of traffic, tours, and tipping. The other Europe was a private world of sun-drenched villas, stately chateaux, and casitas in more remote areas. Renting a villa in this other Europe was a happy solution for families who preferred enjoying a leisurely overseas holiday, relaxing in the country of their choice, rather than being jostled through it.[24] Restated with slight variations in many pieces, this formula became something of a mantra.

By the 1980s, At Home Abroad reflected this language as it presented possible rentals in the Provence hills. A report announced, "One property in Provence is hidden among a dozen acres of vineyards and scented pine. Tranquility is guaranteed, what with mountains that rise on the horizon and a river flowing nearby."[25]

Of course, there was some pushback against all the positive treatments of renting abroad, for, at some level, it posed a problem for the existing travel industry. For agents set to deal with hotels operating on a different scale, finding a unique villa or an apartment for a client abroad likely meant something of a nuisance. It carried many more variables than a Hilton Hotel and required individual negotiations. In 1966, when a reporter for the *National Observer* inquired about renting abroad at the American Society of Travel Agents, he found the association was "unable to locate the names of any companies handling such vacation properties for rent."[26]

Perhaps speaking for the trade in 1984, a piece in *Travel & Leisure* considered both the lure of renting abroad and its risks. The delights were unmistakable. "Staying put. Settling in. All mellow phrases for a new kind of vacation away from home—the unhurried, unharried holiday. . . . Ease into the place, slow down to catch the nuances, create the comforting illusion that you live there, even for a brief moment."[27] Nonetheless, what followed was less encouraging. Julie Wilson, the author of the article, did not focus on particular companies but rather on the bewilderment of the potential renter caught in an ambiguous world lying somewhere between real estate and travel. She suggested that the seeker of a villa home call travel agents, airlines that have tie-ins, or the travel editor of the local newspaper, though "it helps, of course, if your local newspaper is the *New York Times*." She damned the French *gîtes* with faint praise, as "simple, inexpensive accommodations, scattered around the French countryside. . . . probably not the stuff that dreams are made of."[28]

The article raised doubts about agencies for renting villas abroad, reminding readers of travelers who had been scammed and warning that scoundrels had entered the business. It suggested ways of judging the reliability of brokers, such as checking with the consulate of the chosen country, questioning how recently the property had been seen by someone in the firm, and determining how many questions the company asked of the client. It also cautioned about the hidden costs of renting abroad—for food, tipping, and the company's commission. The best bet, it suggested, was the "word-of-mouth network." And it offered a zinger, bound to put off the ordinary reader—"the best way to rent an affordable dream house may still be to discover a friend of a friend with a 10-bedroom villa on the coast of Tuscany."[29]

Since the mid-1980s, much has changed for those seeking vacation houses and apartments to rent, especially the use of the Internet. For a long time Packman held to her established ways of doing business. In 2002, when *Fortune* listed the top twenty-five villa agents, it said of At Home Abroad, "Claire Packman does business the old fashioned way, personalized service rather than high technology."[30] But as times have changed, so has At Home Abroad. Although Packman stated in 2012 that she had scaled down to making arrangements only for established clients and their offspring, she nonetheless was maintaining a strong online list of properties available for rent, including high-end villas in Provence.

At the same time that the Internet has opened for public view the offerings of established agencies, such as At Home Abroad, it has, for some travelers, eliminated the need for an intervening human agent. Companies maintaining websites are essentially Internet bulletin boards: all arrangements are made between the prospective renter and the owner. Charges for posting are invisible to the renter, for the property owner pays an annual fee for the online service. HomeAway, one of the largest of these companies, of which Vacation Rental By Owner (VRBO) is now a part, currently offers extensive listings of properties, with description and photographs, normally accompanied by users' reviews. At present writing, in Lourmarin, a tiny village in the Luberon, with a population slightly over 1,000, HomeAway lists fifty-four properties for weekly rental.[31]

Close on its heels is Airbnb, growing exponentially as I write. The company no longer simply offers rooms for rent; now it makes available apartments and whole villas in Provence, displayed online, some for stays as short as one night. Listings come complete with photographs of interiors and exteriors, detailed reviews, and the promise of immediate contact with the friendly host pictured on the website.[32] Were he with us today, Joseph Wechsberg would certainly be surprised.

SIXTEEN

Along Came Mayle

In 1989, British writer Peter Mayle published *A Year in Provence*. It became a phenomenon, catching the zeitgeist in a way few books about living abroad have done. Mayle told the simple tale of an ad man and his wife leaving the rat race to live out the dream life in the South of France. Mention the word Provence today, and Peter Mayle immediately comes into the conversation.

What interests me is not only his book but also how Americans became prepared to read it. Over the course of the 1960s and 1970s, as well as being known for its unique light and air (and Roman ruins), Provence had come to mean tasty food and fresh ingredients, lavender covered landscapes, special products and goods, and opportunities for weekly or monthly stays. In addition, there emerged a new lure bringing American travelers to the hills of Provence—the joy of doing nothing at all. An early hint came in the 1974 piece by Sean O'Faolain praising Provence for its serenity and quiet, its sense of age, and ultimately its gift of the simple pleasure of strolling. Within a few years discussions of what the era came to call "stress" began to appear in travel literature. In February 1979, *Travel & Leisure* dedicated an issue to "getting away from it all."

The lead article, "The Art of Doing Nothing" by Don Gold, offered the rationale. Gold wrote about his recent vacation. It was ideal. "I could not see another person. It was warm. . . . I was per-fectly at peace." He had traveled, as he put it, "to do nothing." He was not seeking sloth, but silence. He wrote, "I did not want to hear a golf ball clicking off into space or the whirring zip of a tennis racket or the hum of voices in a museum or the rattling of dice at a casino." His goal was "to tranquilize" his senses, "long abused by the assaults of urban life." He could perhaps do so at home by med-itation or yoga, "but it is difficult to find an outdoor hammock in Manhattan or an abandoned beach in Los Angeles. Inevitably, the telephone rings. The mailman comes." Thus Gold recommended getting away from it all. His particular vacation spot was in the Caribbean, not the South of France, but he offered a range of other options—a rural cottage in Ireland, a hotel in a small town in Mex-ico, or "an isolated house in rural France." In such a place it is pos-sible "to consider our lives, to purify and simplify our pleasures," and ultimately "to know who we are with a clarity that cannot be duplicated, on the run, at home."[1]

Gold's language struck notes that resonated in the broader cul-ture of his time. David Brooks was later to characterize—and gently mock—this mood and moment in his 2000 book *Bobos in Paradise*. His take allows insight into a significant group of Americans who by the end of the 1970s were finding their way to Provence. Rela-tive to those traveling to London and Paris, their numbers always remained small. But these eager adopters were a telling group—they were among those Brooks labeled "bourgeois bohemians."[2]

Writing at the turn to the twenty-first century, Brooks had a dif-ferent approach to the "new class" discussed by his fellow conser-vatives. They had used this label to denigrate the emerging elite of educators, writers, and technocrats who were involved in the cre-ation and production of knowledge and culture. Castigating them as "rootless players in the system of production, owning neither property nor labor but only their skill in the manipulation of sym-bols," authors such as Irving Kristol saw them as a class "structur-ally hostile to capitalism."[3] In a more lighthearted but nonetheless trenchant mode, Brooks examined them not as left-leaning political actors but as style setters. They had political beliefs, certainly, but in this report, these remained implicit or hidden.

As Brooks looked at them (and likely, at aspects of himself), they had climbed the ladder of American success by using their wits, not the family connections of the elite who preceded them. Getting into college by demonstrating merit, not the blueness of their blood, they had graduated to professional lives. Their stock-in-trade was information and ideas, not corporate bonds of the old establishment. Although they attained positions with good incomes, they did not want to join the stuffy ranks of the country club. They imagined themselves, despite their driven work lives, as free spirits, even rebels.

As consumers, they could do this because a world of commerce had emerged to serve their needs. The counterculture had spawned its own businesses. In the area of food, there were not only co-ops and farmers' markets but coffee shops and restaurants. Brooks wrote about the new seriousness with which food was taken: "We use the word *guilt* more often in connection with unhealthy foods . . . than in any other context." Local news touted the couple who left the fast lane with a desire to bake the perfect jasmine bread, struggled, and then found success. Important in these stories was the pursuit of a personal passion, or as Brooks put it, life as "an extended hobby."[4] Alice Waters's creation of Chez Panisse was everyone's dream.

Clusters of these businesses thrived in towns that had been the centers of the counterculture, such as Berkeley, California, and Burlington, Vermont. As some local products became corporate— Celestial Seasonings, the Gap, REI—these emerging companies knew the customers they served. Their ads touted thinking "outside the box." To wear, eat, drink, or use their products allegedly took one outside the world of production and distribution. They projected themselves as against the establishment and the style epitomized by Brooks Brothers. The Nike swoosh said it all.[5]

In this world of anticonsumption consumption, everything bought had to be for some use or some good. Objects were better if they were old and textured. It was worthy to spend money on tools or the kitchen. These style setters took exercise seriously and sought equipment of "professional quality." And travel? One ventured away from home to learn, to experience, and to restore one's inner self. One admired indigenous peoples practicing their crafts.[6]

Other authors, such as Dean MacCannell, have seen this kind of travel as a search for authenticity, a critical aspect of the late twentieth century's reconciliation with modernity.[7] But David Brooks and Don Gold seem closer to the mark in explaining what travelers as early as the 1970s were seeking in the hills of Provence— simplification and stillness. Although never directing his attention specifically to Provence, Brooks caricatured the language used to describe these new regions of desire—the ways of their people are "connected to ancient patterns and age-old wisdom. Next to us, these natives seem serene. They are poorer people whose lives seem richer than our own." Authenticity here translated into living in the moment. One traveled not for the impact of the Grand Canyon or the Swiss Alps. One sought only the small things, a way "to spend a part of each day just savoring." But then David Brooks delivered the kicker: "The pace of life is so delicious in such places. But the lease on the vacation rental only goes for two weeks."[8]

And thus, the dream of more, the second home. It was, as he put it, a dream to "build Eden." Brooks imaginatively explored this possibility: It is summer, and "for hundreds of miles around, content[ed] couples are just settling into the creaky divans of their B&B's and cracking open books by writers who have moved to Provence, novels that are like pornography to the overstressed."[9] Brooks did not envisage for a moment the difficulties of home owning in Provence, something that Walter Wells was quick to admit.[10] But rather he moved implicitly with his imagined couples to direct his own readers to Peter Mayle, the writer of one of the most popular travel books ever written, the spur to many travelers' desire for Provence.

A Year in Provence (1989) sold more than six million copies worldwide, becoming an international best seller. With its simultaneous publication in the United States, the book fired the imaginations of American readers to follow Mayle's path to Provence—if not for a life or even a summer, at least for a week or two.[11] As any ad man knows, timing is all, and Mayle's book hit the moment when the desire for a retreat from stress had maximum appeal to many in the baby-boom generation. Ah, to be like Patrick Campbell in 1970 and leave the hurly-burly behind. Updated at the end of the 1980s, the central task was less booze than food, accompanied, of course, by good French wine. Mayle touted many simple pleasures as well—sunsets to see and a swimming pool to float in.

There were adjustments to be sure, for Provence provided a new world of mysterious customs. But what a world! A sun-filled sky over a rural landscape, interesting and amusing neighbors, markets and bakeries. And to give the book something of a narrative arc, there emerged a major task to accomplish—adapting an old house originally restored for summer use to one for year-round living.

We have seen this plot line before, for house renovation was a driving theme of Mary Roblee Henry's *A Farmhouse in Provence,* published in the late 1960s. Mayle's book is different from hers, however, in ways that he likely understood. He once declared *Vogue* "the world's most cloyingly pungent magazine,"[12] and he knew well how to avoid not only Henry's elitism but also her long-windedness and seriousness. Mayle began his writing career in advertising in the 1960s; he later talked of the value of those fifteen years of training, some of it in New York. "You are obliged to stick to the plot—to be concise, informative and if possible entertaining."[13] He left advertising and took off on his own, writing sex education and advice books, some best sellers, and—immediately prior to *A Year in Provence*—the words for a series of illustrated humor books featuring Wicked Willie, a cartoon penis.[14]

What keeps the reader going to the end of *A Year in Provence* is Mayle's carefully honed comic voice. His wit is usually gentle. He knew how to turn a phrase to lift up a paragraph at the end, and he did so on almost every page. He was willing to be a bit naughty, in a subdued sort of way that recognized that he and his readers were adults who could handle a word such as *syphilis*. He offered a few longer riffs, such as the hilarious imagined course of "café deport-ment" for the young women at the university in Aix, which pro-vided instruction in sunglass usage and hair flinging.[15] Occasionally he turned his wit on himself. Mayle had a few enemies on his list—mainly tourists who invaded his territory, uninvited visitors who abused his hospitality, and Parisians. But most of the time he kept his persona as a genial, pleasure-seeking man of middle age enjoy-ing his meals and his wine.

And such meals and such wine! One of the book's appeals is that alongside all this good humor comes rich description of restau-rant meals, course by course. With this Mayle distilled consider-able inside dope, largely about food and drink. A sleuthing reader can learn the best time to arrive at a weekly outdoor market, the location of a hidden restaurant enjoyed by truck drivers, the name of the most delightful café in Aix, and the unadvertised places to sample wines. These nuggets were not announced with stars, but conveyed off the cuff as part of the stories Mayle had to tell.

All was done with a light touch as Mayle offered his memoir of settling into and adapting a house. His *A Year in Provence* allows use as a travel book, for it conveys what it is like to be in a strange place. Alongside descriptions of the landscape and the pleasures of the sunset, he presented the customs and quirks of the locals.

Mayle's precedent here is *Perfume from Provence* by Winifred Fortescue. It had not featured in the American imagination when it appeared in the 1930s but was a big hit with great staying power in Mayle's own country, in part perhaps because of its author's celeb-rity. Fortescue was a noted actress and designer who famously married an older distinguished British military historian who was librarian of Windsor Castle. *Perfume from Provence* was perhaps the earliest book in the English-speaking world on buying and reno-vating a derelict Provençal farmhouse. Its cited "charm" included lovely passages about the landscape, engaging pen portraits, and lively incidents. Nonetheless, the book dripped with condescension when Fortescue portrayed the local Provençaux, who seemed to admire her and serve her well. "I had grown to love these excitable emotional men of the South and to regard them as my children— for they were little more. They were perfectly maddening, entirely without initiative, and quite irresponsible, but they were most lovable."[16]

Mayle was much more respectful of his Provençal neighbors than was Fortescue, but he did deal with the conflicts with them that inevitably arose. Despite good intentions and the desire to fit in, the cultures of a British couple with money in Provence and the artisans they employed did clash at moments. And in Mayle's writing on Provence are literary traces held over from Fortescue's era, characterizations of the locals whose roughness and narrowness make them easy marks for humor.

Mayle developed his narrative in strings of anecdotes that offer readers a way to get partially inside village life. Some involved local customs, such as an annual fête or a goat race. Others opened up the world of truffle hunting, with its use of pigs and specially trained dogs. Mayle shared the principal prejudice of his neighbors, hatred of the Parisians with second homes in Provence. His glee was unabashed when the sudden arrival of the winds of a summer mistral flung food onto the all-white clothing of Parisian guests at an elegant outdoor dinner party. Occasionally Mayle mocked the locals, as in digressions on the hunting season that described their love of costume and gear. This led some reviewers to call his portrayal patronizing. It is in spots, but Mayle proved to be self-deprecating as well, as when he noted his huffing and puffing on his bicycle while men decades older sailed past.

What proved irresistible to readers was Mayle's overarching story of the pleasures of a new life. Hard-working men and women chained to their jobs could read of giving up the clock and the calendar. They, too, could hope for a life measured not by money made or work accomplished but by the ebb and flow of days and seasons close to the land.

Close, but not too close, for what Mayle offered was the promise of getting away from it all while sustaining the upper middle-class life with all its pleasures and privileges. He had a vineyard and enjoyed its reward of vast amounts of wine, but it was his share-cropping neighbor, Faustin, who performed the hard work of tend-ing the vines. Mayle watched as Faustin and his wife picked the grapes, but he did not run to assist. For a considerable period Mayle was forced to endure a dust-filled world while the central heating system was being installed, but he never had to give a hand to the work. And unlike those he employed, he could jump into his pri-vate swimming pool just outside his door whenever it pleased him.

By 1989 Mayle could find his dream in Provence. And Americans reading of it in the 1990s could hope to follow him there. The food route was deep. Garlic, now more than accepted, had become a health food. There were not only articles in food magazines tout-ing Provençal cuisine, there were successful cookbooks and even cooking schools established by Americans in the region. Enough old stone *mas* had been reconstructed and new suburban-style houses built to offer an infrastructure of vacation rentals. Agencies such as At Home Abroad could assist in booking and making all arrangements. Middle-class Americans could imagine themselves Peter Mayle—at least for a week or two during a summer vacation. And, if not this summer, then next? They bought his book to dream his dream.

SEVENTEEN   The Beaten Path

Peter Mayle's success with *A Year in Provence* was the beginning of a small tidal wave. Book after book followed, courtesy of writers eager to recount the experience of buying and renovating a house in Provence and of publishers hoping to ride on Mayle's hit.[1] Each author imagined having a unique story to tell, but the rules of the genre were clear. As Anthony Campbell, an independent book reviewer, wrote regarding *The Olive Farm: A Memoir of Life, Love and Olive Oil in the South of France* (2001) by the British actress Carol Drinkwater, "We get the tortuous business of purchasing the new home, comic encounters with rustic locals who are sometimes helpful, sometimes not, struggles with the language, misunderstandings of local customs, and near-disasters which are eventually triumphantly overcome or occasionally not." As the reviewer of her follow-up book, *The Olive Season* (2003), noted, "There's no inherent book-length interest in Britons pushing off to live in the sun."[2] Such sentiments didn't prevent others from the United Kingdom and the United States from trying.[3]

Mayle himself could not resist his own returns to mine the vein that made him a very rich man. Yet, unlike the efforts of many of his followers, Mayle moved away from house reconstruction with some success. In *Toujours Provence* (1991) and *Encore Provence* (1999), he focused on the many aspects of Provence that amused,

TODAYS SPECIALS
SOUP: YANKEE BEAN
FRENCH ONION
ENTRÉE: LAMB
BREAD....S.
PRIME RIB+VEG
POTATO
CHICKEN À LA KING
ROAST CHICKEN +
VEG POTATO
HUNGARIAN GOULASH

Victoria Roberts

"A year nowhere near Provence."

10 Cartoon, "A Year Nowhere Near Provence," Victoria Roberts, The New Yorker Collection/The Cartoon Bank.

delighted, or angered him. His essays again allowed the play of his ready wit.

They also gave him the chance to take on his critics and those denigrating the region. One object of his scorn was Ruth Reichl, who in the late 1990s was the restaurant critic for the *New York Times.* In a scorching piece in 1998, pushing back against the enthusiasm Provençal food was then engendering, she declared, "Like many Americans, I had romanticized the place. Sparked, I suppose, by the author Peter Mayle as much as by the notion of Mediterranean cooking, I had been dreaming of a Provence that never existed."[4]

She remembered what she had once known about Provence— the rough region filled with "clever peasants who lead a difficult existence, drinking big, rough wines and eking out a living from the land." She recalled the films of Marcel Pagnol and contrasted their portrayal to the world that now greeted travelers, a "fantasy Provence" of lavender and Souleiado prints sold in every market. Spying on the home cooking of her neighbor, she saw "sturdy soups and stews" with "no resemblance to the herb-sprinkled grilled fare being served as Provencal cuisine across America."

Reichl went on to complain about the quality of restaurant food and of ingredients found in the markets. She hated the local baker's bread: "The crusts were tough, the interiors cottony." She found the coffee served to be sour. She returned from a trip to the weekly market with vegetables of poor quality—there were no good tomatoes to be found, and all the green beans were tired. In the town shops every butcher was out of lamb. Even two superb meals at fine restaurants failed to blunt her anger and sense of loss. At one, housed in an old tavern, she learned to her disappointment that the restaurant's proprietor was not the relic from the past she had imagined but a banker who had escaped from urban life. Lured by the dream of Provence, he had opened his restaurant only fifteen years before. Writing in April 1998, Reichl concluded, "He made his dream come true, but I don't have the time. This year, I think I'll try Italy."

In 2000, Peter Mayle responded to Reichl's attack head on. After sarcastically cataloging the food catastrophes that beset Reichl, Mayle soberly remarked, "There is no doubt that you can find indifferent food in Provence, but to find it everywhere you look suggests carelessness or a profound lack of local knowledge." Despite her great connections and intense engagement with food, Reichl seems not to have sought appropriate guidance. Why had she not consulted Patricia Wells, then the food writer at the *International Herald Tribune,* well known, as Mayle put it, for her "intimate and informed knowledge of Provence"? Why had she not learned that she must arrive at the market when it opened in order to get good tomatoes and find lamb at the butchers? Had she not found out that she should turn to small shops for the bread, wine, oil, and good produce and use a supermarket only for staples? Had she not ventured to Les Halles in Avignon, perhaps the best food market in existence, very close to where she was staying? Did she not read restaurant reviews before setting off for meals in Avignon?[5]

Perhaps the real difficulty was that her sources were wrong.

Rather than being inspired by the real guides to the region—here Mayle noted Ford Madox Ford and M. F. K. Fisher—Reichl was hoping to live out the films of the "overwrought and fanciful" Pagnol. According to Mayle, that was like a tourist coming to the United States and expecting the country to look like the movie sets of Frank Capra. Picking up on Reichl's offhand remark that she was drawn to the market "because it was not quaint and not touristed," Mayle blasted, "Tourists, of course, are always other people; never us. We are different. We are *travelers*."[6] Here Mayle was playing on a distinction centuries old that defined a traveler as a venturesome loner, seeking out the authentic to learn from it. A tourist, by contrast, was part of a herd merely guided to a distant place for pre-packaged pleasure.

Reichl's attitude offended him, for he found it condescending and inaccurate. "If you travel away from home for pleasure, you're a tourist." With that, he declared, "I consider myself a permanent tourist." Tourism in Provence had the positive value of boosting the local economy and enabling the region's great restaurants to survive. Then in a straightforward way, without a touch of humor, Mayle gave his personal list of bests that included markets, small food shops in the region, and the guidebook he trusted for dining out.[7]

It turned out, however, that Mayle himself came to have his limits regarding tourists. He found that his Provençal life ceased to be quite so pleasing when the summer people he had helped to attract arrived for their vacations. With the rise of Provence to broader consciousness, these folk were now being directed by one of his least favorite publications, the American *Vogue*. It had recently declared the Luberon, the mountainous region surrounding Ménerbes where he had settled, to be "the secret south of France" and, contradictorily and simultaneously, France's "most fashionable area." The French *Vogue* took a different tack, at the same time stating that Provence was both "finished" and the play place of the rich and famous, complete with a map to track celebrities' whereabouts. All of this led Mayle to instruct the reader about real estate and agents selling it, as well as about changes being wrought by tourists.[8]

"I recently heard Provence being enthusiastically promoted by an agent as 'the California of Europe,'" he wrote in 1991, because of its climate and lifestyle. Disbelieving (despite the evidence provided by *Vogue*), Mayle was told he must see Gordes, and he returned to the perched village that he had admired sixteen years before. Then it was "unspoiled" and its center had only what the village needed: "a butcher, two bakers, a simple hotel, a seedy café, and a post office run by a man recruited, we were sure, for his unfailing surliness."[9]

Mayle now found Gordes still beautiful, but only "from a distance," for it had become overwhelmed by concessions for tourists. A tarmacked car park stood at the approach to the town proper, a new hotel had joined the old, and there was a fast food establishment and a Souleiado boutique. The café had gotten a face lift. Gordes was now "turned into a place for visitors rather than inhabitants. Official Gordes T-shirts can be bought to prove you've been there."[10]

Mayle turned philosophical, noting that this phenomenon was really nothing new. "People are attracted to an area because of its beauty and its promise of peace, and then they transform it into a high-rent suburb complete with cocktail parties, burglar-alarm systems, four-wheel-drive recreational vehicles, and other essential trappings of *la vie rustique*." As many others have found, there is a life cycle to the discovery of an "authentic place."[11] Similar to Santa Fe or the Cotswolds, such a place is initially off the beaten path. It offers accommodations and even housing that is surprisingly affordable. Then it becomes the object of travel writing adorned with alluring images and simultaneously attracts the attention of agents and developers. As new residents and visitors swarm in, prices go up, crowds appear, and the path is now well traveled.

The villagers in Provence don't mind, for they get work in construction and services. Those with land make a killing. As Mayle put it, "Cultivating tourists is much more rewarding than growing grapes."[12] Nonetheless Mayle came to find August a difficult month, for it was then that swarms of French tourists, including those hated

Parisians, arrived to take their summer vacations in the sun of his region. Mayle's situation turned out to be a special case, however. *A Year in Provence* (and the subsequent miniseries on British television) made him such a celebrity that his house became the object of touristic interest. As cars and even buses pulled up for a view, photographers hid in the bushes and Italians tried out his swimming pool. Life in the Luberon lost its charm. Mayle sold his house in Ménerbes and moved to Southampton on Long Island, near children and grandchildren.[13]

Even from a distance, Mayle's animus against Parisians remained a staple of his humor. In his 1999 *Encore Provence,* he returned to them, delighted that his deep antipathy was shared by many Provençaux natives. "A derogatory word—*parisianisme*—is now creeping into the local language to describe their insidious and unwelcome influence on certain aspects of Provençal life," Mayle wrote. Regarded as foreigners by the locals, "they are renowned for their arrogance, for their condescending attitude, for their fashionable clothes, for their shiny cars, for buying all the bread in the bakery, for just being Parisian." They had the presumptuousness in one village to call the local mayor to request action against the *cigales*, or cicadas, whose noise was disturbing their afternoon naps.[14]

Imagining the mayor's likely response gave Mayle a segue to one of his more amusing riffs, the choreography of the "full shrug" executed by a native Provençal to demolish a Parisian. It begins with the local man giving an initial frown and a tilt of the head. The Parisian thinks the man is "deaf, or Belgian, and therefore confused by his sophisticated accent." The full shrug comes when the local pushes out his jaw, cocks his eyebrows, raises his shoulders, spreads his hands out palms upward, and emits "a short, infinitely dismissive sound—something between flatulence and a sigh."[15]

Parisians could hardly answer the "full shrug" directly, dependent as they were on the locals for services and assistance. But one can think of a cinematic event in the 1980s as an extended indirect one. In 1986, Claude Berri adapted one of Pagnol's novels into two

films, *Jean de Florette* and *Manon des Sources.* In contrast to the trilogy of Pagnol films from the 1930s, whose second life in the 1960s
inspired Alice Waters with its affectionate portrayals, this duet of
French films was payback. Highly admired in France and England,
Berri's productions were screened in art houses in the United
States. *Jean de Florette,* especially, was praised and likely found an
audience among those primed for a subtitled French-language picture set in the hills of Provence in the 1920s. Its specific location was
Mirabeau, a tiny village near Pertuis in the Vaucluse.[16]

Gérard Depardieu plays Jean Cadoret, a tax collector from
Marseille. Kind, enthusiastic, robust, and handsome despite his
hunchback, he comes to claim his inheritance, a rural farmhouse
bequeathed to him by his mother, Florette, a former resident of
the village. Cadoret sees the property as offering him a chance to
leave his life-destroying urban existence and to embrace the good
life of the land. With his wife, Aimée, and young daughter, Manon,
he arrives wearing a silk vest and carting possessions that mark the
family as bourgeois. The Cadorets' cultured life is enhanced by
Jean's melodious harmonica and the voice of Aimée, a former opera
singer. The land they come to is magnificent, with all the emblems
that signal Provence in the popular imagination. Jean announces
on his arrival, "Look at these giant thistles, those olive trees. That
wild Rosemary. Ancienne Provence. Zola's paradise. It's even love-
lier than Paradise."[17]

Unknown to him, at the moment of his arrival, a villager—
complete with bad teeth, unshaven face, and a crooked nose—is
wreaking destruction on the roof tiles of the house that Jean is
coming to repossess. The villain at work, played by Daniel Auteuil,
is Ugolin Soubeyran, a young man returned from military service
who wants to drive Jean away, largely by depriving him of water
from the spring on his land. In this Ugolin is strengthened by his
uncle, nicknamed "Papet," played by Yves Montand, whose primary motivation is the age-old peasant desire to maintain the family holdings and name into future generations.

The film sets up a contrast between the romantic Jean, who is also a literate modernizer, and the brutal realism and backward thinking of the Provençal peasants. When Ugolin inquires why Jean has chosen to settle on this piece of land, Jean answers, "It's because I've decided that my happiness lies in returning to nature. I'm here to cultivate the authentic! . . . Yes. I want to eat vegetables from my garden, collect oil from my olive trees and eggs from my hens, and drink wine from my vineyard." In addition to growing vegetables for the family and for the market, Jean plans to raise rabbits, a well-loved source of food in the region.

In the course of the film, Jean becomes a broken man. Throughout his trials, the men of the village drink pastis and talk of him as an urban outsider. Playing *pétanque*, they deliberately throw a ball in the mud to spatter Aimée's good clothes. No one conveys to Jean what they know and suspect, that Ugolin and Papet have secretly blocked Jean's spring and covered up the traces.

Set in the 1920s, the film offers the downside of Provence as perceived by Parisians in the 1980s. Enveloped by glorious landscape and surrounded by fertile earth bathed by the sun, cultivated city dwellers dream of the good life in Provence. But once there, they must face its inhabitants. As portrayed, the men of the village are the negative versions of the eternal Provençaux going back at least to the nineteenth-century characterizations of Alphonse Daudet. In the real world of the 1980s, however, the buyer of a second home had to depend on them as construction workers and vineyard managers. The renter also encountered them as artisans and tradesmen carrying on their own lives despite their clients and customers. Often treated with affection in films and books, as in the case of Peter Mayle's works, the Provençaux in *Jean de Florette* are to a person rough, venal, and narrow minded.

Four years after trying life in the United States, Peter Mayle returned to Provence. He stated that he missed "an entire spectrum of sights and sounds and smells and sensations that we had taken for granted in Provence, from the smell of thyme in the fields to the swirl and jostle of Sunday-morning markets. Very few weeks went by without a twinge of what I can best describe as homesickness." This time he returned with the considerable wealth his success as a writer gave him and bought a great eighteenth-century house on fourteen acres outside Lourmarin.[18]

With his move he turned to film, one in marked contrast to *Jean de Florette*. Mayle wrote *A Good Year*, a novel designed to be adapted into a movie. He collaborated with Ridley Scott, an acquaintance with a nearby house in Provence. Their 2006 movie, taking the same title as Mayle's novel, follows the redemption-by-scenery path of *Under the Tuscan Sun* that preceded it by several years. This time the person in need of mellowing in the light is not a nubile female but rather Max Skinner, grown into a vicious British bond trader played by Russell Crowe, who as "next of kin" has inherited his uncle's property in Provence.

Mayle's Lourmarin appears on the checks that, as a child, Max Skinner writes for his uncle Henry in *A Good Year*. Max hasn't exactly been the good nephew, having neglected his uncle for a decade. He begins his Provence career similarly egotistical and uncaring, thinking only of selling the property and displacing the loyal local who tends the vines. In talking to his real estate agent and friend on his cell phone in his rental car, he fumbles for his dropped phone and hits a female bicyclist but fails even to notice. She, of course, turns out to be a restaurant owner, a beautiful spitfire who will provide the love interest to keep the plot going. In the meantime Uncle Henry's unknown illegitimate daughter from the Napa Valley in California turns up, threatening Max's claim to the property.

Nothing really prepares the viewer for Max's transformation into a decent human being who decides to stay in Provence, restart his romance with the beautiful restaurateur, keep his uncle's house and vineyards, and welcome back Max's daughter (who turns out to have the know-how to restore the estate's undrinkable wine to greatness); but that was probably not the point of the film. The intended star is the beautiful property in the Provence hills. The moviegoer gets spectacular views of it and the surrounding scene, the landscape as appealing in our time as Betty Grable's legs were in hers.

Although *A Good Year* was severely taken to task by a number of well-regarded reviewers, it nonetheless sold more than enough tickets and DVDs to repay the investments of its makers.[19] The actual setting for Henry Skinner's estate was Chateau La Canorgue, a winery outside Bonnieux just north of Lourmarin in the hills of the Luberon. The film became a point of advertisement for real estate in the Luberon, the winery that served as the primary location, and likely for the pricey wine, Le Coin Perdu, that was ultimately portrayed in the film as beyond delectable.

Nevertheless, an undertow to Provence's emergence as a place of desire began at about the same time as the publication of Mayle's *A Year in Provence.* One can catch it not only in Reichl's piece but also in the last work of Lawrence Durrell, *Caesar's Vast Ghost: Aspects of Provence,* published in 1990. Near the end of his long life, Durrell offered this pastiche of memoir, poetry, history, and travel writing. But within its over-luxuriant descriptions and unreliable historical statements lies one honest moment. A resident of the greater historic region since 1957, Durrell juxtaposed the Provence of his dream world and memory with the reality around him.

After a paean to the air and the light—"the special wounded blue" found at times in the skies of the Renaissance paintings of Andrea Mantegna—came Durrell's anger at change. In addition to the dormitory suburbs outside the walls of cities that resulted from the housing crisis following the Algerian war, "the motor-car has swallowed us whole!" He damned the new auto routes that have "subdued and banalized much wild country." Engineers, in widening the older roads, cut down one side of their allées of plane trees, "giving the landscape a sad, defrocked look." They made the roads look "like handsome women with heads half shaved waiting in a cancer ward for a brain operation."

These roads were widened for travelers seeking what he loved, the air, the sun, and the fresh produce of the markets. They included not only French vacationers but Brits like himself, a large number of northern Europeans, and a contingent from North America. Although Durrell had to temper his prose with reminders of the region's eternal beauty, his full judgment came with these words: "All history," he wrote, "has been compromised by the deliberate policy of transforming the backward sections of Provence into tourist playgrounds of a sophistication to match Nice and Monte Carlo."[20]

In 2011 Peter Mayle sold his Lourmarin property for $8 million and bought a hidden one in the tiny village of Vaugines, whose reminders of an older Provence had made it the location of key parts of *Jean de Florette*.[21] Perhaps he, too, was looking for a lost past. Lourmarin had indeed changed.

And along with it, much of Provence and what the French call *la France profonde*. The transformation of the agricultural regions of provincial France had been happening for many decades. When Laurence Wylie spent his year in Roussillon, the agrarian world still constituted one-third of the French population. By 1990, it had been reduced to only 5 percent. And by then, as one historian summed up, "this social fragment bore no resemblance to the historic class called 'peasants.'" Over half of the individual farms had disappeared—while the land was still used for agriculture, these "cherished family units" had been consolidated, ending the centuries-old life of peasants on the land. Whatever this meant for individual agricultural families and a region, at the national level, the approach was successful. France emerged as a major participant in a global food market and became by the 1980s the second greatest exporter of food in the world.[22]

In a place such as Provence, life goes on. Newcomers take the places of those who leave. Those who stay, adjust, the young choosing occupations that enable them to make a living in the new order. If rebuilding old houses and ruins pays, then they enter construction or become plumbers. If the wealthy want artisanal food, then they raise goats and learn to make cheese. The markets return each week (plate 15). Who knows if the tomatoes are local? But the lavender soap smells sweet, and the honey tastes good.

Once again, in 1987, on the occasion of another anniversary of *Village in the Vaucluse,* Laurence Wylie returned to Roussillon to inquire about the place and to write up his findings. Once the isolated farming village of his first description, it had now transformed itself into a center of tourism, second homes, and retirement. An older resident challenged Wylie's queries: "Why do you care so much for the old Roussillon? It doesn't exist any more than the old cars you photographed in 1950! There isn't any more Roussillon." But, of course, there was. Roussillon had simply been turned to new purposes, with new people. What took the place of farming was "the sun, the picturesque scenery, the quaintness of historical sites . . . the pure air." Its new life as a resort arose out of "the unpredictable fads of the fad-making element of society which chose to make this part of Provence fashionable."[23]

Wylie went through the town demonstrating the changes. Roussillon had gone the way of Cortona in Tuscany, Santa Fe in New Mexico, and other relatively "undiscovered" places that received wide media attention and by it were transformed. Most striking to him was the rise in the price of real estate. He remembered the promise of the cheap property available in 1950. He could have bought the house in town that he lived in with his family for $3,000. It was now restored and had a swimming pool in the place of the shed that had earlier blocked a beautiful view of the valley. At the time of Wylie's return, a celebrated French writer owned it and had received an offer for it of $1 million.[24]

The old artisans of Roussillon were gone, as were most of the old establishments. In their stead an abundance of cafés and shops sprang up to serve the day-trippers who flooded the little town. Few from the families Wylie had known in 1950 remained, but several had profited by the new economy. Previously a broker who picked up and transported farm crops, Louis Bonerandi operated a trailer camp and received rent on a filling station; his brother drove a grocery truck to deliver provisions and the bread he still baked to outliers. Believing that the ochre cliffs might not be enough to continue to attract visitors, Roussillon's mayor had begun to promote an international golf course to boost the town's economy.[25] For better or worse, the people who inhabited Provence and the communities that sustained them had entered into the present world.

Yet, nonetheless, in Roussillon as elsewhere in Provence, much still looked the same. The sun still shown, and the mistral still blew. Areas of the landscape remained in protected beauty. Eyes could still take in the hills, the perched villages, the low-lying towns, the vineyards, the fields of poppies. For many across the globe, including some Americans, Provence still called.[26]

EIGHTEEN   *Au Revoir* and *Bonjour*

In 1992, Julia Child, age eighty, walked the short distance from La Pitchoune to the house of the late Simone Beck to deliver the keys to Simca's heirs. Paul Child was still living, though in a nursing home. With Simca gone and Paul no longer by her side, Julia had lost the reason for the second house in Provence. The agreement had always been that the Childs could build the house on the Becks' property in Plascassier and live in it as long as they chose, but ultimately it would revert to Simca's family. Julia's niece watched her, looking for emotion. There was none. It was simply over.[1]

Did this signal the end of Provence as a place of desire for American travelers? By no means. In 2013, 18 million travelers visited the PACA region.[2] Eighty-one percent of them were French, with the majority coming from outside the region. Of the 19 percent left, Italy and the United Kingdom led the way, each with 3 percent, followed by Belgium, Germany, and the Netherlands, each with 2 percent. The United States offered the largest contingent outside of Europe, amounting to 1 percent, or roughly 180,000.[3] Oddly, Asia was completely left out of these official figures—hard to understand given the numbers that I saw on the streets and coming out of tour buses in places such as Arles in late spring 2014. The difficulty with these figures, however, is that they do not disaggregate those visitors to the hills of Provence from summer travelers to the Riviera or winter skiers in the French Alps. Thus, interesting as the numbers and proportions appear to be, they fail to reveal the number of American travelers to inland Provence, especially those making longer stays.

Undoubtedly, Provence has changed since its reinvention in the 1960s and selling in the 1970s. The succession from discovery to popularity to "beaten path" is an established one. And with it, in some circles, comes a sense of déjà vu. In part, this may be the effect of publicity itself. Once a new place is encountered or understood in a new way, it is written about and advertised to potential travelers. But as they venture there in significant numbers, the destination becomes transformed to receive them. The "pre-touristic" stroll that Sean O'Faolain wrote about is changed by the publication of his very writing.

Firsthand reports suggest that some owners of second homes from the United States are aging out, no longer willing to maintain the upkeep on houses they seldom use, and that their places may not be filled by Americans. In addition, generational forces may also be at work, causing destinations that offered adventure or style to parents to become outdated in their children's eyes.

But that doesn't mean that Provence's time is over. It continues to present to travelers rich variety, protected landscapes, and abundant places for getting away from crowds. It pleases the senses with its scents and flavors. Its large stock of second homes still tempts Americans to linger. Its markets are still vibrant, and good restaurants abound. Grandchildren may have a desire to enjoy pleasures their parents choose to skip.

Thus travel to Provence for shorter stays, as well as weekly and monthly rentals, is still on the calendar for many from the United States. They are outnumbered by Italians, Brits, Belgians, Dutch, and Germans, whose enviable closeness to Provence in the Eurozone makes the region an easy reach for vacations. The sun of the summer months has great appeal to Australians during their winter.

11   Arles market scene, 2014. Photograph by author.

On the streets of villages and towns one now sees sizable groups of tourists from Japan, Korea, and China.

Among the urban French themselves, both property owners and paying guests, enthusiasm for the hills of Provence remains strong. The words of Serge Robin, a designer with a shop in Paris, present a point of view widely shared: "It finally came home to me at the beginning of the year," he wrote, contrasting his experience in sunny Saint-Rémy-de-Provence with his life in Paris. In the South of France, while having lunch with friends, he observed "interesting, amusing people, all of them with houses nearby." He was sitting outside, "surrounded by all this marvelous Provençal food and wine. And suddenly I thought: That's it, there's nowhere like it. You've got the climate, you've got the people, you've got the food. Provence simply has to be the best place on earth."[4]

At times, this love of the French mingles with disdain for those foreigners who have intruded. In Roussillon, once Laurence Wylie's backward place of no future, Dorothée d'Orgeval fumed about what had happened to her beloved second home. In an interview with author Christopher Petkanas, she related that although she herself lived mainly in Paris, she did not see her own retreat to Roussillon as part of the village's transformation. She dated the great change far later than had Wylie, putting it in 1982 with the opening of France's fast train to the south. As Petkanas paraphrased, the TGV "changed the face of the Lubéron forever." D'Orgeval had loved Roussillon when it was a backward place. Imbibing his subject's prejudices, Petkanas wrote that with the new ease of travel, "The whole area became chic, perilously expensive and even slightly sinister."[5]

Yet, ironically, the presentation of her small *cabane* in the hills in Petkanas's huge and lavish book on French homes is just the sort of advertisement to lure others to Roussillon and Provence, prompting them to cook her menu of Grand Aïoli followed by goat cheese and peeled peaches and to look for old bottles and pottery such as crowd her shelves.

Fiction has helped keep Provence in mind for many Americans. In *The Dream of Scipio* Iain Pears juxtaposes three men as they faced crisis and loss in three eras of Provence—the Roman Empire in the fifth century, medieval Avignon during the time of the Papacy, and twentieth-century Vichy. The French writer Pierre Magnan offers mystery in such tales as *The Murdered House*. Peter Mayle has tried his hand with *A Good Year* and *Hotel Pastis*. Jane S. Smith has written a clever send-up of contemporary American summer sojourners in *Fool's Gold,* set in and around Gordes.[6]

Provence has kept much of its drawing power to the French (and to their European neighbors) because it is both real and nearby. It is also kept alive as a theme threading through French cinema. Daniel Auteuil, honored for his role in *Jean de Florette* and still a great star in France, has ironically become one of its promoters. Newspapers recently announced that he has remade Pagnol's *Marius* and is likely to take on the whole trilogy. This follows his 2011 return to the screen to write, direct, and act in another Pagnol film, *The Well-Digger's Daughter.* Set in Provence around World War I, the film presents families torn by personal turmoil and conflict. But unlike the representation of the local population in *Jean de Florette,* these Provençaux ultimately demonstrate dignity and humanity. And the sun shines, for it is Provence.

An ocean away, something different and interesting has happened in the United States. To some degree Provence has detached itself in time and place from the real land of the hills and the mistral to emerge for Americans as a stand-in for the good life. One can see this as early as the late 1980s in the wine country in California. When Claude Rouas, a San Francisco restauranteur, decided to build Auberge du Soleil in the Napa Valley, he asked his architect and designer to capture the "Provence feeling," first in his dining room and then later in the villas he added for guests seeking to stay on the grounds. He explained to them that he was not after a Hearst Castle, for which materials were actually brought "beam by beam, stone by stone," but rather something more elusive, an atmosphere. He was after a re-creation of the delights associated with Provence.[7]

Looking very recently at a group of eighteen expensive townhouses along both sides of Provence Village Lane (with a small crossing named Avignon Lane) in Charlotte, North Carolina, I could see something of these associations (fig. 16).[8] These large dwellings, built in 2007 on a small street off a major roadway, promise in a contemporary resale ad "French Provincial Style." Their high peaked roofs and walls of seemingly buff-colored stone look like design elements taken from the cover of the 1974 *Travel & Lei-*

12   Sign for Provence Village, Charlotte, North Carolina. Photograph by author.

sure issue featuring Provence. The ad pictures old stone buildings, suggestive of a chateau, presumably from Provence. In the upscale housing market of this national banking hub, Provence is a signifier of what is elegant and desirable.[9]

These associations are perhaps the reason that Provence has continued to keep its place as a visible part of retail. In suburban shopping malls and reviving downtowns, one can see stores offering bits of Provence for sale. They tend to be easy to spot, for the yellow and blue featured in many of Souleiado's 1970s fabrics often serve as markers. Within "country stores" in a range of vacation spots—some as unlikely as Cooperstown, New York—one can find Provençal nooks, where goods are gathered in attractive, recognizable displays. Provençal cloth even makes a splash on Broadway, in booths at street fairs in New York City. Provence was also the theme of a Henri Bendel window display on Fifth Avenue in autumn 2014.

April Cornell, an outlet conveying the Provençal style, closed for a while, but it has returned after a restructuring with a modest number of stores and an online presence. The descriptive copy for a tea cozy offered for sale at this writing includes these words: "Instantly transport yourself to the south of France. In the village of Bonnieux,

13 Provence within a suburban shop in the East Bay, California. Photograph by author.

14 Provence in an outdoor market, Broadway in New York City. Photograph by author.

15 Provence high style in a Henri Bendel window, New York City. Photograph by author.

life seems almost perfect: the sky is always sunny, the people always smiling and the croissants always fresh from the oven."[10]

Today Williams-Sonoma and Sur La Table remain important retailers of specialty cookware in the United States.[11] In neither store at present is there an emphasis on Provence, but there are recognizable Provençal products available that continue to associate Provence with possession of luxury goods associated with the kitchen and table.

Although travel writing about Provence has subsided somewhat in the twenty-first century, it has hardly died. Such writing continues the project of connecting Americans to the goods and food of Provence. Within the last decade, for example, *Travel & Leisure* guided its readers to the many shops of L'Isle-sur-la-Sorgue and the Saturday market at Villeneuve-lès-Avignon.[12] Established food magazines still feature Provençal cuisine at regular intervals. *Saveur,* founded in 1994 to celebrate the world's food, has from its first issue found Provence to be an important subject.

And then there is the Internet, which has changed travel in many ways. Sociologist Chris Rojek has offered a compelling way to understand how tourists now comprehend sites. He uses a computer metaphor of "dragging" to describe the ways that contemporary individuals either contemplating future travel or just engaging in armchair tourism shape their own images of faraway places. Online and on television are "files" about tourist sites, such as the Eiffel Tower, that can be entered; the viewer mentally "drags" material from these files to create a personal synthesis of "images, symbols, and association" that works in the unconscious to redefine and give new meaning to the explored site.[13]

Rojek's understanding corresponds to my own experience, as do the practical uses of the Internet. This powerful tool offers online access to airlines, rental cars, hotels, restaurants, and vacation rentals. It has changed the relationship between services and customers, as Trip Advisor, Yelp, blogs, and other sites allow consumer reviews to break through promotional material to provide ratings and report experiences.[14]

The Internet tantalizes as well. As I seek to close my writing of this book, "A Walk in Provence" comes across my screen. I was actually looking for opera in Italy when I was referred to this alternative, courtesy of Times Journeys, a new feature of the *New York Times.* Pictures scroll across the top: a lavender field in the forecourt of the Abbaye de Sénanque, a perched village in the sun, an allée of plane trees along a country road. And then, the text, "The word 'Provence' evokes images of rolling hills and mountains, vineyards and farms, the scent of lavender and idyllic French country villages. Experience all that and more while walking off the beaten track, in the steps of Van Gogh and countless wanderers, for a unique view of this timeless land."

Everything in this advertisement has been familiar to Americans since the 1962 presentation of "The Eternal Appeal of Provence" in *Look* magazine and the selling of travel to the region in the 1970s. As is the final statement of Times Journeys, right after mentions of Châteauneuf-du-Pape to be savored at the wine's source, restaurant dining, and villages and sites to be visited—"you'll understand why this is one of the world's most romantic and popular destinations."[15]

One particular company promotes the appeal of Provence, with both a strong presence on the Internet and physical stores. L'Occitane offers constant reminders of its goods and regular promotions and currently produces *Fantastic Provence,* an online magazine, with features on places, restaurants, and festivals as well as its own promotional ads. Its images of lavender fields and articles on places, restaurants, and events offer compelling lures to the region. The tour of its factory and museum in Manosque has itself become a draw.[16] The brick-and-mortar presence of L'Occitane has grown. It is currently a chain with more than 1,500 shops spread throughout the world.[17] Its great expansion in Asia may be an important source of inspiration for the many visitors coming from that continent. In

16   L'Occitane in an upscale shopping district, Walnut Creek, California. Photograph by author.

the United States, the ubiquitous mustard-yellow storefront can be found on city streets and within shopping malls and airports, selling perfumes, soaps, and creams, elegantly packaged and set in artfully designed shops.

And that is where I began this journey, rushing to a L'Occitane store in the Dallas/Fort Worth airport. Without knowing it, I, too, was beginning to dream the dream of Provence.

Acknowledgments

One of the pleasures of a journey, particularly one with long stays, is friendship. One often needs necessities and information about where to go and how to get help. At an early stage, Laura Shapiro helped me find my way, introduced me to others, and then continued to offer sound advice. Justin Spring pushed me in good directions, offering more introductions, solving problems, sharpening my prose while never letting me feel that the trip was an extravagance. Barbara Ketcham Wheaton was a generous companion and guide, and her seminar at the Schlesinger Library, "Reading Historic Cookbooks: A Structured Approach," opened new doors. Bertram Gordon offered encouragement and aid along the way. Kimberly Marlowe Hartnett helped me land safely with ideas to brighten my writing.

I am grateful to those I met during these travels. Dana Polan extended a kind hand and offered general support as well as knowledge of *The French Chef.* Martha Rose Shulman shared her Provence experiences along with the recipes. Kermit Lynch answered many questions and enabled me to interview the incomparable Lucie Peyraud. Many wonderful and busy persons gave me time, encouragement, and information about Provence, American travel, and taste. My thanks to Shelley Bennett, Herrick Chapman, Christopher Endy, Sarah Farmer, Allan Glube, Sarah Hanley, Rita and Yale

Kramer, Henry Lefkowitz, Mitchell Owens, Lucie Peyraud, Veronique Rougeot Peyraud, Jeffrey Pilcher, Lia G. Poorvu, Richard K. Popp, Daniel Ravier, Carol and François Rigolot, Rosalind Rosenberg, Jane S. Smith, Nathalie Sotkine, Matthew Smyth, Jean Vallier, Patricia Wells, and Walter Wells.

Libraries and archives matter in a work such as this, both for their rich materials and the invariably helpful members of their staff. Close to home is the great Schlesinger Library of the Radcliffe Institute with its astounding cookbook collection, the Harvard University Archives, Widener Library, and the Boston Public Library. Farther afield are the Special Collections Research Center at Syracuse University, the Harry Ransom Center at the University of Texas, the New York Public Library, and the Huntington Library in California. In France is CIRET with its bibliography of travel materials ably managed by René Baretje-Keller. I had the boost of a summer return to the Radcliffe Institute in 2014 and am grateful to the staff and the other fellows for their assistance, good company, and useful comments at my presentation.

Help with photographs came via the capable hands of Carole Frohlich/The Visual Connection Image Research. I also had assistance from many other sources. Graphic designer Mary Stoddard proved to be a miracle worker as well as a wonderful friend. The Irving Penn Foundation was encouraging and generous. Keith Luf, Lynn Mason, and Leah Weisse at WGBH were kind, skilled, and helpful. In Provence, John Steel rose to the challenge at an important moment with excellent skill. Gail Skoff responded to my request for a photograph with great kindness. Diana Carey at the Schlesinger Library pointed to the library's generous policies. Paula Wolfert, Tom Oppenheimer, and most of all photographer Claire Bloomberg made it possible for there to be a daubière pictured. Dan Horowitz was patient while I snapped photographs at every turn.

More important, Dan went along for the full journey and offered constructive criticism on what must have seemed to him an infinite number of revisions. Sarah Horowitz, assisted by her husband, Lucien Fielding, helped when translation was needed. All family members were supportive, including the two to whom this work is dedicated.

I owe a special debt of gratitude to my agent, Alia Hanna Habib of McCormick Literary, for going well above and beyond her professional role to bring this work into being. I am grateful also to those readers for the University of Chicago Press whose sound advice pushed me in the right ways. Editor Timothy Mennel read and commented with care as he shepherded the manuscript into print; his speed in answering questions and that of his able assistants, Nora Devlin and Rachel Kelly, helped bring the book into being. Jenni Fry's careful attention saved me from errors both grammatical and substantive. Isaac Tobin contributed his special gifts to the book's design. A book comes into being as the result of many pairs of hands and eyes, some of them unknown to the author: my thanks to all at the University of Chicago Press.

Notes

1. Patricia Wells, preface to Winifred Fortescue, *Perfume from Provence* (New York: Hearst Books, 1993), viii; the original was published in 1935.
2. James Pope-Hennessy, *Aspects of Provence* (London: Longmans, Green, 1952), quote 5.
3. John Murray (firm), *A handbook for travellers in France: being a guide to Normandy, Brittany, the rivers Seine, Loire, Rhône, and Garonne, the French Alps, Dauphiné, Provence, and the Pyrenees, the island of Corsica, &c. &c. &c., their railways and roads*, vol. 2 (London: J. Murray, 1873), 485. For the importance of Murray's guidebooks, see James Buzard, *The Beaten Track: European Tourism, Literature, and the Ways to Culture* (Oxford: Oxford University Press, 1993), 166.
4. Harvey Levenstein, *Seductive Journey: American Tourists in France from Jefferson to the Jazz Age* (Chicago: University of Chicago Press, 1998), 250–51; Michael Nelson, *Americans and the Making of the Riviera* (Jefferson, NC: McFarland, 2008); Deborah Rothschild, ed., *Making It New: The Art and Style of Sara and Gerald Murphy* (Berkeley: University of California Press, 2007).
5. Olga A. Carlisle, "Provence Still Life," *Holiday* 45 (June 1969): 26–31, 86–88; quote 30.
6. Richard K. Popp, *The Holiday Makers: Magazines, Advertising, and Mass Tourism in Postwar America* (Baton Rouge: Louisiana State University Press, 2012), 38–41.
7. Bertram M. Gordon, "The Evolving Popularity of Tourist Sites in France: What Can Be Learned from French Statistical Publications?" *Journal of Tourism History* 3 (2011): 91–107.
8. The most comprehensive data are available from a 2014 study, but it tabulates domestic and foreign travelers to PACA, a region that includes not only what was once the province of Provence but also the Côte d'Azur, the area around Avignon known as the Comtat Venaissin, and in the Alps, part of the former province of Dauphiné ("Chiffres Clés, Provence-Alpes-Côte d'Azur," download obtained via the official tourism site of the Provence-Alpes-Côte d'Azur [PACA] region: http://www.infotourismepaca.fr/tendances-et-chiffres-cles/chiffres-cles/). Gard, the region around Nîmes, is not a part of PACA.
9. Tourism studies as a field has typically focused on the economic or operational aspects of travel. This work follows the lead of *Touring Cultures* to focus instead on

"unpacking the orientations that people bring with them" and "tracing some of the mythologies of escape involved when people go touring or dream of touring" (Chris Rojek and John Urry, "Transformations of Travel and Theory," in *Touring Cultures: Transformations of Travel and Theory*, ed. Chris Rojek and John Urry [New York: Routledge, 1997], 1–19, quote 2).

10. Harvey Levenstein, *We'll Always Have Paris: American Tourists in France since 1930* (Chicago: University of Chicago Press, 2004).

11. David Lodge, *Paradise News* (New York: Penguin, 1991), quote 62.

12. Among the works I've consulted are Chris Rojek and John Urry, eds., *Touring Cultures* (New York: Routledge, 1997); Tom Selwyn, ed., *The Tourist Image: Myths and Myth Making in Tourism* (New York: John Wiley and Sons, 1996); Nigel Morgan and Annette Pritchard, *Tourism Promotion and Power* (New York: John Wiley, 1998); Graham M. S. Dann, *The Language of Tourism: A Sociolinguistic Perspective* (Wallingford, UK: CAB International, 1996). A useful summary of the field up to 2001 is provided by Nelson H. H. Graburn with Diane Barthel-Bouchier, "Relocating the Tourist," *International Sociology* 16 (June 2001): 147–58. In addition to Graburn's contributions, this article cites the influential work of Judith Adler, Graham M. S. Dann, Dean MacCannell, Chris Rojek, and John Urry, among others. H-TRAVEL@h-net.msu .edu, facilitated by the always helpful historian Bertram M. Gordon of Mills College, has opened a meaningful channel of communication and made me aware of current avenues of research in the field.

13. Noel B. Salazar and Nelson H. H. Graburn, eds., *Tourism Imaginaries: Anthropological Approaches* (New York: Berghahn, 2014), see esp. Introduction, 1–28.

14. Culinary tourism has become an important subject of study, especially among sociologists. Among the most interesting discussions are the essays in Lucy M. Long, ed., *Culinary Tourism* (Lexington: University of Kentucky Press, 2004); Lisa M. Heldke, *Exotic Appetites: Ruminations of a Food Adventurer* (New York: Routledge, 2003); and Jeffrey M. Pilcher, *Planet Taco: A Global History of Mexican Food* (New York: Oxford University Press, 2012).

15. Horace Sutton, *Footloose in France* (New York: Rinehart, 1948), 189.

16. Lawrence Durrell, *Caesar's Vast Ghost: Aspects of Provence* (London: Faber and Faber, 1990), 9.

17. This Roussillon is a region west of the Rhône, not to be confused with the village of Roussillon in Provence.

18. William Brustein, *The Social Origins of Political Regionalism: France, 1849–1981* (Berkeley: University of California Press, 1988), 56–64.

19. Shanny Peer, *France on Display: Peasants, Provincials and Folklore in the 1937 World's Fair* (Albany: State University of New York Press, 1998). Only in quite recent times has some regionalism returned administratively to France. Beginning in 1972, departments were aggregated into regions for economic development. With that the region of Provence-Alpes-Côte d'Azur (PACA) came into being. Initially they were advisory bodies, but they attained certain powers in the 1980, with regional prefectures and assemblies.

20. Eugene Weber, *Peasants into Frenchmen: The Modernization of Rural France, 1870–1914* (Stanford, CA: Stanford University Press, 1976), quote 207. The level of integration of Provence and other rural areas has been disputed by Graham Robb in *The Discovery of France* (London: Picador, 2007), but his conclusions in this book are highly contested.

21. For a broader discussion and the example of Brittany, see Patrick Young, *Enacting Brittany: Tourism and Culture in Provincial France, 1871–1939* (Burlington, VT: Ashgate, 2012); earlier French efforts to encourage tourism in the provinces are portrayed in Peer, *France on Display*. Susan Rogers has considered the long-standing

tension between France as a unified nation centered in Paris and France as rooted in traditions related to the soil of "highly diverse rural societies" (Susan Carol Rogers, "The 'Peasant' in Contemporary France," *Anthropological Quarterly* 60 [April 1987]: 56–63; quote 56).

22. Alphonse Daudet, *Letters from My Mill: To Which Are Added Letters to an Absent One* (Boston: Little, Brown, 1900), 2; Stephen Heath, *César* (London: British Film Institute, 2004), 64.

23. "Thomas A. Janvier, the Author, Dead," *New York Times*, June 19, 1913; Caroline Hazard, "Mrs. Janvier's Varied Life," letter to the editor, *New York Times*, August 5, 1922. Under the author's name on the title page of Thomas A. Janvier, *An Embassy to Provence* (New York: Century, 1893) is "Sòci dòu Félibrige."

24. Anne-Marie Thiesse, *Écrire la France: Le Mouvement littéraire régionaliste de langue française entre la Belle Époque et la Libération* (Paris: Presses Universitaire de France, 1991)

25. This and other common quotations appear in "Frédéric Mistral," *Wikipedia*, http://en.wikipedia.org/wiki/Fr%C3%A9d%C3%A9ric_Mistral#Quotations.

26. Bertram M. Gordon, "The Mediterranean as a Tourist Destination from Classical Antiquity to Club Med," *Mediterranean Studies* 12 (2003): 203–26, esp. 209.

27. At an important stage in my work, I benefitted greatly from the three-volume work under the direction of Pierre Nora, *Realms of Memory: Rethinking the French Past*. I used the English language edition, edited and with a foreword by Lawrence D. Kritzman, and translated by Arthur Goldhammer (New York: Columbia University Press, 1996–98). Also helpful in understanding France since World War II has been John Ardagh, *The New France* (Harmondsworth: Penguin, 1973); and John Ardagh, *France in the New Century* (Harmondsworth: Penguin, 2000).

PART I

1. Thomas Jefferson to Madame La Comtesse de Tesse, March 20, 1787, in *The Writings of Thomas Jefferson*, vol. 2, ed. H. A. Washington (New York: Cambridge University Press, 1853), 131.

2. For Thomas Jefferson's travels in Provence see William Howard Adams, *The Paris Years of Thomas Jefferson* (New Haven, CT: Yale University Press, 1997), 108–114; and Marie Goebel Kimball, *Jefferson: The Scene of Europe, 1784–1789* (New York: Coward-McCann, 1950), 184–201.

3. Kimball, *Jefferson*, quote 188.

4. Jefferson to William Short, March 27, 1787, quoted in Kimball, *Jefferson*, 191.

5. Adams, *Paris Years*, 110; Charles-Louis Clérisseau, *Monumens de Nismes* (Paris: P. D. Pierres, 1778).

6. Jefferson to La Comtesse de Tesse, *Writings of Thomas Jefferson*, 134.

7. Jefferson to La Comtesse de Tesse, *Writings of Thomas Jefferson*, 131–32.

CHAPTER TWO

1. Henry James to William James, October 15, 1882, in *The Correspondence of William James*, vol. 1, ed. Ignas K. Skrupskelis and Elizabeth M. Berkeley (Charlottesville: University Press of Virginia), 334.

2. He called these bullfights "shabbily and imperfectly done" (Henry James, *A Little Tour in France* [Boston: Houghton Mifflin, 1884], 182).

3. James, *Little Tour*, 180.

4.   James, *Little Tour*, 171.

5.   James, *Little Tour*, 183.

6.   James, *Little Tour*, 168.

7.   James, *Little Tour*, 168.

8.   James, *Little Tour*, 172. John Urry has written eloquently about the importance of paintings and photographs in preparing travelers for what they see in their travels (*The Tourist Gaze: Leisure and Travel in Contemporary Societies* [London: Sage, 1990]).

9.   James, *Little Tour*, 189.

10.   James Woodress, "Willa Cather and Alphonse Daudet," in *Cather Studies*, vol. 2, ed. Susan J. Rosowksi (Lincoln: University of Nebraska Press, 1993), http://cather.unl .edu/cs002_daudet.html.

11.   Originally published on October 19, 1902, this piece was reprinted in Willa Cather, *The World and the Parish: Willa Cather's Articles and Reviews*, vol. 2 (Lincoln: University of Nebraska Press, 1970), 946–52, quotes 948.

12.   A. Hyatt Mayor, travel diary "I Tatti, Provence, Burgundy," unnumbered pages, box 3, A. Hyatt Mayor papers, Special Collections Research Center, Syracuse University, Syracuse, New York. Information on Mayor's life comes from the finding aids to his papers and those of the Huntington family. Unless otherwise noted, all Mayor quotes are from this travel diary. Mayor did rely on the train for covering greater distances and escaping the rain.

13.   "A. Hyatt Mayor," *Dictionary of Art Historians*, ed. Sorenson Lee, http://www.dictionary ofarthistorians.org/mayora.htm. For an understanding of Mayor's background and access, see Shelley M. Bennett, *The Art of Wealth: The Huntingtons in the Gilded Age* (San Marino, CA: Huntington Library, 2013). I am grateful to Shelley Bennett for help in finding material relating to Mayor.

14.   Catherine Berthol Avenir has written of bicycling and the other modes of transport along with descriptive writing about travel in *La Roue et le stylo: Comment nous sommes devenus tourists* (Paris: Odile Jacob, 1999).

15.   Frank Schoonmaker, *Through Europe on Two Dollars a Day* (New York: Robert M. McBride, 1927), 28.

16.   Paul Cummings, oral history interview with A. Hyatt Mayor, March 21–May 5, 1969, Archives of American Art, http://www.aaa.si.edu/collections/interviews/oral-history -interview-hyatt-mayor-13146#transcript.

17.   For example, Anne Merriman Peck, *A Vagabond's Provence* (New York: Dodd, Mead, 1929), 170–71.

18.   The writing on Ford is immense. I have profited most from Dominique Lemarchal and Claire Davison-Pégon, eds., *Ford Madox Ford, France and Provence* (New York: Rodopi, 2011), especially Julian Barnes, "Ford and Provence," 153–63; Martin Stannard, "Going South for Air: Ford Madox Ford's *Provence*," 243–50; and Max Saunders, "Ford's Thought-Experiments: Impressionism, Place, History, and 'the Frame of Mind That Is Provence,'" 259–76. A new collection contains a fine essay by Christine Reynier, "Mapping Ford Madox Ford's Provence in *Provence*" (*Provence and the British Imagination*, ed. Claire Davison et al. [Milan: di/Segni, 2013], 193–202).

19.   Ford Madox Ford, *Provence: From Mistrals to the Machine* (Philadelphia: J. B. Lippincott, 1935), 13.

20.   Angela Thirlwell, "Ford's Provence: A Pre-Raphaelite Vision," in Lemarchal and Davison-Pégon, eds., *Ford Madox Ford, France and Provence*, 199.

21.   Ford, *Provence*, 79.

22.   Ford, *Provence*, 33.

23.   Perhaps more than many of his contemporaries, Ford was positioned to see the growing horror in Germany and the threats that nation posed.

24. Ford, *Provence*, 86.
25. Ford, *Provence*, 88.
26. Ford, *Provence*, 21.
27. Ford, *Provence*, 170.
28. Ford, *Provence*, paraphrases and quotes 46, 41, 90, 99, 110, 111, 112.
29. Ford, *Provence*, 305.
30. That a mistral took his money is likely true, but it did not lead him to write, for he had been working on *Provence* all during his time of subsistence farming (Jason Andrews, "In Provence: The Life and Work of Ford and Biala," in Lemarchal and Davison-Pégon, eds., *Ford Madox Ford, France and Provence*, 189).
31. Noel Sauvage, "An Admirer's View of Provence," New York Times, March 24, 1935.

PART II

1. Marcel Monmarché, *Provence, Côte d'Azur* (Paris: Hachette), 1948, 107; Laurence Wylie, *Village in the Vaucluse*, 3rd ed. (Cambridge: Harvard University Press, 1974), v.
2. Laurence Wylie, *Village in the Vaucluse*, 1st ed. (Cambridge: Harvard University Press, 1957), 153.
3. Wylie, *Village*, 1st ed., 163, 151.
4. Wylie, *Village*, 1st ed., 206–12, quotes 206, 208.
5. Wylie, *Village*, 1st ed., 266.
6. Wylie, *Village*, 1st ed., 267.
7. Wylie, *Village*, 1st ed., 138.
8. These are the words Wylie ascribed retrospectively to his own earlier mood in the second edition of *Village in the Vaucluse* (Cambridge: Harvard University Press, 1964), 341.

CHAPTER THREE

1. The name Commissaire General au Tourisme was at one time translated into English as the French National Tourist Office, but by 1957 it was generally called the French Government Tourist Office, the name that has persisted.
2. Ad, French Government Tourist Office, *Holiday* 21 (May 1957): 115.
3. Ad, French Government Tourist Office, *Holiday* 27 (April, 1960): 20–21. The hotel was located north of Toulon in Var, one of the six departments that today constitute the PACA region of which Provence is a part.
4. Brooke L. Blower, *Becoming Americans in Paris: Transatlantic Politics and Culture between the World Wars* (New York: Oxford University Press, 2011), 57.
5. Christopher Endy, *Cold War Holidays: American Tourism in France* (Chapel Hill: University of North Carolina Press, 2004).
6. Richard K. Popp, *The Holiday Makers: Magazines, Advertising, and Mass Tourism in Postwar America* (Baton Rouge: Louisiana State University Press, 2012), 38–41.
7. Ad, French National Tourist Office, *Holiday* 2 (December 1947): 131.
8. "Memo To: The American Woman Headed for Europe; Subject: Clothing," *Holiday* 2 (April 1948): 136–43.
9. Horace Sutton, *Footloose in France* (New York: Rinehart, 1948), vii–viii; details of his life from Frank J. Prial, "Horace Sutton, 72, Magazine Columnist and Travel Author," *New York Times*, October 28, 1991.
10. Sutton, *Footloose*, vii.
11. For background on travel to France here and elsewhere, see Harvey Levenstein, *We'll*

Always Have Paris: American Tourists in France since 1930 (Chicago: University of Chicago Press, 2004).

12. Endy, *Cold War Holidays*, 61–62.
13. Endy, *Cold War Holidays*, 7.
14. This was more than value of all goods exported from France to the United States that year. Levenstein, *We'll Always Have Paris*, 121. The contemporary figure derives from the MeasuringWorth.com Purchasing Power Calculator measure, http://www.measuringworth.com/uscompare/.
15. Endy, *Cold War Holidays*, 59.
16. Levenstein gives an able depiction of American movies set in Paris in *We'll Always Have Paris* (160–63). In 1970 France welcomed over 1.3 million Americans (Endy, *Cold War Holidays*, 8).
17. *Holiday* 9 (February 1951): 67.
18. Endy, *Cold War Holidays*, 128–8; Levenstein, *We'll Always Have Paris*, 107, 183. Nonetheless, for those with less money, the costs of air transport remained prohibitively high for many travelers.
19. *Holiday* 21 (April 1957): 12–13.
20. Mary Roblee, "In the Jet Set, New York to Paris in a Boeing 707," *Vogue* (December 1958): 79.
21. Roblee, "Jet Set," 79.
22. Levenstein, *We'll Always Have Paris*, 183–84.
23. Levenstein, *We'll Always Have Paris*, 127, 191.
24. Endy, *Cold War Holidays*, 55–65; Levenstein, *We'll Always Have Paris,* 179–82.
25. *Holiday* 21 (April 1957).
26. Popp, *Holiday Makers*, 101.
27. David Dodge, "The Charmed Country," *Holiday* 21 (April 1957): 86–97, 99–102, 104, photo 91. Dodge mentioned Arles but only as a gateway to the Côte d'Azur, 96.
28. Edward M. Strode, "Europe's Still There," *Holiday* 1 (April 1946): 49–55, quote 53.
29. George Millar, "Voyage of the *Truant*," *Holiday* 2 (March 1947): 103–108, quote 107.
30. Ludwig Bemelmans, "Mademoiselle Regrets," *Holiday* 4 (October 1948): 117–20, quote 117.
31. Bemelmans, "Mademoiselle Regrets," quotes 119, 120. Bemelmans's drawing 116.
32. Sutton, *Footloose*, 189.
33. Sutton, *Footloose*, 200–1.
34. Sutton, *Footloose*, 321, 208; The restaurant garnered three stars in *Le Guide Michelin, 1950*.

CHAPTER FOUR

1. Jocelyne Rotily, *Au Sud d'Eden, Des Américains dans le Sud de la France* (Marseille: Association Culturelle France-Amérique, 2006), 57–89; Marsden Hartley, *Somehow a Past: The Autobiography of Marsden Hartley* (Cambridge: MIT Press, 1997), 140–41.
2. Art Institute of Chicago, *Cézanne: Paintings, Watercolors & Drawings* (Chicago: Art Institute of Chicago, 1952).
3. Meyer Shapiro, "Foreword," *Cézanne: Loan Exhibition* (New York: Wildenstein, 1959), n.p. This exhibit was under the patronage of Mrs. Dwight D. Eisenhower and Hervé Alphand, France's Ambassador the United States.
4. Douglas Cooper to Francis Steegmuller, February 14, 1968, Douglas Cooper–Francis Steegmuller Papers, box 1, folder 2, Getty Research Institute, Los Angeles, CA. Douglas Cooper moved to Provence in 1950.
5. James Pope-Hennessy, *Aspects of Provence* (London: Longmans, Green, 1952), 28.

6. Pope-Hennessy, *Aspects*, 160, 13.
7. Pope-Hennessy, *Aspects*, 76, 77.
8. Pope-Hennessy, *Aspects*, 78.
9. Pope-Hennessy, *Aspects*, 9, 11, 149.
10. Pope-Hennessy, *Aspects*, 153.
11. Pope-Hennessy, *Aspects*, 160.
12. Pope-Hennessy, *Aspects*, 7.
13. Pope-Hennessy, *Aspects*, 97.
14. Reprinted in *The Lawrence Durrell Travel Reader*, ed. Clint Willis (New York: Carroll & Graf, 2004), 392–96.
15. Richard K. Popp, *The Holiday Makers: Magazines, Advertising, and Mass Tourism in Postwar America* (Baton Rouge: Louisiana State University Press, 2013), 90–93, quote 90.
16. Lawrence Durrell, "Ripe Living in Provence," *Holiday* 26 (November 1959): 71–74, 184–93 passim.
17. Durrell, "Ripe Living," 74, 184.
18. Durrell, "Ripe Living," 184.
19. Durrell, "Ripe Living," 185.
20. Lawrence Durrell, "Laura, a Portrait of Avignon," *Holiday* 29 (February 1961): 58–63, 108–9, quotes 108, 109.
21. Lawrence Durrell, "In Praise of Fanatics," *Holiday* 32 (September 1962): 66–74, quotes 68, 70.
22. Durrell, "In Praise," 72, 74.
23. Mitchell Goodman, "Provence—Another Name for a Traveler's Dream," *House Beautiful* 101 (September 1959): 156–57, 193–97, quote 157.
24. Goodman, "Provence," 193.
25. Goodman, "Provence," 197.
26. *To Catch a Thief*, 1955. Quotations are from my transcriptions taken from viewing the film.

PART III

1. "The Eternal Appeal of Provence," photographs by Irving Penn, produced by Patricia Coffin, *Look* 26 (April 10, 1962): 66–67.
2. "Eternal Appeal of Provence," 60, 71.
3. "Eternal Appeal of Provence," 60–71, quote 71.
4. "Eternal Appeal of Provence," 71.

CHAPTER FIVE

1. Olga A. Carlisle, "Provence Still Life," *Holiday* 45 (June 1969): 26–31, 86–88, quote 26.
2. For an important new discussion of the role of the senses in travel writing, see Stephanie Malia Hom, *The Beautiful Country: Tourism and the Impossible State of Destination Italy* (Toronto: University of Toronto Press, 2015), esp. 50–51.
3. *Life* 65 (December 27, 1968).
4. "Lust for Life (film)," *Wikipedia, the Free Encyclopedia*, https://en.wikipedia.org/w/index.php?title=Lust_for_Life_(film)&oldid=684348761.
5. *Lust for Life*, directed by Vincente Minelli (MGM: 1956); all quotations are from my transcriptions taken upon viewing the film.

6.   Bosley Crowther, "Screen: Color-Full Life of van Gogh; 'Lust for Life' Tells Story through Tints: Kirk Douglas Stars in Film at the Plaza," *New York Times*, September 18, 1956.

7.   What did prove a commercial success in this same time was the 1961 film version of the Broadway musical *Fanny*. This nod to Marcel Pagnol's great trilogy of the 1930s gave Marseille full play in glorious images. While it offered its viewers a beautiful port city, it allowed, as had Hitchcock's *To Catch a Thief*, only a tease of the Provence hills at the end of the film. Although viewers see the grand house where Fanny lives with her husband and child, supposedly on land high above the port, this estate bears no distinctive markers of Provence—it could exist almost anywhere.

8.   "Eternal Appeal of Provence," 60.

9.   "Eternal Appeal of Provence," 64–65; cf. "A Page of History," l'Oustau de Baumanière website, http://www.oustaudebaumaniere.com/en/esprit-baumaniere/a-page-of -history.

10.   "Eternal Appeal of Provence," 68–69.

11.   "Eternal Appeal of Provence," 69.

12.   A number of books have explored the ways that tourists learn about what they want to see and how to see it from paintings and photographs. Notable among them are John Urry, *The Tourist Gaze: Leisure and Travel in Contemporary Societies* (London: Sage, 1990), and Orvar Löfgren, *On Holiday: A History of Vacationing* (Berkeley: University of California Press, 1999).

13.   Carlisle, "Provence Still Life," quote 28.

14.   Carlisle, "Provence Still Life," quotes 30, 31.

15.   Carlisle, "Provence Still Life," quote 86.

16.   Mitchell Goodman, "Provence," *Atlantic Monthly* 214 (August 1964): 110–12.

17.   Goodman, "Provence," quotes 110.

18.   Goodman, "Provence," quotes 110.

19.   Goodman, "Provence," quote 111.

20.   Goodman, "Provence," quote 110

21.   Goodman, "Provence," quotes 112. The contemporary figure derives from the MeasuringWorth.com Purchasing Power Calculator measure, http://www.measuring worth.com/uscompare/.

22.   Within a few years, Mitchell Goodman gained a very different reputation, as a prominent antiwar activist.

23.   Horace Sutton, "In Provence with Baedeker and Bismuth," *Saturday Review* 44 (December 2, 1961): 44, 51–53.

24.   Sutton, "In Provence with Baedeker and Bismuth," quotes 51.

25.   Sutton, "In Provence with Baedeker and Bismuth," quote 53.

CHAPTER SIX

1.   Laurence Wylie, "Social Change at the Grass Roots," in Stanley Hoffman et al., *In Search of France* (Cambridge: Harvard University Press, 1963), 159–234, quote 164.

2.   Laurence Wylie, *Village in the Vaucluse*, 2nd ed. (Cambridge: Harvard University Press, 1964), 343.

3.   John Murray (firm), *A handbook for travellers in France: being a guide to Normandy, Brittany, the rivers Seine, Loire, Rhône, and Garonne, the French Alps, Dauphiné, Provence, and the Pyrenees, the island of Corsica, &c. &c. &c., their railways and roads* (London: J. Murray, 1873), vol. 2, 486; Horace Sutton, *Footloose in France* (New York: Rinehart, 1948), 189.

4.   Jean-Laurent Rosenthal, "The Development of Irrigation in Provence, 1700–1860:

The French Revolution and Economic Growth," *Journal of Economic History* 50 (September 1990): 615–38, esp. 617.

5. Robert L. Frost, "The Flood of 'Progress': Technocrats and Peasants at Tignes (Savoy), 1946–1952," *French Historical Studies* 14 (Spring, 1985): 10–20.

6. For an excellent source, with a map of the historic canals and one of the post-dam Durance, the canal system, and the power stations, see A. S. P. Manasseh, "Changes in the Lower Durance Region," *Geography* 58 (July 1973): 250–54; EDF Group, Thai and Lao Governments (Contact, Laurent BELLET, EDF Hydro), "From Serre-Ponçon to Nam Theun 2: Back to a Sustainable and Multi-purpose Future Integrating Water, Energy and Food Needs," http://www.water-energy-food.org/en/practice /view__593/from_serre-pon%C3%A7on_to_nam_theun_2_back_to_a_sustainable _and_multi-purpose_future_integrating_water_energy_and_food_needs.html.

7. Bertrand Hervieu, "Un impossible deuil: à propos de l'agriculture et du monde rural en France," *French Politics and Society* 10 (Fall 1992): 41–59.

8. Susan Carol Rogers, "Which Heritage? Nature, Culture, and Identity in French Rural Tourism," *French Historical Studies* 25 (Summer 2002): 475–503, quote 475. See also the evocative essay by Armand Frémont, "The Land," in *Realms of Memory: Rethinking the French Past*, directed by Pierre Nora, vol. 2, ed. Lawrence D. Kritzman, trans. Arthur Goldhammer (New York: Columbia University Press, 1996), 3–35.

9. A vivid exhibition of these paintings is included in "Neo-Impressionism and the Dream of Realities: Painting, Poetry, Music," Phillips Collection, Washington, DC (personally viewed November 26, 2014).

10. Ellen Furlough, "Making Mass Vacations: Tourism and Consumer Culture in France, 1930s to 1970s," *Comparative Studies in Society and History* 40 (1998): 247–86. In 1982, France's *congés payés* became five weeks. Furlough added, "By the 1980s over 60 percent set off for the beaches, countryside, or their second homes" during July or August. They could do this because France had quite consciously developed its transportation system, infrastructure, and tourist industry not only for international travelers but also for its own citizens. Many vacationers took themselves to the new facilities for mass tourism built along the beaches in Languedoc, Aquitaine, and Corsica, stimulated by state initiatives combined with private industry. But some French nationals found their way to inland Provence (247–86, quote 250).

11. Restoration meant higher taxes: see Helena Maxwell, *Beyond the Riviera* (New York: C. Scribner's Sons, 1936), 45.

12. H. D. Clout, "*Résidences Secondaires* in France," *Second Homes: Curse or Blessing?*, ed. J. T. Coppock, (Oxford: Pergamon, 1977), 47.

13. Clout, "*Résidences Secondaires* in France," 51, 50.

14. Françoise Gribier, "Les résidences secondaires des citadins dans les campagnes françaises," *Études rurales*, fascicules 49–50, 52 (1973): 181–204, specific reference 184. Early in my work Professor Sarah Farmer of the University of California, Irvine, generously allowed me to read her conference paper on second homes in France, and it helped me begin to think about the subject. The revised paper has now reached published form as "The Other House: The Secondary Residence in Postwar France" (*French Politics, Culture & Society* 33, no. 1 [Spring 2016]).

15. Clout, "*Résidences Secondaires* in France," 55. This is not to say that there weren't complications in buying an older structure. One indication is the guidebook by Robert Landry written in 1970 for French seeking second homes in the country, *Guide des villages abandonnés* (Paris: Balland, 1970).

16. Gribier, "Les résidences secondaires," 185.

17. Wylie, *Village in the Vaucluse*, 2nd ed., 341.

18. Map, Gribier, "Les résidences secondaires," 186.

19. Benjamin Stora, *Algeria, 1830–2000: A Short History*, trans. Jane Marie Todd (Ithaca, NY: Cornell University Press, 2001).

20. Alistair Horne, *A Savage War of Peace: Algeria, 1954–1962* (New York: New York Review of Books, 2006).

21. Advertisement, *New Yorker*, February 4, 1961, 9; commentary quote, Hal Stebbins, "You Can't Beat Realism," *Printer's Ink*, June 16, 1961, 34.

22. *New Yorker*, February 4, 1961, 9. By the end of the twentieth century, tourism accounted for more than half the income in southern France, an area larger than but inclusive of Provence (Bertram M. Gordon, "The Evolving Popularity of Tourist Sites in France: What Can Be Learned from French Statistical Publications?" *Journal of Tourism History* 3 [August 2011]: 91).

CHAPTER SEVEN

1. My understanding of food history in the United States has been greatly enriched by many, including Harvey Levenstein, *Revolution at the Table: The Transformation of the American Diet* (New York: Oxford University Press, 1988) and *Paradox of Plenty: A Social History of Eating in Modern America* (New York: Oxford University Press, 1993); Laura Shapiro, *Perfection Salad: Women and Cooking at the Turn of the Century* (New York: Farrar, Straus and Giroux, 1986) and *Something from the Oven: Reinventing Dinner in 1950s America* (New York: Viking, 2004); and Donna Gabaccia, *We Are What We Eat: Ethnic Food and the Making of Americans* (Cambridge: Harvard University Press, 1998).

2. Priscilla Parkhurst Ferguson, *Accounting for Taste: The Triumph of French Cuisine* (Chicago: University of Chicago Press, 2004).

3. Stephen L Harp: *Marketing Michelin: Advertising and Cultural Identity in Twentieth-Century France* (Baltimore, MD: Johns Hopkins University Press, 2001), 241–42. Curnonsky and Marcel Rouff, *La Provence*, (Paris: Rouff, n.d.).

4. J.-A.-P. Cousin's series Voyages gastronomiques au pays de France, as discussed in Harp, *Marketing Michelin*, 244.

5. Stephen L. Harp, "The Michelin Red Guides: Social Differentiation in Early-Twentieth Century French Tourism," in *Histories of Leisure*, ed. Rudy Koshar (New York: Berg, 2002), 191–214, esp. 201–5.

6. *Guide Michelin France*, 1937, 32–33. The Boston Public Library holds a large number of these guides.

7. Harp, "Michelin Red Guides," 205.

8. Ford Madox Ford, *Provence: From Mistrals to the Machine* (Philadelphia: J. B. Lippincott, 1935), 33.

9. Shapiro, *Something from the Oven*, 198, 197.

10. M. F. K. Fisher, *Serve It Forth* (New York: Harper, 1937), 52.

11. Fisher, *Serve It Forth*, 78–79.

12. Fisher, *Serve It Forth*, 250.

13. Fisher, *Serve It Forth*, 118.

14. Mimi Sheraton, "Earle MacAusland Is Dead at 90," *New York Times*, June 8, 1980, offers information and insights into MacAusland's life and career.

15. Earle R. MacAusland, "Introduction," in Samuel Chamberlain, *Bouquet de France: An Epicurean Tour of the French Provinces* (New York: Gourmet, 1952), vii.

16. Samuel Chamberlain, *Etched in Sunlight: Fifty Years in the Graphic Arts* (Boston: Boston Public Library, 1968), 111.

17. Chamberlain, *Etched in Sunlight*, 152–56, quote 154.

18. Samuel Chamberlain, "Mediterranean Provence, including the Comté de Nice," *Gourmet* 10 (March 1950): 10–12, 33–40, quotes 11.

19. Chamberlain, *Etched in Sunlight*, 161.

20. Chamberlain, *Bouquet de France*, quotes 191, 192, 193.

21. Waverley Root, *The Food of France* (New York: Knopf, 1958).

22. Root, *Food of France*, 315, 323.

23. Root, *Food of France*, 327–30. It should be remarked that the tomato was not introduced into the region until the late eighteenth century.

24. When he turned to the wine, his praise grew fainter, except, of course, for Châteauneuf du Pape (Root, *Food of France*, 343).

25. Leslie Charteris, "The Provençal Touch," *Gourmet* 19 (May 1959): 14–15, 70–71, quote 71.

26. Isabella Beeton, *The Book of Household Management* (New York: Ward, Lock, 1888), 1,036.

27. In these paragraphs, the writer is citing personal experience and quotes words that once came out of her mother's mouth.

28. The discussion of food scares in this and the following paragraphs comes from personal experience buttressed by Warren Belasco, *Appetite for Change: How the Counterculture Took on the Food Industry, 1966–1988* (New York: Pantheon, 1989).

29. Harvey Levenstein, *Fear of Food: A History of Why We Worry about What We Eat* (Chicago: University of Chicago Press, 2012).

30. Samuel Chamberlain, "France Revisited: Provence," *Gourmet* 25 (December 1965): 24–26, 32, 34, quotes 25. The land he described had been recently transformed by a great hydroelectric project that helped control the Durance River and provided irrigation.

31. "France Revisited: Provence," *Gourmet*, quotes 24–26.

32. David's best biography is Artemis Cooper, *Writing at the Kitchen Table: The Authorized Biography of Elizabeth David* (London: Michael Joseph, 1999).

33. Elizabeth David, "Fast and Fresh," *At Elizabeth David's Table: Classic Recipes and Timeless Kitchen Wisdom*, compiled and introduction by Jill Norman (New York: HarperCollins, 2010), 20.

34. Elizabeth David, "Provençal Cookery," *Mademoiselle* 52 (March 1961): 132.

35. Ruth Reichl, "Preface," *At Elizabeth David's Table*, 7.

36. Craig Claiborne, "Down a Rustic Road in Provence: French Cuisine Retains Its Pride," *New York Times*, May 10, 1966; "The Flavor of Provence," *New York Times*, October 2, 1966.

37. *New York Times Cookbook*, ed. Craig Claiborne (New York: Harper, 1961).

38. Simone Beck, Louisette Bertholle, and Julia Child, *Mastering the Art of French Cooking* (New York: Knopf, 1961); Craig Claiborne, "Cookbook Review: Glorious Recipes," *New York Times*, October 18, 1961.

39. *As Always, Julia: The Letters of Julia Child and Avis DeVoto*, ed. Joan Reardon (Boston: Houghton Mifflin Harcourt, 2010).

40. Shapiro, *Something from the Oven*, 213–30; Dana Polan, *Julia Child's "The French Chef"* (Durham, NC: Duke University Press), 2011.

41. Laura Shapiro, *Julia Child* (New York: Viking, 2007), 111. I was happily present on October 22, 1999, when Smith College honored Julia Child and a host of others. Child's distinctive "bon appétit" soared in the college gymnasium filled with 2,000 dinner guests and caused their enthusiastic applause.

42. "Boeuf Bourguignon," *The French Chef*, episode 1, aired January 1, 1963.

CHAPTER EIGHT

1. Preface, Jean-Noël Escudier and Peta J. Fuller, *The Wonderful Food of Provence* (Boston: Houghton Mifflin, 1968), viii.

2. The version given by Richard Olney, the expatriate gastronome and food writer, is

likely closer to the truth. Yes, Rebstock was from Toulon, but he was a publisher who had gathered together "a collection of recipes culled from local restaurants, amateur cooks, gazettes and books." Olney described two 1966 lunch meetings, one at each of their dwellings, that called into question Rebstock's knowledge and experience with food and its preparation (Richard Olney, *Reflexions* [New York: Brick Tower Press, 1999], 98–99). Additionally I was unable to find Rebstock in any directory listing French notables. Whatever his pedigree, Rebstock/Escudier nonetheless continued to garner praise from knowledgeable gastronomes. In *Great Feasts of Provence*, Robert Carrier called his cookbook a "great classic of Provençal cooking" ([New York: Rizzoli, 1993], 36).

3. Jean-Noël Escudier, "La Cuisine de Provence, I: The Heritage," trans. Peta J. Fuller, *Gourmet* 27 (February 1967): 23–24, 58–61, quote 58.

4. Nika Hazelton, "For Pyromanic and Pasta-Lover," *New York Times Book Review*, December 1, 1968, 28.

5. Escudier and Fuller, *Wonderful Food of Provence*, 7.

6. Craig Claiborne, "Garlic Galore," *New York Times*, August 24, 1969.

7. "Cooking with James Beard: French Christmas Food," *Gourmet* 29 (December 1969): 40, 58.

8. Mary Roblee, "In the Jet Set, New York to Paris in a Boeing 707," *Vogue*, December 1958, 79. Roblee had something of a romantic history. While a writer for *Vogue* in the mid-1950s, she had a well-published affair with screen actor Tyrone Power, then married to Linda Christian. Less public at the time was her relationship with the conductor Herbert von Karajan after Roblee interviewed him for *Vogue* during his first visit to New York with the Berlin Philharmonic in 1955. His love letters to Roblee following their meeting surfaced at auction only in 1990, after his death (Susan Heller Anderson, "Chronicle," *New York Times*, May 17, 1990). The letters have since disappeared from the record.

9. Mary Roblee Henry, "6000 Bottles of Wine," *Atlantic Monthly*, 223 (May 1969), 69–71.

10. Mary Roblee Henry, 1967–69, folder 3, box 499, Alfred A. Knopf Collection, Harry Ransom Center, Austin, Texas.

11. Mary Roblee Henry, "Réveillon at la Sérafine," *Gourmet* 29 (December 1969): 26–27, 46, 51, 52, 54, 56.

12. Henry, "Réveillon," 46.

13. Henry, "Réveillon," 51, 52.

14. Henry, "Réveillon," 52.

15. Henry, "Réveillon," 56.

16. Mary Roblee Henry, *A Farmhouse in Provence* (New York: Knopf, 1969).

17. Henry, *Farmhouse*, 17–18.

18. Henry, *Farmhouse*, 20–21.

19. Henry, *Farmhouse*, xiv.

20. Henry, *Farmhouse*, 56–57.

21. Henry, *Farmhouse*, 105.

22. Henry, *Farmhouse*, 67, 72.

23. Henry, *Farmhouse*, 143.

24. Henry, *Farmhouse*, 181, 189.

25. Judith Jones, *The Tenth Muse: My Life in Food* (New York: Knopf, 2007), 151.

26. Laurence Wylie to Alfred A. Knopf, July 29, 1969, Laurence Wylie Papers, Harvard University Archives, Cambridge, Mass.

27. "A Farmhouse in Provence," by Mary Robee Henry, *New York Times*, June 8, 1969. In this review, Henry's maiden name was consistently misspelled as "Robee," something she may have felt was de trop.

28.   Diana Vreeland to "Mary," undated, Mary Roblee Henry, 1967–69, folder 3, box 499, Alfred A. Knopf Collection, Harry Ransom Center, Austin, Texas.

PART IV

1.   For full understanding of these segments, see Dana Polan, *Julia Child's "The French Chef"* (Durham, NC: Duke University Press, 2011), quote 223–24.
2.   "Apple Desserts," *The French Chef*, episode 215, aired January 13, 1971.
3.   "Spinach Twins," *The French Chef*, episode 203, aired October 21, 1970.
4.   "Bouillabaisse a la Marseillaise," *The French Chef*, episode 201, aired October 7, 1970.
5.   "Apple Desserts." *The French Chef*.

CHAPTER NINE

1.   Patrick Campbell, "How to Live the Sweet Life in the South of France, *Holiday* 47 (June 1970): 52–53, 68–69, 84, quote 69. In the French game of boules, or *pétanque*, each player stands in place and throws a heavy, generally metal, ball; the object is get closest to the small wooden ball that has been placed in the playing area, which is generally any flat surface in a public part of a village or town.
2.   Rosamond Bernier, "Cote d'Azur: Artists' Choice," *Travel & Leisure* 1 (April/May 1971), 50–57, quote 51.
3.   Bernier, "Cote d'Azur," quotes 57, 51.
4.   Bernier, "Cote d'Azur," *Autour de Vence* 50, quote 53.
5.   Bernier, "Cote d'Azur," quote 56.
6.   In her book *Some of My Lives: A Scrapbook Memoir* (New York: Farrar, Straus and Giroux, 2011), Bernier gives a sense of her larger career; in it she elaborates on this encounter with Matisse, 93–96; Bernier, "Cote d'Azur," quote 54.
7.   Bernier, "Cote d'Azur," quote 56.
8.   Bernier, "Cote d'Azur," quote 56.
9.   This article was one of his last before his untimely death. He died in April 1971, just as this issue hit the stands.
10.   Michael and Frances Field, "Provencal Cuisine," *Travel & Leisure* 1 (April/May 1971): 65–7, quotes 65. There is no cedilla in the title.
11.   *Travel & Leisure* 1 (April/May 1971): Insert, 28. In this promotion Cezanne carries no accent aigu.
12.   "French Provincial Cooking, Part 1: The Cuisine of Provence," *Bon Appétit* 15 (Sept/Oct 1970): 20–25, quote 22.
13.   "French Provincial Cooking, Part 1," quotes 21, 22; Frogs Legs Provencale photograph 24.
14.   "*Gourmet*'s Menues: Provençal Dinners," *Gourmet* 33 (March 1973): 46–54.
15.   Doone Beal, "Auberges à la Provençale," *Gourmet* 35 (March 1975): 24–7, 68, quotes 24, 68.
16.   Elisabeth Lambert Ortiz, "*Gourmet* Holidays: Provence—I," *Gourmet* 36 (August 1976): 17–18, 69–73, quotes 17.
17.   Sean O'Faolain, "The Good Life in Provence," *Travel & Leisure* 4, (May 1974): 18–23, 44–46, quotes 20, 21.
18.   O'Faolain, "Good Life in Provence," quote 20.
19.   O'Faolain, "Good Life in Provence," quote 22. Ironically, on the opposite page a Texas Instruments ad promoted new electronic calculators.

20.   O'Faolain, "Good Life in Provence," quotes 44, 45.
21.   O'Faolain, "Good Life in Provence," quotes 45.

CHAPTER TEN

1.   Paul D. Zimmerman, "A 'Castle' in France for the Price of a Beach Cottage," *New York Times*, March 14, 1971. Earlier pieces in the *New York Times* had treated renting abroad, but on the real estate pages, not the travel ones.
2.   Soon after his time in Provence, Zimmerman became a screenwriter, and his *The King of Comedy* has seemed to later critics to anticipate the zeitgeist of the early 1980s.
3.   But, let it be said, that the potential is not always the actual. Over time, the great growth of traffic has eroded the promise of the A7. During the great escapes of the summer, traffic jams and delays on it have become legendary.
4.   "Paul Zimmerman, 54, Book and Film Writer," obituary, *New York Times*, March 6, 1993.
5.   Jon C. Teaford, *The American Suburb: The Basics* (New York: Routledge, 2008), 31.
6.   Bruce J. Schulman, *The Seventies: The Great Shift in American Culture, Society, and Politics* (New York: Free Press, 2001), quotes 78–79.
7.   Richard K. Popp, *The Holiday Makers: Magazines, Advertising, and Mass Tourism in Postwar America* (Baton Rouge: Louisiana State University Press, 2012), 104.
8.   Don Gold, "The Art of Doing Nothing" *Travel & Leisure* 9 (February 1979): 43–44, quote 44.
9.   Harvey Levenstein has written well about these food trends in *Paradox of Plenty: A Social History of Eating in Modern America* ([New York: Oxford University Press, 1993], esp. chapter 14).
10.   Warren Belasco, *Appetite for Change: How the Counterculture Took on the Food Industry, 1966–1988* (New York: Pantheon, 1989), 38.
11.   Belasco, *Appetite for Change*, quotes 44, 37.

CHAPTER ELEVEN

1.   Biographical information on Alice Waters from Thomas McNamee, *Alice Waters and Chez Panisse* (New York: Penguin, 2007).
2.   David Kamp, *The United States of Arugula* (New York: Broadway, 2006), 130.
3.   Alice Waters, "Foreword," in Marcel Pagnol, *My Father's Glory and My Mother's Castle*, trans. Rita Barisse (San Francisco: North Point, 1986), 7.
4.   Stephen Heath, *César* (London: British Film Institute, 2004), 28–29, 34, 64.
5.   Waters, "Foreword," 7.
6.   The rescuers were Gene and Tom Opton; Waters, "Foreword," 7.
7.   McNamee, *Waters*, 104–6.
8.   Richard Olney, *The French Menu Cookbook* (New York: Simon and Schuster, 1970), 22.
9.   Peyraud family history comes from Richard Olney, "Domaine Tempier: The Vineyard and the Peyrauds," *Lulu's Provençal Table: The Exuberant Food and Wine from Domaine Tempier Vineyard* (New York: HarperCollins, 1994), 1–24.
10.   Author interview with Lulu Peyraud, Domaine Tempier, June 5, 2014.
11.   McNamee, *Waters*, 183–84.
12.   Richard Olney, *Reflexions* (New York: Brick Tower, 1999), 191 (entry for July 10, 1975).
13.   Olney, *Reflexions*, 195.
14.   Here I must thank Kermit Lynch not only for his willingness to talk with me in Octo-

ber 2012 but also for his continued helpfulness over e-mail, including his assistance with arrangements for my visit to Domaine Tempier in June 2014.

15. Kermit Lynch, *Adventures on the Wine Route: A Wine Buyer's Tour of France* (New York: Farrar, Straus and Giroux, 1988), quote from 16.

16. Richard Olney, "Preface," in Lynch, *Adventures on the Wine Route*, ix.

17. Lynch, *Adventures on the Wine Route*, 16.

18. Olney, "Preface," x.

19. Olney, "Preface," x.

20. Adam Sachs, "Provence: Its Transportive Rosé Wine," *Travel & Leisure*, August 2011, http://www.travelandleisure.com/articles/provence-its-transportive-rose-wine. The original title in the print edition was "La Vie en Rosé."

21. Lynch, *Adventures on the Wine Route*, 15, 16–17.

22. Olney treated Lynch almost as one of his abundant, ever-visiting family members, seeing him often, noting in his diary all the important occasions such as Lynch and Skoff's marriage and the births of their children.

23. Kermit Lynch, *Inspiring Thirst: Vintage Selections from the Kermit Lynch Wine Brochure* (Berkeley: Ten Speed, 2004), 93.

24. Lynch, *Inspiring Thirst*, 23.

25. Lynch, *Inspiring Thirst*, 97–98.

26. Lynch, *Inspiring Thirst*, 157.

27. Olney, "Domaine Tempier," quote 23.

28. See "Menu for 'Northern California Regional Dinner,'" McNamee, *Waters*, 128.

29. Mark Blackburn, "It Was the Festival of the 'Stinking Rose,'" *New York Times*, July 18, 1979; McNamee, *Waters*, 153–55. In 1979 the festival was enshrined along with that of Gilroy, California—the "garlic capital of the world"—in Les Blank's film documentary *Garlic Is as Good as Ten Mothers*.

30. Lynch, *Inspiring Thirst*, 389–90. Until the closing of Café Fanny in 2012, this was an annual event.

31. Alice Waters, *Chez Panisse Menu Cookbook* (New York: Random House, 1982), esp. 18, 35–39, 131, 263.

32. Olney, *Reflexions*, 339.

33. Waters, "Foreword," quotes xii.

34. Waters, "Foreword," quotes xiii–xiv.

35. Waters, "Foreword," xiv.

36. Olney, "Domaine Tempier," *Lulu's Provençal Table*, quote 1–2.

CHAPTER TWELVE

1. Paula Wolfert, "Introduction," Jean-Noël Escudier and Peta J. Fuller, *The Wonderful Food of Provence* (New York: Perennial Library, 1988), quote v.

2. Wolfert, "Introduction," quote v.

3. Florence Fabricant, "Food Notes," *New York Times*, February 24, 1988.

4. In 1971 Craig Claiborne's *International Cook Book*, published by the *New York Times*, had a lengthy section on France (taking up more than 200 of its 565 pages), including many dishes from Provence.

5. This knowledge was gleaned at the seminar led by Barbara Wheaton at the Schlesinger Library, June 2013, for which I am very grateful. Her method of research and much of her approach is now available in Barbara Ketcham Wheaton, "Cookbooks as Resources for Social History," *Food in Time and Place: The American Historical Association Companion to Food History*, ed. Paul Freedman et al. (Oakland: University of California Press, 2014), 276–97.

6. As Priscilla Ferguson has put it, following the Revolution, France's "national identity emerged from a complex interaction of center and periphery, a negotiation between Paris as the center of a culture and the provinces as repository of that culture" (Priscilla Parkhurst Ferguson, *Accounting for Taste: The Triumph of French Cuisine* [Chicago: University of Chicago Press, 2004], 124).

7. There are Provençal recipes in French cookery books of the eighteenth century, and there is a collection from 1839, but it was Reboul's book that was to be the influential one.

8. As one mid-twentieth-century cookbook writer put it, daube is "le plat le plus traditionnel de la Provence terrienne, comme la bouillabaisse est celui de la Provence maritime," which roughly translates as "the most traditional dish of the Provençal countryside, comparable to the bouillabaisse of the Provençal seashore" (Louis Giniès, *Cuisine provençale* [Paris: Éditions Montsouris, 1963], 61).

9. To understand Provençal cookbooks and *boeuf en daube*, I examined forty-eight such books in the culinary collection of the Schlesinger Library, Cambridge, Massachusetts.

10. Jean-Baptiste Reboul, *La Cuisinière Provençale*, 12th ed. (Marseille: Librairie P. Ruat, 1927), 179–80. This is the last edition produced under Reboul's direction, before his death in 1926.

11. Auguste Escoffier, *Le guide culinaire: Aide-mémoire de cuisine practique* (Paris: Flammarion, 1921), 456, first published 1903. Escoffier did include a recipe for Daube à la Provençale that is very close to that of Reboul, using red wine and no cognac, in a cookbook for domestic cooks (Auguste Escoffier, *Ma cuisine: 2,500 recettes* [Paris: Flammarion, 1934]).

12. René Jouveau, *La cuisine provençale de tradition populaire* (Berne: Éditions du Message, 1963).

13. Elizabeth David, *French Provincial Cooking* (London: M. Joseph, 1960), 539–41.

14. Richard Olney, *French Menu Cookbook* (New York: Simon and Schuster, 1970), 413–15.

15. I am struck by the similarities and differences between Provence and Mexico, as each cuisine entered into the American consciousness in the post–World War II era. Jeffrey M. Pilcher has summarized this in "From 'Montezuma's Revenge' to 'Mexican Truffles': Culinary Tourism across the Rio Grande," in *Culinary Tourism*, ed. Lucy M. Long (Lexington: University Press of Kentucky, 2004), 76–96.

16. Mireille Johnston, *The Cuisine of the Sun* (New York: Random House, 1976), M. F. K. Fisher quote, back cover of Vintage paperback edition, 1979. Sheraton review, *New York Times*, March 13, 1977.

17. Julian More, *A Taste of Provence: The Food and People of Southern France with 40 Delicious Recipes*, with photographs by Carey More (New York: Henry Holt, 1988), quote 10.

18. *A Taste of Provence*, quote 18, photo of the daube 78.

19. Leslie Forbes, *A Taste of Provence: Classic Recipes from the South of France* (Boston: Little, Brown, 1987), 103.

20. Martha Rose Shulman, *Provençal Light* (New York: Bantam, 1994).

21. Louisa Jones, *The New Provençal Cuisine* (San Francisco: Chronicle, 1995), 101. Let it be said that not all books published in this decade offered valuable food advice. For example, *Pedaling through Provence Cookbook*, written by a bicycle-group guide, was a small artsy-craftsy book filled with cutesy drawings. Its recipe for Demi-Daube bore only a fleeting relation to its semi-namesake: designed to be cooked in half the time, it used sirloin steak (Sarah Leah Chase, *Pedaling through Provence Cookbook* [New York: Workman, 1995], 145–50).

22. Patricia and Walter Wells, *We've Always Had Paris . . . and Provence* (New York: HarperCollins, 2008).

23.   Patricia Wells, *At Home in Provence* (New York: Scribner, 1996), 253–54, photo 252.

24.   Richard Olney, *Lulu's Provençal Table: The Exuberant Food and Wine from Domaine Tempier Vineyard* (New York: HarperCollins, 1994), 196–98.

CHAPTER THIRTEEN

1.   John Urry, *The Tourist Gaze: Leisure and Travel in Contemporary Societies* (London: Sage, 1990); *The Media and the Tourist Imagination: Converging Cultures*, ed. David Crouch, Rhona Jackson, and Felix Thompson (London: Routledge, 2005); Stephanie Malia Hom, *The Beautiful Country: Tourism and the Impossible State of Destination Italy* (Toronto: University of Toronto Press, 2015), esp. 50–51.

2.   Richard Olney, *Reflexions* (New York: Brick Tower Press, 1999), 331.

3.   *Provence the Beautiful Cookbook*, recipes and food text by Richard Olney, regional text by Jacques Gantié (San Francisco: Collins, 1993), photos 36–37, 123.

4.   "The Eternal Appeal of Provence," photographs by Irving Penn, produced by Patricia Coffin, *Look* 26 (April 10, 1962), unnumbered pages following 71.

5.   "Eternal Appeal of Provence," 71.

6.   Adam Lewis, *Van Day Truex: The Man Who Defined Twentieth-Century Taste and Style* (New York: Viking, 2001), discussion of the renovation 216–18, quote 218. See also Christopher Petkanas, "Van Day Truex: Master of Understatement" *House & Garden* 165 (January 1993): 72–75, 119.

7.   Jeanie Puleston Fleming, "Shopper's World: France's Colorful Country Fabrics," *New York Times*, April 6, 1986; Wendy Moonan, "Antiques: A Lasting Imprint on Fabrics," *New York Times*, July 6, 2001; Pierre Moulin, Pierre LeVec, and Linda Dannenberg, *Pierre Deux's French Country* (New York: Clarkson N. Potter, 1984), 24–35.

8.   Matthew Smyth, personal communication, August 16, 2013.

9.   Moulin, LeVec, and Dannenberg, *Pierre Deux's French Country*. Linda Dannenberg followed up the book with an informative article, "In Pursuit of the Provençal," *Departures* (November/December 2003), http://www.departures.com/articles/in -pursuit-of-the-provencal/.

10.   Susanne Stephens, "The Treasures of Provence," *Architectural Digest* 47 (March 1990): 94–101, quote 96.

11.   "Eternal Appeal of Provence," 60–61; Olga A. Carlisle, "Provence Still Life," *Holiday* 45 (June 1969): 26–31, 86–88, quote 26.

12.   Pierre Magnan, *The Essence of Provence: The Story of L'Occitane*, trans. Richard Seaver (New York: Arcade, 2003).

13.   What Hom states about the Mercato market in Dubai has resonance for L'Occitane stores, if one substitutes Provence for Italy: such a place "mythologically resolves contradictions and contemporary anxieties about globalization by activating Italy as a referent for tradition" (Stephanie Malia Hom, *The Beautiful Country: Tourism and the Impossible State of Destination Italy* [Toronto: University of Toronto Press, 2015], 173).

14.   Information on Williams and Williams-Sonoma comes from Arlyn Tobias Gajilan and Chuck Williams, "From Pots to Poachers, I Searched for Tools That Would Transform American Kitchens. Along the Way, I Discovered That Good Taste Can Build a Business," *Fortune Small Business*, September 1, 2003, http://money.cnn.com /magazines/fsb/fsb_archive/2003/09/01/350785/index.htm.

15.   Christopher Petkanas, *At Home in France* (New York: Rizzoli, 1990).

16.   Petkanas, *At Home in France*, 92–101.

17.   Petkanas, *At Home in France*, 14–27.

18.   Petkanas, *At Home in France*, quote 25.

19.   Patricia Wells, *Patricia Wells at Home in Provence* (New York: Scribner, 1996).

20.   Moulin, LeVec, and Dannenberg, *Pierre Deux's French Country*, 35; Julian More, *A Taste of Provence: The Food and People of Southern France with 40 Delicious Recipes*, with photographs by Carey More (New York: Henry Holt, 1988), kitchen photo 94, Lucien Peyraud photo 95. Olney, *Provence the Beautiful Cookbook*, 228.

21.   Richard Olney, *Lulu's Provençal Table: The Exuberant Food and Wine from Domaine Tempier Vineyard* (New York: HarperCollins, 1994), photo 70–71.

22.   Olney, *Lulu's Provençal Table*, photos 110, 126, 163, 253.

23.   Olney, *Lulu's Provençal Table*, photo 337.

PART V

1.   Patricia Wells, *Patricia Wells at Home in Provence* (New York: Scribner, 1996), 11.

2.   Wells, *At Home in Provence*, 13.

3.   Mary Roblee Henry, *A Farmhouse in Provence* (New York: Knopf, 1969), 12–13. Le Hameau de la Reine was the private quarters of Marie Antoinette that included a farmhouse and other agricultural buildings; I have capitalized Hameau.

4.   Patricia Wells and Walter Wells, *We've Always Had Paris . . . and Provence* (New York: HarperCollins, 2008), 170.

5.   Wells and Wells, *We've Always Had Paris*, 184.

6.   Wells, *At Home in Provence*, 12.

7.   I am grateful to Patricia and Walter Wells for a visit to Chanteduc and conversation, May 12, 2013, and to Rita and Yale Kramer for their kind invitation that led to conversation in New York with them and Patricia Wells on October 19, 2013.

CHAPTER FOURTEEN

1.   Laurence Wylie, *Village in the Vaucluse,* 3rd edition (Cambridge: Harvard University Press, 1974), 378.

2.   Laurence Wylie, "The New French Village, *hélas*," *New York Times*, November 25, 1973, Sunday Magazine, 62–63, 65–67, 70, 72, 77, 79–80, 82.

3.   Wylie, "New French Village," 77, 79.

4.   Wylie, "New French Village," draft, pp. 13–14, box 12, f. NY Times article, Laurence Wylie Papers, Harvard University Archives, Cambridge, MA.

5.   Wylie, "New French Village," 79–80. There is a difficulty with the TimesMachine version of this issue of the *New York Times*, which gives the pages here, as the advertising pages following 79 were copied, leaving out the content page, 80; the PDF version has no page numbers.

6.   Wylie, "New French Village," 79.

7.   *Blue Guide: The South of France: Provence and the French Alps,* ed. Stuart Rossiter (London: Ernest Benn, 1966); M. B. Shaw and D. W. Pitt, *Your Guide to Provence* (London: Alvin Redman, 1966).

8.   Henry Buller and Keith Hoggart, *International Counterurbanization: British Migrants in Rural France* (Aldershot: Avebury, 1994), 12.

9.   This number is derived from those holding the *carte de séjour,* the residence permit once required by the French government for stays longer than three months. It did not, however, include those who evaded registration or who inhabited French second homes for less than the three-month period. At present, for those within the European Union, the *carte de séjour* is no longer required. Since 2009 residency by US citizens of up to a year requires only a valid visa.

10.   Keith Hoggart and Henry Buller, "Geographical Differences in British Property

Acquisitions in Rural France," *Geographical Journal* 161 (March 1995): 69–78, esp. 70–71, 72, 76.

11. Rosalind Rosenberg, personal communication, October 28, 2013.

12. Alice Kaplan has written of this in *Dreaming in French: The Paris Years of Jacqueline Bouvier Kennedy, Susan Sontag, and Angela Davis* (Chicago: University of Chicago Press, 2012). For a comprehensive history of study-abroad programs, see Whitney Walton, *Internationalism, National Identities, and Study Abroad* (Stanford, CA: Stanford University Press, 2010). Harvey Levenstein, making rich use of the diaries and letters written during Junior Year Abroad by Smith College and Mount Holyoke College students, noted that as early as 1931 some of them took their Christmas vacation in the South of France and Italy; and that the experience of Aix and Arles in the 1950s also felt transformative (*We'll Always Have Paris: American Tourists in France since 1930* [Chicago: University of Chicago Press, 2004], 29–30, 175–76, 178). Corroborating these works is the personal testimony received from Lia G. Poorvu about the intellectual pleasures and scenic delights of being in Aix for six weeks in 1954, at the start of the Smith Junior Year Abroad program.

13. Mary Ann Caws, *Provençal Cooking: Savoring the Simple Life in France* (New York: Pegasus, 2008), 16–19.

14. Caws, *Provençal Cooking*, 39, 37.

15. Caws, *Provençal Cooking*, 78–79.

16. Helen C. Griffith, "Provençal Retreat: A Secluded Seventeenth-Century French Farmhouse Beckons Atlanta's Ann Cox Chambers to Return Again and Again," *Southern Accents* 15, no. 4 (1992): 102–10, quote 109.

17. Jean Rafferty, "Rebuilding with Style in a Year in Provence," *New York Times*, October 26, 2006; Jack Smith, "A Place in Provence," Robb Report, quotes, http://robbreport.com/Home-Design/A-Place-In-Provence.

18. Griffith, "Provençal Retreat," quotes 109–10.

19. Smith, "Place in Provence"; Rafferty, "Rebuilding with Style."

20. Magher's style is most fully seen in Joni Webb, "News about Ginny Magher," *Cote de Texas* (blog), November 2, 2012, http://cotedetexas.blogspot.com/2012/11/news-about-ginny-magher.html; Quote from "Perfect 18th Century Provencal Farmhouse Restoration," Andreas von Einsiedel Interior Photography, http://www.einsiedel.com/?collection=234.

21. Wells and Wells, *We've Always Had Paris . . . and Provence* (New York: HarperCollins, 2008), quotes 170–71, 169.

22. Patricia Wells, *Patricia Wells at Home in Provence* (New York: Scribner, 1996), quotes 11–13.

23. Wells and Wells, *We've Always Had Paris*, quote 187. Her Provence cooking classes began in 1995; in 1998, she also began teaching cooking classes in Paris (252, 256).

CHAPTER FIFTEEN

1. Joseph Wechsberg, "Rent a House? On the Continent," *Atlantic Monthly*, February 1957, 93–95, quotes 93.

2. Wechsberg, "Rent a House?" quotes 94, 94–95.

3. Wechsberg, "Rent a House?" 94, quote 95.

4. Wechsberg, "Rent a House?" quote 95.

5. Patrick Campbell, "How to Live the Sweet Life in the South of France, *Holiday* 47 (June 1970): 52–53, 68–69, 84.

6. "A Place in Provence" in "Holiday Travel Handbook," *Holiday* 47 (June 1970): 78.

7. Gîtes: "Gîtes de France," *Wikipédia*, http://fr.wikipedia.org/wiki/G%C3%AEtes _de_France#Historique; Kelby Carr, "Gites de France: A Splendid Option for a Memorable Stay in France," *About Travel*, http://gofrance.about.com/od/lodging /a/gites-de-france.htm.

8. The first article giving a friendly mention to *gîtes* that I found in a mainstream American magazine came in 2001. "If you want to vacation the way the French do, consider *gîtes ruraux,* rustic—often *very* rustic—farmhouses (from $500 per week) that are everywhere in France." The piece then gave contact information ("For Rent: Private Homes in Europe," *Gourmet* 61 [May 2001]: 78).

9. Entrepreneurial British second home owners in France had already begun the process of linking their French houses with vacationing countrymen and women when, in the early 1960s, Americans entered the game.

10. "A Place in Provence," 78.

11. Marylin Bender, "A Housewife Finds Villas for Family," *New York Times,* October 16, 1961. The associate was Stanley Linder.

12. Bender, "Housewife Finds Villas."

13. I interviewed Claire Packman in New York City on October 5 and December 3, 2012. Much of the following comes from these interviews. She brought her scrapbook of clippings, press releases, and brochures with her to the second interview and was kind enough to allow me to photograph them for use in this work. She also gave me some office files to take home. In what follows, many of the clippings in the scrapbook, cut from newspapers and magazines, and some in the files can only be partly cited.

14. Lydia Bickford, "Exotic Vacation Homes from France to Greece," Lafayette (IN) *Journal and Courier,* 1968.

15. Frank Hiteshew, "Castles for Rent: References Required," *Carte Blanche,* Fall 1965, 14.

16. Bruce Jay Friedman, "Villa-renting in Europe," *Playbill* 3 (April 1966). In his memoir *Lucky Bruce,* Friedman writes less glowingly about this summer, which came toward the end of his first marriage. In retrospect, the gain of this summer was the writing of his life-changing play, *Scuba Duba* (Bruce Jay Friedman, *Lucky Bruce: A Literary Memoir* [Emeryville, Ontario: Biblioasis, 2011], 120–22).

17. Bruce Jay Friedman, "Villa-renting in Europe."

18. Reports in the press varied from 2,000 to 3,000 properties during this time.

19. Louis George, "Villas for Rent: Month or Season," *Palm Beach Life,* September/October, 1973.

20. Horace Sutton, "Rent Your Way around the World," *Los Angeles Times,* June 28, 1970.

21. *House and Garden,* 1966.

22. *The Merv Griffin Show,* season 16, episode 102, aired February 14, 1979.

23. "Business Meetings—Vacations in Your Own Villa," *MarketAir Newsletter* 3 (November/December 1967).

24. "Diners Club International News," *Signature,* February 1973.

25. Jerry Hulse, "Find the Perfect Escape in a Private Villa," *Los Angeles Times,* November 2, 1980.

26. Harold H. Brayman, "Renting Villas Abroad for Offbeat Vacations," *National Observer,* April 25, 1966.

27. The Editors, "At Last—A Practical Guide to Villa Vacations, House Swapping and the Joys of Staying Put," *Travel & Leisure,* February 1984, 79.

28. Julie Wilson, "How to Rent a Villa and Other Homes Away from Home," *Travel & Leisure,* February 1984, 80–82, quote 81.

29. Wilson, "How to Rent a Villa," quotes 81.

30. "Before You Book: 20 Questions," *Fortune,* August 12, 2002, quote 164.

31. And, now, at copyediting in November 2015, 103 properties for minimum stays

from 1–14 nights. HomeAway property listings for Lourmarin, France, http://www
.homeaway.com/search/keywords:Lourmarin%2C+France.

32.   "Village apartment, fabulous view," Airbnb, https://www.airbnb.com/rooms
/1780593?s=sWFY.

CHAPTER SIXTEEN

1.   Don Gold, "The Art of Doing Nothing," *Travel & Leisure* 9 (February 1979): 43–44.
2.   David Brooks, *Bobos in Paradise: The New Upper Class and How They Got There* (New
York: Simon and Schuster, 2000).
3.   Daniel T. Rodgers, *Age of Fracture* (Cambridge: Harvard University Press, 2011), 83.
4.   Brooks, *Bobos in Paradise,* quotes 199, 108.
5.   Brooks, *Bobos in Paradise,* chapter 2.
6.   Brooks, *Bobos in Paradise,* 203–8 and chapter 6, esp. 227.
7.   Dean MacCannell, *The Tourist: A New Theory of the Leisure Class* (New York:
Schocken, 1976).
8.   Brooks, *Bobos in Paradise,* 207.
9.   Brooks, *Bobos in Paradise,* 251–52.
10.   Interview with Patricia and Walter Wells, May 12, 2013, Vaison-la-Romaine.
11.   Peter Mayle, *A Year in Provence* (New York: Knopf, 1989); The British edition was
published by Hamish Hamilton, 1989.
12.   Peter Mayle, *Toujours Provence* (New York: Knopf, 1991), 103.
13.   "Peter Mayle: 20 Years in Provence," *The Connexion,* December 2009, http://www
.connexionfrance.com/peter-mayle-interview-a-year-in-provence-20-years-10512
-news-article.html.
14.   At this writing, Amazon lists six of the Wicked Willie books that Mayle wrote in collaboration with the illustrator, Gray Jolliffe, including *Man's Best Friend* (London:
Pan, 1984); I've actually read several.
15.   Mayle, *A Year in Provence,* 106–7; quote 106.
16.   Winifred Fortescue, *Perfume from Provence* (Boston: Houghton Mifflin, 1937), 2–3.
(The British edition was published by William Blackwood, 1935.)

CHAPTER SEVENTEEN

1.   Or it could be Tuscany, as in Frances Mayes's *Under the Tuscan Sun: At Home in Italy,*
a 1996 best seller and later a movie. Its location is often confused with Provence.
2.   Anthony Campbell, review of Carol Drinkwater, *The Olive Farm: A Memoir of Life,
Love, and Olive Oil in the South of France,* http://www.acampbell.org.uk/book
reviews/r/drinkwater.html; Anthony Peregrine, "Book Review: The Olive Season by Carol Drinkwater," *Travel* (July 2003), http://www.telegraph.co.uk/travel
/destinations/europe/france/727864/Book-review-The-Olive-Season-by-Carol
-Drinkwater.html.
3.   One delightful version is by a French-born writer living and teaching in the United
States: Yvone Lenard, *The Magic of Provence: Pleasures of Southern France* (High-
town, NJ: Elysian Editions, 2000).
4.   Ruth Reichl, "Critic's Notebook; My Year in Provence Last August," *New York Times,*
April 22, 1998.
5.   Peter Mayle, *Encore Provence: New Adventures in the South of France* (New York:
Knopf, 1999), 40–41, quotes 40.
6.   Mayle, *Encore Provence,* 42–43.

7.   Mayle, *Encore Provence*, 43, lists 45–51.

8.   Peter Mayle, *Toujours Provence* (New York: Knopf, 1991), 103.

9.   Mayle, *Toujours Provence*, quotes 109, 110.

10. Mayle, *Toujours Provence*, 110–11.

11. Mayle, *Toujours Provence*, 112.

12. Mayle, *Toujours Provence*, 112.

13. Doreen Carvajal, "Glorifier of Provence Seeks Refuge in the Hamptons," *New York Times*, June 18, 1995, http://www.nytimes.com/1995/06/18/nyregion/glorifier-of -provence-seeks-refuge-in-the-hamptons.html?scp=8&sq=Mayle%20Year%20 in%20Provence%20review&st=cse.

14. Peter Mayle, *Encore Provence*, 80.

15. Mayle, *Encore Provence*, 80–81.

16. The British Academy of Film and Television Arts awarded *Jean de Florette* best picture, and Daniel Auteuil, one of the principals in both films, received the César award, the French equivalent of an Oscar, for his performances in both. An interesting take on the impact of the Berri films in Great Britain is Phil Powrie, "'I'm only here for the beer': Post-tourism and the Recycling of French Heritage Films," in *The Media and the Tourist Imagination: Converging Cultures,* ed. David Crouch et al. (London: Routledge, 2005), where he links these films with the beer ads for Stella Artois.

17. *Jean de Florette*, directed by Claude Berri (France: Renn/Films A2/Rai2/DD, 1986). All dialogue is taken from the film's subtitles.

18. Mayle, *Encore Provence*, 5. The most informative article on Mayle is John Grace, "A Year in Provence, 20 Years On," *Guardian,* January 11, 2010; and http://www.connexion france.com/peter-mayle-interview-a-year-in-provence-20-years-10512-news-article. html.

19. Although it only received a low 25 percent on the website Rotten Tomatoes' meter aggregating critical response, the viewers' rating was a more favorable 65 percent (http://www.rottentomatoes.com/m/good_year/).

20. Lawrence Durrell, *Caesar's Vast Ghost: Aspects of Provence* (London: Faber and Faber, 1990), 11–13.

21. "Peter Mayle's Lourmarin Maison Sold: New Home outside the Slumberous Village of Vaugines," *Provence Ventoux* (blog), June 15, 2011, http://provenceventouxblog .com/2011/peter-mayles-lourmarin-maison-sold-new-home-in-the-slumerous -village-of-vaugines/.

22. Richard F. Kuisel, *The French Way: How France Embraced and Rejected American Values and Power* (Princeton, NJ: Princeton University Press, 2012), 365–66, quotes 365. Susan Carol Rogers has warned that the "peasant" has been disappearing by waves since the mid-nineteenth century, but remains an important force, at least rhetorically, capable of use by the political Left and Right ("Good to Think: The 'Peasant' in Contemporary France," *Anthropological Quarterly* 60 [April 1987]: 56–63).

23. Laurence Wylie, "Roussillon, '87: Returning to the Village in the Vaucluse," *French Politics and Society* 7 (Spring 1989): 1–26, quotes 6, 7, 8. My book, however, serves as a partial refutation of Wylie's statement: the fad for Provence didn't just happen; it was created out of many forces.

24. Wylie, "Roussillon, '87," 12. In today's dollars, $3,000 is approximately $30,000; in 1987 it would have been roughly $14,000.

25. Wylie, "Roussillon, '87," 17–18.

26. Despite its attraction to tourists, Provence seems in some quarters to remain a problem area, mainly because of its low level of industrial development. See, for example, Jacques Garnier, *Un appareil productif en mutation: les 50 ans qui ont tout changé en Provence-Alpes-Côte d'Azur* (Paris: Economica-Anthropos, 2011).

CHAPTER EIGHTEEN

1. Bob Spitz, *Dearie: The Remarkable Life of Julia Child* (New York: Knopf, 2012), 482.
2. Comité Régional du Tourisme de Provence-Alpes-Côte d'Azur, *Chiffres Clés*, January 2014, http://www.infotourismepaca.fr/wp-content/uploads/2012/08/Chiffres -cl%C3%A9s-2014.pdf. In my search for information on historical and current statistics on American travel to Provence, I've made determined efforts, initially using the traditional methods of historians. I've turned to newer approaches, contacting the always helpful M. René Baretje-Keller, the guiding hand of CIRET, the International Center for Research and Study on Tourism, in France. I followed up with queries to the appropriate French agencies that Baretje-Keller suggested, with no responses. Additionally I've posted queries on H-Travel and (with the help of Prof. Bertram Gordon) its French analog, Les Clionautes. None of these has yielded any information beyond the above.
3. In July 2014, the Office of Travel and Tourism Industries of the US government published its report on American travel to destinations abroad. France garnered two million, but this included business and professional travelers, as well as those traveling for pleasure. Thus travelers to the PACA region constituted roughly 9 percent of Americans going to France, for whatever reason. http://travel.trade.gov/tinews /archive/tinews2014/20140723.html.
4. Quoted in Michael Peppiatt, "A Designer's Passion for Provence," *Architectural Digest* 57 (December 2000): 92.
5. Christopher Petkanas, *At Home in France* (New York: Rizzoli, 1990), 14–27, quotes 18.
6. Iain Pears, *The Dream of Scipio* (New York: Riverhead, 2002); Pierre Magnan, *The Murdered House,* trans. Patricia Clancy (New York: Thomas Dunne, 1999 [first published in French, 1984]; Peter Mayle, *A Good Year* (London: Time Warner, 2004); Peter Mayle, *Hotel Pastis* (London: Hamish Hamilton, 1993); Jane S. Smith, *Fool's Gold* (Cambridge, MA: Zoland, 2000). Presented here is only a sampling of the fiction set in Provence; the Internet offers lists of many more books with Provence as the locale.
7. Bruce David Colen, "Napa Valley's Auberge du Soleil: A Touch of Provence in Northern California," *Architectural Digest* 43 (March 1986): 116–23, 200.
8. Hom considers a much larger development in the eastern reaches of the East Bay, Sorrento, at Dublin ranch in California (Stephanie Malia Hom, *The Beautiful Country: Tourism and the Impossible State of Destination Italy* [Toronto: University of Toronto Press, 2015], 180–81).
9. Property description as advertised on Zillow.com, http://www.zillow.com /homedetails/8812-Provence-Village-Ln-Charlotte-NC-28226/83965381_zpid/, and YouTube, https://www.youtube.com/watch?v=HckP7bE_Lp0, in January 2014.
10. "Rosehip Tea Cozy," April Cornell website, http://www.aprilcornell.com/product /Rosehip-Tea-Cozy-GFROSTCU-Yellow/linens-kitchen-attic-clearance.
11. Williams-Sonoma and Sur La Table were the two largest retailers of specialty cookware in 2003, as discussed in Arlyn Tobias Gajilan and Chuck Williams, "From Pots to Poachers, I Searched for Tools That Would Transform American Kitchens. Along the Way, I Discovered That Good Taste Can Build a Business," *Fortune Small Business* (September 1, 2003), http://money.cnn.com/magazines/fsb/fsb _archive/2003/09/01/350785/index.htm.
12. "Antiques-Hunting in Provence," *Travel & Leisure* (August 2007), http://www.travel andleisure.com/articles/antiques-hunting-in-provence.
13. Chris Rojek, "Indexing, Dragging and the Social Construction of Tourist Sights," in *Touring Cultures: Transformations of Travel and Theory,* ed. Chris Rojek and John Urry (New York: Routledge, 1997), 52–74, quote 54. Rojek also considers how this can lead to "distortion . . . myth and fabrication" (55).

14.   Nicolai Scherle and Ralph Lessmeister, "Internet Cultures and Tourist Expectations in the Context of the Public Media Discourse," in *Mediating the Tourist Experience: From Brochures to Virtual Encounters,* ed. Jo-Anne Lester and Caroline Scarles (Burlington, VT: Ashgate, 2013), 91–103, esp. 96–99.

15.   "A Walk in Provence," *Times Journeys,* http://www.nytimes.com/times-journeys/travel/a-walk-in-provence/?action=click&region=body-main&version=homepage-postcard&module=learn-more.

16.   "Factory & Museum Visit," L'Occitane website, http://usa.loccitane.com/factory-museum-visit,82,1,34672,0.htm?gclid=CjwKEAiA9uaxBRDYr4_hrtC3tW8SJAD6UU8GPtwq9UMdoJ21m0BbBZTv9Fg-u8qWrRFHgbXMF4bseh0C7xbw_wcB. In 2012 visiting the headquarters and museum of L'Occitane was a highlight of a day trip of neighboring guests staying in a villa turned into rental apartments in Lourmarin.

17.   Claire O'Connor, "The Billionaire behind L'Occitane's Asian Expansion," *Forbes.com*, March 23, 2011, http://www.forbes.com/forbes/2011/0411/features-billionaire-behind-loccitane-asian-expansion.html.

Index